MW00803837

Meanings of Ripley

Meanings of Ripley:
The *Alien* Quadrilogy and Gender

Edited by

Elizabeth Graham

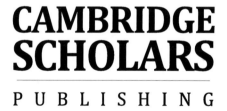

CAMBRIDGE
SCHOLARS
PUBLISHING

Meanings of Ripley: The *Alien* Quadrilogy and Gender,
Edited by Elizabeth Graham

This book first published 2010

Cambridge Scholars Publishing

12 Back Chapman Street, Newcastle upon Tyne, NE6 2XX, UK

British Library Cataloguing in Publication Data
A catalogue record for this book is available from the British Library

ISBN (10): 1-4438-2339-2, ISBN (13): 978-1-4438-2339-5

TABLE OF CONTENTS

ACKNOWLEDGEMENTS

There are many people that I need to thank for their work and support throughout the development and completion of this book. First and foremost, I want to thank the contributors for their ideas and insights that come together to offer readers a variety of interpretations of such a complex and significant filmic character as Ellen Ripley. Their hard work, patience, and perseverance are greatly appreciated. Also, a very special thanks to George Moore who went beyond the role of contributor and provided invaluable assistance with the Introduction and Appendices for this collection.

I also want to thank Amanda Millar, my editor at Cambridge Scholars Publishing. She worked with me to successfully resolve some serious issues that nearly destroyed the project. As the project moved forward, Amanda was always available providing whatever information I needed. Her support and assistance is very much appreciated.

In addition, I must thank Brandon University, especially the Brandon University Research Committee, for the financial and resource support that I received while working on this book. The ability to hire a student assistant, Catherine Taylor, was one form that support took. Catherine conducted preliminary searches, dealt with interlibrary loan requests, and photocopied material. This was perhaps the least stimulating component of the project so I thank Catherine for working so diligently.

Finally, I want to thank my family and friends for their support and encouragement. In particular, I need to thank my sister, Leona Graham, for creating the artwork for the cover of this collection. Her artistic ability is something I have always admired and so I was very happy when she agreed to become involved with this project. I also must thank my partner, Michael Manson, for his unfailing professional and personal support as I worked on this collection. Having a partner who is a retired professor of English Literature has advantages when one is working on a book. Michael was a tremendous help as I began proof-reading the final manuscript. However, his personal support and encouragement were just as valuable to me. I am very thankful that he is in my life.

INTRODUCTION

ELIZABETH GRAHAM

There is no doubt that the *Alien Quadrilogy* has received considerable popular and academic attention over the past thirty years. Much of this attention is perhaps due to the belief that it signalled a rebirth of science fiction and horror films. The films mark a course alteration away from the collapse into self-parodies originating with the 1950s invasion films. Much of the literature concentrating on the *Alien* films has been devoted to interpretations of the films, individually or collectively, or the aliens and what they represent. The films have been described as classic westerns in space having clear delineations between the heroes and the villains. They have also been interpreted as social commentaries on war, colonialism, AIDS, and other socially charged issues of the mid to late twentieth century. Mullhall argues that the significant attention the films have received is a consequence of the many issues explored in the films themselves:

> these movies are preoccupied, even obsessed, with a variety of interrelated anxieties about human identity—about the troubled and troubling question of individual integrity and its relation to the body, sexual difference and nature. (2002, 1)

As the central human character in the films, Ellen Ripley has received considerable attention and has become an iconic figure in the science fiction community as well as academic circles. Due to the longevity of her iconic status, many have posed the question, directly or indirectly, across the kitchen table, and in popular and academic publications, what is the Meaning of Ripley?

Ripley has come to represent many things to many people. Her complexity across four films has allowed for varied and contradictory interpretations of what she and the films represent. As a woman she was both a challenge to the established androcentric genre of science fiction/horror and also to established patriarchal societal norms regarding gender. At the same time, however, she can also be read as a female character who reinforced gender expectations. She has been discussed as a feminist hero, a substitute for the Old West male hero, a patriarchal mother, a monster, and a Final Girl, to mention only a few interpretations. Given these variations, it is interesting that so many individuals writing about the *Alien* films, and Ripley in particular, discuss *the* meaning of a film or scene, *the* intentions of the writer or director, *the* impressions left *upon* the audience as if audience members are blank receivers with no worldview or control over their thoughts (see Williams 2006). This underlying assumption that there is some objective reality in relation to a science fiction/action/horror film is quite interesting to say the least. My point is that it is unusual to find in the literature dealing with these films any recognition that the meanings derived from a film are the result of a multitude of factors interacting with each other in a given social context.

Within the Interactionist Traditions of Sociology, individuals are viewed as simultaneously products and producers of the society in which they live. We are products created from the totality of our lived experiences. We are producers of the social world in that our conformity to established social patterns maintains the status quo, and changes in our behaviours can disrupt the status quo, ultimately resulting in social change. To understand the relationship between individual and the social context, and how these two interact in society, aspects of C. Wright Mills' work and Blumer's thoughts on the role of films in this relationship are useful to consider.

In his now classic piece, "The Promise," Mills explains:

> By the fact of his [her] living [s]he contributes, however minutely, to the shaping of this society and to the course of its history, even as [s]he is made by society and by its historical push and shove. (1993, 167)

He argues that an understanding of this relationship is essential for any inquiry intended to explore who we are or how we see the world in which we live.

While it may initially seem inappropriate to rely on a work as dated as Herbert Blumer's 1933 book, *Movies and Conduct*, his insights remain valuable, and unfortunately

> Hollywood film has been neither the subject of sustained analysis nor the center of an accumulating tradition of scholarship [in sociology].... Apart from a handful of sociologists working within the postmodernist rump of symbolic interactionist groups [a group that neither I nor this book represent]... the fictional nature of film and literature continues to place these products of human creativity and social organizations on a terrain

that is beyond the range of routine sociological concern. (Dowd 1999, 325-326)

In addition, Blumer's primary concern with the influence of film on the individuals seems particularly relevant to the underlying assumption of this collection that in general the social context in which films, as with all products, are created and observed or interpreted is worthy of attention in any attempt to understand the meanings of the films.

As part of that endeavour to understand the influence of film, he necessarily needed to explore why different individuals can be influenced differently by the same film. He claims,

> There is a wide variety in what people may select out of a picture. Its influence, consequently, is dependent not solely upon its content but also upon the sensitivity and disposition of the observer. (1970 [1933], 179-180)

He elaborates by stating that these differences among individuals are more than consequences of sex or age, although these are important; "cultural background and personal character" and "the interests of one's group" also need to be considered.

> The implication is that if one is to foretell the effects of a motion picture one must know, in general, something of the interests and experience of those to whom the picture will be shown. (191)

In general, Blumer's point is not inconsistent with that found in recent feminist and film criticism literature dealing with intersectionality—multiple aspects of individuals and the contexts in which they exist need to be considered in order to reach a fuller, more complete understanding of what is happening. With a primary focus on oppression and inequality, intersectionality calls our attention to the interconnections of gender, race/ethnicity, social class,[1] and there is no doubt that such an approach would be worthwhile in an examination of Ripley. The various interpretations of her presented in this collection imply the need for considering the complexities discussed in that literature. That one character can be understood in so many seemingly diverse ways indicates not just the complexity of the character in terms of the intersections among gender, race, class, but also the complexity of the audiences as they engage

---

[1] Among the other factors considered in discussions involving intersectionality are sex, sexuality, and nationality.

with such a character. However, as Jennings points out, by exclusively favouring such plural positions

> there are dangers involved for the future of political organizations and critical arguments against oppressions that still face us, both individually and collectively. (1995, 193-4)

If such pluralistic approaches are not used in conjunction with approaches concentrating on these factors individually, there is the potential of destroying any sense of collectivity among individuals who have in common experiences of oppression and subjugation tied to one of these factors. Having no sense of shared experiences with others effectively works to discourage any type of action that could challenge structural inequality.

In addition, a number of the contributions to this collection do not have only issues of oppression as their concern. They also explore the ways in which the fictional Ellen Ripley is able to move beyond or overcome the oppressive elements that she encounters in her worlds.

This collection does not explore the "cultural background and personal character" of the contributors. Nonetheless, taking up Blumer's comment about the audience members, it is worth noting that many of the differences among these contributors, discussed below, are part of the collection's strength because they illustrate the relationship between the individual and society and how elements of uniqueness for each individual allow us to exist in similar social contexts, observe the same things, and still come to very different conclusions about meanings.

As most readers are aware, Ellen Ripley first appeared in *Alien* in 1979 and last appeared in 1997 in *Alien Resurrection*. Following the logic of C. Wright Mills, to attempt understandings of her as a social artifact produced by individuals, as well as others' interpretations of her requires that the social context leading up to and during her presence in society be understood in conjunction with at least some understanding of those doing the interpreting.

There is no doubt that prior to and during the time period referred to here questions about gender were being discussed in society. In fact, *scientific* discussions about the connection between biology and gender have a very long history. In the early 1900s, the belief in male intellectual superiority was advocated by individuals such as Cattell and Thorndike. Fausto-Sterling claims that such views

were so congenial to the economic and political establishment of the period
that rational, scientific challenges to their work were studiously ignored.
(1985, 17-18)

Interestingly, while this view seemed to dissipate in the late 1930s, its
rebirth, with no new facts, came about not long before the release of *Alien*
in 1979. In fact, just one year before the film was released, Edwin Wilson
wrote:

> It pays males to be aggressive, hasty, fickle and undiscriminating. In theory
> it is more profitable for females to be coy, to hold back until they can
> identify the male with the best genes.... Human beings obey this biological
> principle. (in Fausto-Sterling 1985, 156)

While individuals like Wilson, supporting the patriarchal status quo,
argued the biological imperative of masculine and feminine characteristics
or claimed male superiority, others, like Simone de Beavoir, attempted to
dismantle such biological determinism, and still others such as Mary Daly
and Adrinne Rich attempted to subvert that argument, attacking patriarchy
sometimes in favour of separatism. A vast array of gender inequalities in
Western societies were debated—everything from a woman's right to vote,
to accessible birth control, to women holding positions of authority over
men, to sexual assault, and much more. Responses and participation in the
ongoing debates differed in a variety of ways at the individual and societal
levels, in political and academic arenas. As time passed, more detailed and
diverse positions regarding the gender questions were put forward
reflecting the interdependent relationship between biography and history
discussed by Mills and the variability inherent in that relationship—
individual biographies brought into the discussion about gender offered
varied interpretations, insights, and queries.

   Within such a social context inundated with tremendous uncertainty
and disagreement about gender and yet still dominated by patriarchal
ideology,

> What could be more unexpected than making the sole protagonist and
> survivor a woman?... women as heroic survivors was a concept alien
> enough to constitute a surprise for the audience while at the same time not
> so foreign that it would put mainstream audiences off. (Gallardo and Smith
> 2004, 17)

   The chapters in this collection reflect the uncertainty and disagreement
about gender as well as the importance of the relationship between
biography and history in that they illustrate that there is not a singular

meaning of Ripley but rather multiple meanings that are consequences of the creators of the series and their social contexts, the audience members and their social contexts, and the relationships between these two groups.

This collection offers discussions of Ripley with particular attention to feminism, autonomy, and sexual agency in relation to the context of gender during the time period in which the films were released. As a whole, it is multidisciplinary and, therefore, augments debates and discussions not only in film criticism but also popular culture, philosophy, sociology, and Gender and Women's Studies. In planning this book, I had in mind an audience of undergraduate students studying in these areas. Consequently, while the book is intellectually stimulating, it does not fall victim to the overuse of discipline-specific jargon that would frustrate those who are unfamiliar with the terminology. Rather it invites them, as well as the general population, to see that there are commonalities across disciplines.

Ripley is presented as a product of Second Wave, Radical Feminism, as a traditional woman and mother under patriarchy, as Other who, in refusing to be used by the Company or by the alien ultimately transcends to an authentic self, as an individual who poses sexual agency, and as an autonomous individual who is not limited by the constraints of gender role expectations. The varying interpretations are rooted in the varied backgrounds of each contributor—some are female and some are male, some are Canadian and some are American, some are junior scholars while others have established careers, and four distinct disciplines (or groups) are represented. As can be seen in the following pages, each of these individuals is quite conscious of their own biographical relationship to history and that it has influenced what they see and how they interpret.[2]

The collection begins and ends with chapters that specifically point to the importance of the social context in relation to gender while Chapters Two, Three, and Four focus on Ripley as reflective of social circumstances within the contexts of the films with particular attention to ideas of motherhood, femininity, and sexual agency.

Chapter One, *Alien Feminist*, by George Moore, examines the first film in the quadrilogy, *Alien*. Moore, who teaches English Literature and published a book length study on the feminist, Gertrude Stein, readily admits that

> the changes in the feminist movement during the Seventies were part of the larger social changes that influenced me a tremendous amount... my

---

[2] The contributors have provided brief statements that offer the reader insights about their approach in analyzing Ripley.

critical approach is simply a way of me evaluating my own past and my changed perspective on it.

In this chapter, Moore takes up the question of whether Ripley is a feminist as the concept was understood in the 1970s and 1980s. He identifies the importance of the social context when attempting to understand the creation of *Alien* and the development of Ripley's role.

> Ripley's role, and the film's general attitude toward women, are products of a changing feminist awareness... the point might... be made that the film helps historicize the movement's concerns during this particular period of upheaval.

In Chapter Two, "Redressing Ripley: Disrupting the Female Hero," Peter Wood is undoing the idea of Ripley as a feminist hero in *Aliens* and argues that she is consistent with patriarchal ideas of woman and motherhood. In his chapter, he states that the film

> essentializes Ripley in ways that reinforce the fundamental, natural, and intrinsic connection between being female and having a lower social status than males, as well as the fact that being female means being, always already, a mother.

However, his objective in putting forth this claim is to reveal, through attention to the often neglected elements of the film, that hero status does not ensure escape from oppression:

> In a larger sense, I wanted to reinforce the idea that being an action hero does not immediately and easily do away with all traces of sexism. Indeed, some films, like *Aliens*, can present a strong female character and yet still offer a conservative message of what it means to be a woman.

Eva Dadlez, who teaches Philosophy and Women's Studies, explores the parallels between Ripley's struggles in *Alien³* and Simone de Beaviour's notion of the *myth of the feminine* and Ripley's transcendence in Chapter Three, "Paradox and Transcendence in *Alien³*: Ripley Through the Eyes of Simone de Beauvoir." Making use of de Beaviour's work is a perfect fit for Dadlez. She sums up the rationale behind her approach by saying that she

> Love[s] Simone de Beaviour! Always thought of her as a feminist touchstone that exposed cultural hypocrisy, as it's exposed in *Alien³*.

In her chapter, Dadlez explains that the film "embodies many of the insights inherent in de Beauvoir's *myth of the feminine*.

> This particular fiction does so... by affiliating its heroine Ripley with the alien, a true Other... and then by stressing the difference and alienness of Ripley's sex in presenting her against the backdrop of the almost exclusively masculine world... Next, it does so by presenting Ripley in paradoxically incompatible roles... Finally, the film conveys de Beauvoir's insights by showing us Ripley's transcendence.

In Chapter Four, "Getting off the Boat: Hybridity and Sexual Agency in the *Alien* Films," Sarah Bach and Jessica Langer argue that there is a visible progression of Ripley's sexual agency across the four films. Through their examination of the quadrilogy, they reveal the process by which Ripley is able to shed patriarchal control in some respects but is ultimately not able to defeat patriarchy itself. Bach and Langer explain that by the end of *Alien Resurrection*:

> She no longer needs to take part in heterosexual sexual exchange in order to succeed within the system of patriarchy, but instead this line foreshadows her breaking of the system itself, utilizing her newfound human-alien hybridity to place herself outside the system and bring it down from without. This chapter will trace the development of Ripley's sexual agency throughout the *Alien* films in her relationships with aliens and with other humans – and, ultimately, within her own hybridity and that of the aliens.

For Sarah Bach, it was not just her background in Cinema Studies that brought her to examine the character of Ellen Ripley:

> Thanks to my mother, 'Aliens' has been one of my favourite movies since I was six years old. At first I identified most strongly with Newt, but as I grew older and my understanding of feminism and our culture expanded, I saw that development mirrored in the changes that Ripley undergoes through the series. Ripley has been a source of inspiration for as long as I can remember.

Her co-author, Jessica Langer, explains that there is a parallel between their examination of Ripley and her earlier work:

> Although most of my academic work focuses in various ways on postcolonialism and science fiction, I have always found it interesting to explore how systems of oppression—such as colonialism and patriarchy—

can be so similar and are often intertwined both in history and in cultural production.

Finally, in Chapter Five, *"Aliens'* Ellen Ripley: Ambiguous Interpretations and Her Autonomy," I explicitly return to the notion of social context arguing that it must be taken into account when considering interpretations of Ripley. As someone who teaches Sociology and Gender and Women's Studies, my interest in the social context, and the relationship between the individual and society should not be surprising. In my chapter, I point to three common interpretations of Ripley that are reflective of a social context influenced by Second Wave Feminism and the backlash against it—the monstrous feminine, the woman in man's clothes, and the traditional woman and mother.

> In addition, accepting that feminist scholars "need… to also study change and equality when it occurs rather than only documenting inequality" (Risman 2004, 435), I also offer an alternative interpretation of Ripley that reflects societal changes related to gender.

I offer my own view of Ripley as an autonomous individual; an interpretation that reflects both my roots in Second Wave Feminism and my move away from it:

> While it [Second Wave Feminism] is part of who I am and how I see the world, I have become more and more dissatisfied with feminism's reluctance to see women as anything other than victims of patriarchy.

All of the contributors in this collection not despite but because of their differences offer valuable interpretations of Ripley and her societies, as well as our societies. It is, therefore, my hope that as a whole the collection will foster discussions and debates not just about women in science fiction/action/horror films but about the ongoing issues regarding gender in Western societies.

In addition to the five chapters, this collection includes five appendices and a selected bibliography[3] that can be used as resources for those unfamiliar with the films, the pairing of *Alien* and *Predator* films, the work of the *Alien Quadrilogy* creators, and the extensive literature. In

---

[3] This bibliography includes all the sources used in the following chapters that specifically centre on Ripley and the *Alien Quadrilogy* as well as sources not used in this collection.

general, these appendices and bibliography provide further insight into the contexts from which the films emerged.

The first four appendices are summaries of the *Alien* films with specific notations to indicate where and how the Director's Cut/ Special Edition of each film differs from the Theatrical Releases. I made this decision because in some instances the two versions of each film vary in significant ways and have resulted in noteworthy interpretative differences. Recognizing, as this collection does, the importance of context in interpreting meaning, it seemed necessary to outline these variations. For example, whether someone is commenting on the climactic scene in *Alien*[3] when Ripley, "Cruciform arms extended, obviously Christlike… falls backwards into the light" (Dadlez), or the scene in the altered Theatrical Release in which Ripley embraces the alien queen that has exploded from her chest as she falls backward into the flames of the furnace will, without question, affect the meanings that are ultimately attached to the film. Appendices E is meant to offer the reader peripheral information that while not directly related to the content of the four *Alien* films is part of the context. It begins with a brief overview of *Predator I* and *II*, but is primarily a summary of the *Alien vs Predator* films which were intended to revitalize the *Alien* franchise but failed.

That the contributors come from a variety of disciplines and few specialize in film studies but have come together in this collection to create a work focusing on the trail blazing character of Ellen Ripley, demonstrates her continued significance approximately thirty years after her first appearance in *Alien*. In addition to the varied contributions of these authors about the *Meanings of Ripley* and the resources provided in the Appendices, it is worth noting that this collection also ventures outside of the prevailing arguments found within the established field of film criticism.

I hope that as a collection this book which largely represents perspectives of those outside film criticism will open discussions to a more general audience and encourages others to look to the past as well as the present when formulating their assessments of an iconic character such as Ripley. The complex and contradictory facets of her character encourage investigation, discussion, and repeated revisiting of previous conclusions. In addition, Ripley, like other fictional characters, has the potential to further our understandings of ourselves and our societies when we explore how and why we come to specific conclusions about *Meanings of Ripley*.

References

Blumer, H. 1970 [1933]. *Movies and conduct*. New York: Arno Press.

de Beauvior, S. [1952] 1989. *The second sex*. (Translated and edited by H. M. Parshley). New York : Knopf.

Dowd, J. 1999. Waiting for Louis Prima: On the possibility of a sociology of film. *Teaching Sociology* 27: 324-342.

Fausto-Sterling, A. 1985. *Myths of gender: Biological theories about women and men*. New York: Basic Books, Inc.

Gallardo C., X. and C. J. Smith. 2004. *Alien woman: The making of Lt. Ellen Ripley*. New York: Continuum.

Mills, C. W. 1993. The promise. In *Readings in social psychology: perspective and method*, ed. B. Byers, 166-172. Boston: Allyn and Bacon.

Mullhall, S. 2002. *On film: Thinking in action*. London: Routledge.

Mulvey, L. 1989. Visual pleasure and narrative cinema. In *Visual and other pleasures*, 14-28. Bloomington: Indiana University Press.

Williams, E. 2006. Birth kills, abortion saves: Two perspectives by incongruity in Ridley Scott's *Alien*. In The rhetoric of alien abduction. *E-Clectic* 4, no.2 http://abacus.bates.edu/eclectic/vol4iss2/pdf/troaaewf.pdf (accessed April 26, 2010).

CHAPTER ONE

THE *ALIEN* FEMINIST

GEORGE MOORE

Introduction

Lt. Ellen Ripley's individual film images are rarely distinguished today from the journey she takes through the four films of the *Alien* series. She has now become iconic as the subsequent films have inculcated popular reaction to her developing feminist image. This suggests society's need to perpetuate her difference over the decades. But it is significant that the Ripley of the original *Alien* movie creates a much more conflicted image than the one built up through the series of films. Ripley engages the audience as a representative of the women's movement, and particularly its Second Wave struggle for affirmation during the period of the film's production in the late 1970s. The conflicts within the women's movement at the time are themselves reinvented in different ways by a host of writers, producers, directors, and actors, including the two women who act in the film. Sigourney Weaver's first effort as Ripley was a product of a feminist awareness if not of feminist thinking associated with the movement itself, and so the character incorporates both feminist ideas and reactions against feminism. But the strongest context for Ripley is certainly the advent of the Radical Feminists, first emerging during the late 1960s and coming to power within the larger women's movement by the 1970s. Radical Feminism distinguished itself by its call for an abandonment of the old thinking about reconciliation with the enemy, men, and a demand for a newly constructed society based primarily if not exclusively on women's needs. The *radical* element was associated with New Left radicalism in the 1960s, and so also picked up a certain initial adherence to Marxist ideology (Roth 2004, 200-205). Ripley is no Marxist, nor is she fully conceived in the guise of a feminist extremist such as the Radical Feminists themselves came to be seen. *Feminist Practice*, a publication issued in the 1970s, for instance, declares that the word radical:

was used as a term of abuse to corral those aspects of [women's liberation] which most threatened their image of respectability. Radical Feminists became a corporate object of derision which these women and men could then dissociate themselves from. (Rowland and Klein 1996, 10)

If no extremist, Ripley's character shows definite signs of an awareness of changes in the movement during the late 1970s which include its radicalization. This can be attributed, in part, to a general awareness of Radical Feminism and to the film's various writers, producers, and actors who engaged the popular notion of militancy within the movement.

The purpose here is to suggest how Ripley's role and the film's general attitude toward women are products of a changing feminist awareness. Although neither could be conceived as addressing the feminist concerns of the decades since the film's release—in particular, the importance of the social construction of gender and the place of race, class and culture in determining those roles— the point might yet be made that the film helps historicize the movement's concerns during this particular period of upheaval. In the end, it is Ripley's relationship to the emerging conflicts centred around Radical Feminism that best suits her original role in *Alien*, and which best provides a means of exploring the contradictions found in her image as both the product of male discourse (in writers, director and producers) and the society's desire to find in her an image of the liberated woman.

Ripley and Radical Feminism in 1970s America

What happens to Ripley in *Alien* is actually the radicalization of her character through events in the film which expose the patriarchal nature of the Company's plans. The Company represents the nefarious business interests centred on retrieving the alien for possible bio-weaponry purposes. Ripley's radicalization occurs late in the film, whereas early in the film she is much more in line with the women's movement as it was just prior to the first *liberationists*, or women who decided that separate and self-sustaining was better than equal. These women saw that the old promise of gender equality was merely the perpetuation of the more conservative social forces that sought to keep women hopeful but waiting and in check. Within the movement, the debate was between the earlier fight for gender equality and the later call for complete liberation (Berkeley 1999, 39-55). This struggle parallels the film's production period, and can be read through various dimensions of the film's engagement with feminist ideas. In her history of the movement, *Daring to Be Bad: Radical Feminism In America, 1967-1975* (1989), Alice Echols argues that women within the movement were forced to decide between two ideologies, "the ideology of gender equality" or the more radical "ideology of difference" (289). The public view of this difference has a great deal to do with Ripley's role in the film, not just because of its popular image as vocal and self-assertive, but because the new association promoted a more militant stance on women's rights. As Winifred D. Wandersee suggests:

> The radical feminists offered an extreme critique of American society, which, because it did not allow room for compromise, encouraged the *possibility* of separatism rather than activism, and a search for personal solutions to political problems. (1988, xv)

That separatism manifested itself in a new breed of independence and, to some extent, a form of social alienation, both aspects of which seem apparent in Ripley's character.

At its outset, *Alien* presents us with the perfect paradigm (or perhaps parody) of the earlier quest for gender equality. As the single female officer aboard the commercial towing vehicle, the Nostromo, Ripley has achieved her station in the Company's chain of command by hard work, as is indicated by her take-charge attitude toward daily procedures, and her insistence on being included in all discussions that affect the crew's mission and the ship's operation. She strikes audiences as a self-motivated and career-minded woman, conscious of the latent sexism that the system displays when male officers and crew members simply ignore her comments and suggestions. And she deals amiably, if authoritatively, even with these situations, as in the case of the engineer Parker's demands for equitable pay and Ash's nullification of her authority when Dallas, the captain, is off the ship. Parker complains that he and his assistant, Brent, deserve "equal shares" in the commission of the Company's business. Ripley points out to him that he is already entitled to a "full share," demonstrating that she knows more than he about Company pay scales and contracts. With Ash, there are darker motives involved in his opening the air lock against her direct order. She would not risk infecting the rest of the crew; he would risk it all for a chance to examine an unknown species. But later, she coxes Ash into letting down his guard about his hidden desires, and he shows his strange admiration for the lethal alien that is now onboard. She does this, however, only to point out abruptly his violation of quarantine and the superseding of her authority in the countermanding of her direct order. It seems certain that the audience identifies both of these instances initially with Ripley's adept handling of male chauvinism, and only later, for Ash, with the greater subplot of the Company's desire for the alien. Early on, then, Ripley demonstrates her rank within the hierarchy of the Company's command and would seem to support a position of equal rights, if she can but get the conventions of command and law to support her authority.

Toward the end of the 1960s and into the decade of the film, the women's movement in America focused its efforts on women's rights and equal opportunity in hopes that women's roles would change if they could escape the traditional confines of home and family that had limited their success in the workplace and society (Tobias 1997, 212). The result, by the early 1970s, was an increase of women's positions in business and social organizations, and a more prominent general understanding of women's leadership acumen (Carden 1977, 35). But changes were slow, and the movement itself had to contend with increasing discontent in its ranks with the lack of gains in two decades of struggle. This was the crisis that gave rise to the Radical Feminists, and actually to the resurgence of the word *feminist* generally (Crow 2000, 2). Those who saw themselves as Radical Feminists now demanded something more than occupational role changes; they called for a separate understanding of women's concerns, and saw sexism and women's oppression as the root causes of all other problems facing women of the day (Crow 2000, 2).

The more radical call for independence coincided with the failure to ratify the Equal Rights Amendment (ERA) after years of state by state battles and with a resurgence of conservatism among both men in power and women who were voicing their objections to the radicalization of the women's rights movement. The use of the system to change the system was failing, and it is not surprising that the old Marxist mandates of social reform from the New Left found their way back into the rhetoric of Radical Feminism's demand for an abandonment of efforts to work within the system. In rejecting the capitalist and patriarchal mandates of the society, they began an effort to create a society of their own (Berkeley 1999, 44; Echols 1989, 14). The ideology of difference brought with it more public demonstrations, and soon developed a more militant public image for feminists in the movement, an image that Hollywood and other media would find an easy label (Echols 1989, 289). But it was also natural, according to Kathleen C. Berkeley, that the radical image became popular:

> Women with more flamboyant personalities and styles had little difficulty in capturing and playing to the media attention; and for these women, the more outrageous and radical their stance or action, the easier it became to popularize their political message. (1999, 47)

Radicalism was a response to a frustration some women felt over the failure to accomplish lasting gains. If the women's movement had achieved strategic goals, "job access, the right to a medically assisted abortion, the equal access to credit" (Tobias 1997, 96), there were objectives that continued to elude them, and for many these culminated in the stalled passage of the ERA. But the real split between the radicals and the movement occurred more as a popular image than in the movement itself; as Berkeley suggests:

> the more liberationists pushed the radical button, the easier it became for the media and the public to assume incorrectly that there was a fixed and unalterable division between mainstream, liberal equality feminism... and avant-garde, radical, liberation feminism. (1999, 52)

Political exigencies demanded that the movement remain cohesive (Berkeley 1999, 52-54), but the media persisted in aggrandizing the new radical element. Radical feminism became the bad girl mystique of the movement even as it was legitimately trying to establish a stronger feminine base for the core of the organization. Consequently, the Radical Feminisms were often marginalized even within the movement itself (Bell and Klein 1996, 10). But women had discovered that going along with the system even in order to ultimately change it meant compromising at times their ideals. Co-opted by the very process of their own involvement in trying to reform society, many proclaimed society irredeemable and abandoned political efforts all together (Tobias 1997, 227-228; Crow 2000, 3).

Ripley's character manages to chart some of these changes through her attitudes and decisions in the film, especially as she evolves from a Company woman, dedicated to equal rights and official protocol, to a radical liberationist who in the final scenes destroys the spaceship, Nostromo, ending the Company's commercial and scientific ventures in direct overthrow of her earlier demonstrations of authority. It is significant that her initial *feminist* role would appear more radical to audiences at the time than perhaps it was, but it makes clear that the producers, screenwriters and director, and the film industry generally, were aware of the claims for equality made by the movement. Ripley appears to achieve her rank as third officer by an explicit trust in the hierarchical assumptions of the organization and an investment in the micro-society of the ship. But the sexist nature of the patriarchy there finally overrides the hierarchal structure of command. What at first appears to be merely annoying instances of misogyny in Parker, Ash, and others, turn out to be an underlining ideology of the micro-society and its intentional suppression of one woman's independence. Ripley appears at first to believe in the system in which she has invested time and energy, pointing out infringements of protocol and regulations when others demonstrate neglect and annoyance with official rule, and so she takes on her feminist role in the audience's mind initially through moments of right action and proper office.

Alien suggests the nature of this change toward a radical social awareness in Ripley's final rejection of the Company, an act that reflects a major shift in policy within the women's movement. The ERA spent most of the decade in state houses seeking ratification after U.S. Congressional passage in 1972 (Tobias 1997, 137). The greatest push was in 1972-1982 when equal rights were at the forefront of feminist efforts and of society's awareness. Ripley's self-awareness of her position shows a growing awareness in Hollywood of this situation. Fox Studios had already voiced an interest in stronger roles for women when the script for *Alien* was submitted. Producers were increasingly aware of female audiences and looking for more films with female leads (McIntee 2005, 25). With what looked like a possible victory for the ERA in the late 1970s, women began to assume a different future, and called repeatedly for the end of elitism based on sex (Crow 2000, 1). Advancements in equal opportunity, particularly under Title VII of the Civil Rights Act, for a decade or more had allowed women the legal right to challenge "discrimination based on sex" (Wandersee 1988, 17-18). Ripley takes this new entitlement to heart, and confronts job related chauvinism on a number of fronts. The problem is that the Company represents more than social legitimacy; it represents the inherent inequalities of power. Audiences finally realize the Company for the nefarious force that guides the commercial and capitalist ventures at the core of the crew's missions, while secretly mandating the prerogatives of scientific acquisition by prioritizing the capture of an alien species above any concern for human life. The gender based distinctions coincide with the Company's priorities, that the scientific discovery, and potential capital gain, represented by the alien, outweigh human considerations.

An unseen presence, the Company voices its priorities by means of "Mother," the onboard computer, and by Ash, the science officer, later exposed as an android working in the Company's interest. The hidden dimension of the Company supports the nature of patriarchal power, a given in this microcosmic world of quasi-military command structures. Unfortunately, Ripley's assumptions about authority also derive from this same official order, even though in the end the Company considers the crew "expendable" and shows itself more evil even than the alien. The earlier examples of sexism with Parker and Ash now become more central as examples of the breakdown of the equal rights promise and of the reaction of the working class against the new radicalization of the women's movement.

When Parker attempts to control Ripley by commanding she come back to face him and answer his complaints in the engine room, she ignores him, turning only as she is leaving to say: "Why don't you just fuck off," her words blurred by engine room noise. Then she adds a parting gibe: "I'll be on the bridge if you need me." She confronts Parker's sense of sexual superiority, which is continually frustrated by Ripley self-assurance as an officer. In the year the film was released, Catherine MacKinnon wrote that "Economic power is to sexual harassment as physical force is to rape" (Tobias 1997, 114). Parker's rage over economic inequality has sexual overtones and seems at times to border on physical violence. It may be that this loss of power triggers a violence only partially veiled in his threats and crude sexual innuendoes, as when he jokes about cuntilinguism with Lambert over the group dinner table.

Parker here represents not only the film industry's awareness of the need for racial equality, but also problems associated with the radical feminists' prioritizing gender over race. Critics like James Kavanagh see Ripley's and Parker's mutual efforts against the alien as an indication of the social commonwealth of women's liberation and the working classes. Kavanagh finds minorities at the time struggling to overcome a hegemonic system represented by the computer "Mother" (1990, 77). But the deeper sexual tensions preclude any kind of true sympathy between Parker and Ripley even in the final crisis, a point supported by segments cut from the film where Parker "talks to Brett about his desire to do violence to Ripley" (Kaveney 2005, 135). More to the point, Parker's role simply diminishes after Dallas' death when Ripley finally takes charge. Parker's early role, then, is in direct opposition to Ripley as feminist, aggravated by the fact that his call for wage equity is simply dismissed by her. If the women's movement initially sought to incorporate Marxist ideology from the New Left, it ultimately rejected it in favour of a purely gender-based argument (Roth 2004, 200-205). As Echols points out:

> radical feminists' tendency to subordinate class and race to gender and to speak hyperbolically about a universal sisterhood was in large measure a reaction to the left's penchant for privileging class and race over gender. (1989, 10)

Parker stands out in contrast to Ripley, who maintains her authority specifically in relationship to the ship's hierarchies. It is also apparent that he reacts not so much to authority as to *female authority*, a threat to the last domain of power accessible to him, sexual power. Ripley refuses this, along with his criticisms of the class and wage structure, because her authority is dependent on a system that has, officially at least, been blind to gender. She shows no sympathy with his working class demands, and even ignores his initial complaints. The movement feminists, Echols suggests, were often only "anti-capitalist" by early association with the New Left; radical feminists, on the other hand, "dismissed economic class struggle as 'male' and, therefore, irrelevant to women" (1989, 6-7), and it never became a priority (Richardson 1996, 147).

But Parker also fits another stereotype of the times, and one that plays into the film's sexual tensions. As Shulamith Firestone characterizes the situation with men in the Black Power movement in the 70s by suggesting that black women were:

> merely a buttress for his own (masculine) self-image. The same old trick in revolutionary guise: the male defining himself negatively as man-strong by distinguishing himself from women-weak, through his control of her... achieving a false sense of manhood (power) through domination of all females in his vicinity. (Crow 2000, 440)

The gender domination, the frustrated struggle for male authority, and the working class overtones of the revolutionary struggle are all elements in the make-up of Parker's character. Here, by focusing almost exclusively on Ripley's feminism, many early critics of the film missed the racial stereotype in Parker's character. It appears again in his final display of heroics in stepping between Lambert and the alien in an act of self-sacrifice. Dallas earlier hints that Parker's heroics have been a problem in the past, and he warns him against rash actions. The maleness of Parker's self-image is important, and can be seen at times in his dominance over Lambert (almost as if in retaliation for Ripley's denial of this authority). Ripley prioritizes her own gendered power by refusing Parker's claims to economic equality or sexual authority. She intentionally ignores both race and working class arguments, much as the "White feminists" of the time would, whose

> universalist ideas about the nature of gender oppression grew out of further attempts to argue against others who saw feminism as disruptive and diversionary to radical politics. (Roth 2004, 194)

Ash's threat to her authority is different, although still gender based. He ignores her authority when he opens the air lock explicitly against her command when she would have the infected Kane and landing party go through proper quarantine. Ripley later makes her command role explicit to him, and yet it is clear that Ash's actions are guided not only by his desire to retrieve the alien for the Company, but by his distinct dislike for Ripley *as a woman*. Audiences become aware of Ash's sexism, even as they do of the crew's. At times, Ripley and Ash appear to be competing for Dallas's attentions with Ash taking the side of science and playing up aspects of male bonding as they share a fascination with the nature of the alien, and Ripley by her demands that Dallas recognize the legitimacy of her position as officer and equal. When compared with Ash's obsequious behaviour around Dallas, whose command he questions but never refutes, with Ripley he feigns a concern for Kane's well being, dropping all pretence to scientific protocol. Interestingly, where most critics find Ripley a little inhumane in her strict adherence to protocol at the risk of Kane's life (Kavanagh 1990, 79), few have seen that Ash tries to manipulate Ripley by appealing to her humanity, the "traditional realms" of female understanding. This moment, however, initiates the conflict that will end with Ash's attack on her, and his own exposure as android.

Feminists of the day would recognize their own struggle for equal rights in Ripley's dealings with Parker, Ash, and Dallas, as well as identifying the forces that gave rise to radicalization. Even as Ripley ultimately becomes conscious of the truth of her difference, a faction of women in the movement were realizing what critics Rowland and Klein see as a crucial realization: "Patriarchy is the oppressing *structure* of male domination," and "'emancipation' or 'equality' on male terms is not enough" (1996, 11-12). Involvement with the New Left had shown that all conditions of oppression are systemic, not local. By the early 1970s, Radical Feminism was talking about a totally new kind of society in ways that frightened the more conservative elements in both male and female segments of the culture. But the radical element was also aware that you cannot fight the system from within. As Maren Lockwood Carden suggests:

> In identifying one's interests with those of any power class, one thereby maintains the position of that class. As long as any class system is left standing, it stands on the back of women. (Rowland and Klein 1996, 12)

This growing realization of failure, and the perpetuation of traditional standards, was a turning point. The more the social system proved incapable of accommodating ideas of independence, the more women refused to work strictly within the realm of the equal rights agenda.

Underlying the feminist Ripley, however, are even more basic problems of the male construction of her gender. *Alien's* director, screenwriters and producers—all male—were not simply engaging but reacting to the same ideological shifts in the popular image of feminism described above. In particular, director Ridley Scott, and producers David Giler and Walter Hill, both also secondary screenwriters, were obviously taken with the new, more militant feminist image. Yet these male ideas about feminism are the heart of the problem. Their shared understanding of women's liberation tends toward stereotypes, and their designs seem based on popular, often adverse, responses to Radical Feminism. Their choice of a woman to play the part of Ripley and the focus on her final independence seems to have been a late decision in the film's evolution. According to David McIntee, whose insightful work, *Beautiful Monsters: The Unofficial and Unauthorised Guide to the Alien and Predator Films*, provides a detailed film history, Giler and Hill, in their revisions to Dan O'Bannon's original screenplay, added elements of anti-capitalist and anti-corporate themes (2005, 25-6). But these contrast starkly with Ripley's early insistence on official protocol and her officer status. With their promotion of Ripley as an equal rights crusader, Scott and the others may have hoped to gain sympathy for their hero among female audiences. And yet by aligning her with the officer class they also confuse the nature of her Radical Feminism. The sense of her as a simple reformist seems to be supported by the fact that the role was initially written as a standard sci-fi character type; she was to be the one who questions authority and runs contrary to general accepted opinions (but who inevitably is proven right). Such rebel figures were important to audience identification; the hero's difference is based on insights into the dangers that audiences are sensing (McIntee 2005, 25-7).

In addition, Ripley's role was originally conceived and written by Dan O'Bannon as unisex, and called "Roby." Unisex, of course, meant "male" in screenwriting jargon from the era, and so was initially constructed without any traditional female qualities. "Shussett has admitted that they both thought of the characters as all-male, and just felt that the option of using women would make it more marketable"; and the original script itself reads: "The crew is unisex and all parts are interchangeable for men or women" (McIntee 2005, 22). When her gender was changed by Giler and Hill in their revisions to the script, they have her retain most of the standard character's rebellious assertiveness (McIntee 2005, 25). Ripley begins as outsider, but in part only because the others in the crew are neglectful of their duties and casual about their concerns with the mission. That is, other than Kane, who is quick, alert, and overeager about all things scientific, but he dies first and leaves no one but the robot, Ash, to see the true consequences of the alien's presence onboard ship. This is a horror film, after all, and it must be remembered that suspense is built by having the audience sense what those in the film do not seem to know. Yet Ripley's identity gets mixed in with this, and as filmmakers began to see the uniqueness and marketability of a female protagonist (but also of a women with an attitude), it becomes clear they added her perspective *as a woman* to the standardized anticipation that she will be the sole survivor.

Sigourney Weaver's interpretation of the role goes beyond even the final shooting script in ways that suggest her own participation in feminizing Ripley, but also her sometimes conflicted sense of her role.[1] The film is a complex interaction of artistic forces, and not simply the "product of masculine discourse," as some have suggested (Gallardo and Smith 2004, 3). Scott appears to have been caught off guard at times in interviews by the feminist question, so his comments give us insights into the popular notion of feminism at the time: "My film has strong women simply because I like strong women," he says:

> It's a personal choice. I'm in no way a male chauvinist, nor do I understand female chauvinism—I just believe in the equality of men and women. It's as simple as that. (Knapp and Kulas 2005, 48)

Scott's "female chauvinism" may reflect the popular idea of the Radical Feminists as "anti-male" because of their separatist demands. But it is also obvious that the feminism discussed by the filmmakers was tempered by the early feminist criticisms of it.

It is on the point of equal rights that critics seem to have mostly condemned Ripley's role initially. Robin Wood, for instance, writing in the 70s, finds Ripley's feminism simplistic, a reduction of complex issues to clichés. The film, he complains, does not live up to its own expectations:

> What it offers on this level amounts in fact to no more than a 'pop' feminism that reduces the whole involved question of sexual difference and thousands of years of patriarchal oppression to the bright suggestion that a woman can do anything a man can do (almost). (1985, 218-219)

---

[1] Cf. Walter Hill and David Giler, "Alien" Final Shooting Script. 1978. http://www.dailyscript.com/scripts/alien_shooting.html.

Similarly, Judith Newton sees that:

> what *Alien* offers on one level, and to a white, middle-class audience, is a
> utopian fantasy of women's liberation, a fantasy of economic and social
> equality, friendship, and collectivity between women and men. (1990, 84)

But both these critics read Ripley through what Sheila Tobias calls the
"role equity" phase of the movement, and would perhaps condemn Ripley
specifically for the failures of the movement to achieve more (1997, 96).

Then too, Ripley's destruction of the ship and the Company's
investment may also reflect filmmakers' and audiences' anxieties about a
decade or more of feminist activism (Taubin 1993, 94). As Newton points
out,

> anxieties, aroused by the film's specific fantasy of a redeeming female hero
> and by its more general feminist and utopian content, must be seen as a
> response to feminism as a collective force, as a force disruptive of
> traditional gender roles. (1990, 84)

Whether Scott and others were aware of the radical difference in her
destruction of the Nostromo seems, at times, unclear. But it fits the later
Final Girl scenarios where the last woman alive manages to escape the
monster alone (Kanevey 2005, 131).

Ripley's Contradictions

Ripley continues to be read by critics either in terms of equality
politics or later liberation politics and rarely as a woman undergoing a
process of her own radicalization. It's clear that she realizes the mistake of
playing by men's rules, and yet reaffirms what Shelia Tobias says were the
concerns "that only women who are 'similarly structured' to men—that is,
career- and power-oriented women—would succeed when external
barriers were removed" (1997, 212). At the moment that Ripley decides to
destroy the Nostromo, the very symbol of the patriarchal order that has
betrayed her, she has moved well beyond the role of Company woman.
Yet she remains a controversial figure, in part because even these
independent actions conflict with certain underlying stereotypes of gender
and genre.

Early horror films, known for their sexual victimization of women, use
the female body as a ciborium of innocence and vulnerability (Clover
1993, 76-7; 134). These features in *Alien* complicate feminists' readings of
the film. On the one hand, instances of sexuality in the film are so muted

as to be ambivalent, even though originally there were nudity and explicit sex scenes outlined in the storyboards and unused footage. We might consider how audiences' perceptions of Ripley would change if they were to see, for instance, her sexual liaison with Dallas, or hear her discuss with Lambert the idea of sex with Ash (McIntee 2005, 26). Her independence, and isolation, are certainly enhanced by the absence of such elements. The nudity that is not there in the final production was a prominent aspect of the early film's design (Peary 1984, 162). These elisions go so far as to cause Robin Wood to comment that "The film constructs a new 'normality' in which sexual differentiation ceases to have effective existence—on condition that sexuality be obliterated altogether" (1985, 219). They, of course, reinforce Ripley's autonomy at the same time, and mute questions of sexuality that were even then becoming part of feminism's internal debates.

Ripley's feminism might also be seen as compromised by H.R. Giger's bio-erotic set designs and alien models. Giger's psychosexual fantasies translate at one point into two quasi-vaginal openings through which the crew must climb to reach the derelict ship. The alien itself is not only phallic-jawed, with a toothed phallus projecting from within its mouth, but it uses its tail as a phallic weapon. This latter particularly in the scene with Lambert where it wraps itself around her leg and climbs slowly up between her thighs. The early sexual content included a graphic rape scene that did not finally make it beyond the storyboards (*Movie Mistakes*). Giger's design for the newborn alien that emerges from Kane's chest is what he has called "a baby dinosaur" (McIntee 2005, 31), but what others have referred to as a *penis dentata* and a "little-dick-with-teeth" (Ambrogio 1983, 174; Taubin 1993, 94). With the *egg* shaped larva and the birthing through the chest, these images create a host of possible sexual threats in the film. It is against this that Ripley must establish her gender identity. The problem is that these sexual images are not simply contrasts, but exaggerated horror/sci-fi elements borrowed from earlier exploitation films, and establish a register of retrograde sexual signifiers that simply identify the filmmakers' attraction to somewhat over-determined psychosexual effects.

The conspicuous absence of sex among crew members also plays into Ripley's isolation and independence. Scott decided against earlier planned romantic liaisons because he feared they would prove divisive to the crew's identity (Knapp and Kulas 2005, 19). Ironically, critics have pointed out how selfish and dysfunctional the crew appears (Ambrogio 1986, 171). "It is a mark of 1970s cynicism and despair, perhaps," Newton states, "that Ripley saves only her own humanity" (1990, 84). Without romance, Ripley's intellectual side is allowed to blossom, and the psychosexual imagery becomes more of a threat to her autonomy. The alien's phallic bio-weaponry makes it an ideal monster in a film about a feminist hero, and as the Company's prize, it joins the patriarchal order as its primary sexual symbol.

Of course the key sexual reference in *Alien* is Ash's attempted oral rape of Ripley. He attacks her with a rolled up girlie magazine in a cubical where the walls are covered with nude pin-ups. If anything, the message is a bit over-determined. Many have been attracted to the idea of the robotics and rape, but the primary image is certainly the phallic power of the patriarchy, of which Ash proves to be a mechanical representation. If over-determined, the scene supports Ridley Scott's attempts to play into male sexual fantasies. And even as a common horror film directive, the scene puts into question the idea of the film's feminist criteria. The fact that Ash, the sexless android,[2] is decapitated, and then speared (penetrated?) by Lambert with one of the electrical prods they have used to hunt the alien supports the later images of a more militant feminism. Ash's impotence as an android, however, suggests Ripley's sexual identity is never really threatened, a point that Scott makes clear in interview (McIntee 2005, 26). What is significant in this scene is its obvious effort to make Ripley vulnerable to the horror film's monster; but the monster here is no longer the alien, it is Ash, an extension of the Company.

This rape scene helps emphasize Ripley's transformation from Company woman to Radical Feminist. It is specifically here that Kanevey reads *Alien* as feminist "in its anxieties that a woman like Ripley, who passes as equal in a male-arranged world, will always be at risk of being betrayed or threatened" (2005, 138). The confused sexual symbolism elsewhere works to support the notion that the film was never conceived as a feminist statement of any kind. In truth, female sexuality, inside and outside the movement, was only becoming a critical issue at this precise moment in the society.

Feminist concerns with sexuality included new battle fronts in the areas of rape and pornography, going public with debates on the issues in the early 1970s (Tobias 1997, 112). That feminism was concerned with exactly the kind of exploitation that the film represents seems ironic, but understandable. As a sci-fi/horror film, *Alien* has been read in feminist terms through Ripley's character, but it fails to represent a feminist text as such, except by dangerous omission. Symbols of sexual violence in the

---

[2] Although the film does not concern itself directly with Ash's sex life, it has been the source of lengthy conjectures about the nature of android impotence. See specifically Gallardo and Smith 2004, 50-52.

film suggest that the filmmakers were exploiting sexual imagery common to the horror film genre. A scene mentioned earlier which was cut, has Lambert graphically sodomized by the alien and dangling naked from a set of chains. All that remains in the film is a brief glimpse of her naked leg. If pornography and the problem of rape were major concerns for the movement in the 1970s, they were not universally condemned as yet (Tobias 1997, 183). Although "some early radical feminists contended that pornography caused violence against women" (Echols 1989, 288), and Margaret Atwood even argued more explicitly that it led directly to sexual violence (Tobias 1997, 185), what was new was that feminists were seeing that pornography was directly related to male dominance (Echols 1989, 288). This, of course, is exactly how the threat in *Alien* is manifest. The movement, however, continued to be split over its own anti-pornography position due to the problem of free speech (Berkeley 1999, 70). To argue Ripley's victory over the phallic forces seems anachronistic at best, for the common horror film tactic of exploiting female vulnerability was more likely the objective.

Echols sees pornography in film as a backlash against feminism at this time, and as:

> a reaction to the sexual revolution which increased women's sense of sexual vulnerability by acknowledging women's right to sexual pleasure while ignoring the risks associated with sexual exploration for women. (1989, 289)

But it is also not coincidental," she argues, "that the anti-pornography movement began in the late 70s, a period of intense backlash against feminism" (1989, 289). The exploitation of rape in the film may indeed symbolize the film's strongest anti-feminist position, but it reflects a more general confusion of sexual identities in the society. Men in particular were struggling with the dissolution of traditional sexual roles. The fact that the two planned rapes in the film are carried out by an automaton and an alien goes to support not only the traditional ideas of sexual dominance, but also those of victimization. Marsha McCreadie even argues that the backlash within the film industry against the liberties women had enjoyed in film earlier in the decade may take the form of reactionary re-casting and use of rape to suggest the consequences to women who go too far with their self-defining sexual politics (1990, 15). It must be remembered that many of these radical feminist concerns were only now becoming strategic issues. Winifred Wandersee makes it clear:

The slogan 'the personal is political'.... could well describe the whole decade of the seventies as much as the women's movement itself. Issues that were previously ignored or evaded—including sexual relations, sexual harassment on the job, child abuse, incest, wife battering, rape, and pornography—became public policy issues in the seventies and eighties. (1988, xvi)

The complexity of women's views on feminism at the time is reflected in the casting of roles for the film as well. Sigourney Weaver originally wanted to play Lambert, which she saw as the most interesting character; Veronica Cartwright, with more acuity perhaps, wanted to play Ripley, and only found out she would not the day she arrived on the set to start shooting (McIntee 2005, 29-30; Peary 1984, 159). So it seems Weaver had no real sense of the film's feminist potential before filming. Cartwright only agreed to play Lambert when Scott convinced her she would be the "audience identification character" as a victim, something that says a good deal about his thinking on feminism at the time (McIntee 2005, 30).

Conclusion: The Undressing of Ripley

Ripley's Radical Feminism may only emerge with her decision to destroy the Nostromo. But it is affirmed by our sense of the failures among the male crew: Dallas panics in his final moments in the cramped air duct; Kane falls prey to his own boyish eagerness to discover what's in the egg; Parker *plays the hero* ineffectually; and Ash simply proves himself the primary enemy. Ripley's rise to power can now be read as the result of the demise of male officers. With Dallas' death, she is left in command, but does not have the time to gain the respect of those beneath her because Parker and Lambert are dead within moments. Dallas' death may threaten Parker's own sense of social order as well. With his last attempt to complain, Ripley raises her voice and cuts him off: "Will you just shut up and listen." He acquiesces, and whether audiences realize it or not, this is a strategic change in his character; his role as spoiler and sexist immediately seems to dissipate.

Earlier, with the death of Dallas, Ripley has gained access to Mother. But when she reads the new primary directive that the crew are "expendable," Ash is suddenly behind her. In frustration, she pushes him up against the wall. It marks a rare moment of lost composure for her, but also a physical expression of her anger at the betrayal. We read in this the fatal moment of system failure, and with it Ripley is forced to recognize her own complicity. Her plan now? To blow up the ship with the alien in it. Alert audiences notice that this is an exact verbal echo of Lambert's suggestion disparaged by everyone earlier. Yet, Lambert remains the victimized female character.

Ripley's decision to destroy the Company's nefarious desires for a new bio-weaponry represents her awareness of the failure of equality feminism. It is clear that playing by the rules will not suffice. The social order, its patriarchal intransience, and the blind scientific devaluation of human life—a point Ash makes plain in his final praise of the alien as the "perfect organism," devoid of human morality—are the truths of the corporate/ scientific world. When Ripley restates Lambert's call to abandon the ship, she sides for the first time with the only other women in the crew. But it's that Ripley's character changes dramatically; rather, she realizes if the system will not support her best efforts, she must support herself. Her betrayal by the Company is revelatory.

Initially, feminists were unsure of the *radical* appellative, for fear the New Left would not take them seriously; it becomes prominent only in the 1970s (Crow 2000, 2). But many were already sure about the nature of the changes necessary to sustain the movement. The new consciousness could really be called nothing short of radical. In "The Bitch Manifesto" (1970), Joreen Freeman declares that women who accept the label "Bitch" ("The name is not an acronym"), possess a number of traits that Ripley displays, and which the public would identify with Radical Feminism: "aggressive, assertive, strong-minded, competent, ambitious, loud, brash, strong" (Koedt and Levine 1973, 50). Ripley finally shows an attitude that fits her times, even if critics like Wood complain about "the film's myth of the 'emancipated woman': 'masculine', aggressive, self-assertive" (1985, 219). In the end, the contradictions may be more about historical changes than critical perspectives.

Ripley's destruction of the ship signals her revolutionary stance on the rights of women. It suggests the anti-corporate theme of the film added by Hill and Giler. She reflects a current need to "construct alternate selves that are independent and self-assertive" and "to develop a new dialectic of sex class—an analysis of the way in which sexual identity and institutions reinforce one another" (Berkeley 1999, 166). Ripley's final isolation, her survival alone, suggests the difficulties Radical Feminism experienced by the mid decade.

The final scene of the film, often called Ripley's "striptease," compromises her feminist role again for many. She strips down to her underwear in preparation for hyper-sleep, the alien (and the audience) watching from the wings. The voyeurism of the scene runs contrary to most feminist readings, but not all: "In becoming a woman at the level of the narrative, Ripley is clearly marked as a victim," Vivian Sobchack writes,

> however, in becoming a woman as a fleshy representation of biological difference, Ripley takes on the concrete configuration of male need, demand, desire and fear, and she commands power at a deeper level of the film than that of its story. (1990, 106-7)

Again, this suggests that sexuality can be contextualized in the film in two ways, and that what we have read as the victimization of women has also been seen as the source of their power. Yet it is clear that the scene does more to exploit Weaver's body than it does to strengthen our sense of her independence. Both Weaver and Scott saw the scene as an act of sexual enticement (Peary 1984, 162). Weaver for its voyeuristic aspects, and Scott for its sense of Ripley's vulnerability. Their views embody that persistent contradiction in the film's feminism, addressed again by McCreadie when she argues that films were slow to catch up with Second Wave feminism:

> though political and social events of the late 1960s and early 1970s encouraged independence and autonomy for women, paradoxically women's parts in movies were reactionary or even retrograde. (1990, 2-3)

With a growing awareness of "the feminist superwoman who was beginning to be able to have, and do, it all," McCreadie still finds that "women's images in films lagged languorously behind" (1990, 2-3). In *Alien*, Ripley survives her own victimization to become a reflection of the radical feminist hero. Yet the film presents that hero only through the exploitation of popular notions of feminism, and falls repeatedly back into the sexist standards of the horror film genre. McCreadie could well be characterizing the contradictions we have found in *Alien* itself when she states that late 70s films generally "give mixed messages, ideas that in turn reflect society's confusion over male-female roles, and the position of women in general" (1990, 149). It may be these same contradictions that single out Ripley as a prototype of the new female hero at the very moment of that radical struggle in feminist history.

References

Alien quadrilogy. 2003. Twentieth Century Fox Home Entertainment, Inc. Includes Interviews and Commentary. DVD Box Set 2009847, 2003. ASIN: B0000VCZK2. Beverly Hill.

Ambrogio, A. 1986. *Alien*: In space, no one can hear your primal scream. In *Eros in the mind's eye: Sexuality and the fantastic in art and film*, ed. D. Palumbo, 169-179. Contributions to the study of science fiction and fantasy, Number 21. New York: Greenwood Press.

Bell, D. and K. Renate, eds. 1996. *Radically speaking: Feminism reclaimed*. Melbourne: Spinifex Press.

Carden, M. L. 1977. *Feminism in the mid-1970s: The non-establishment, the establishment, and the future*. A report to the Ford Foundation. New York: The Ford Foundation.

Clover, C. J. 1993. High and low: The transformation of the rape-revenge movie. In *Women and film: A sight and sound reader*, eds. P. Cook and P. Dood, 76-85. Philadelphia: Temple University Press.

Creed, B. 1996. Horror and the monstrous feminine: An imaginary abjection. In *The dread of difference: Gender and the horror film*, ed. B. Keith Grant, 35-65. Austin: University of Texas Press.

Crow, B. 2000. *Radical feminism: A documentary reader*. New York: New York U Press.

Echols, A. 1989. *Daring to be bad: Radical feminism in America, 1967-1975*. Minneapolis: University of Minnesota Press.

Firestone, S. 2000. Racism: The sexism of the family of man. In *Radical feminism: A documentary reader*, ed. B. Crow, 430-442. New York: New York University Press.

Gallardo-C, X. and C. J. Smith. 2004. *Alien woman: The making of Lt. Ellen Ripley*. New York: Continuum.

Greenberg, H. R. 1991. Reimagining the gargoyle: Psychoanalytic notes on *Alien*. In *Close encounters: Film, feminism, and science fiction*, ed. C. Penley, E. Lyon, L. Spigel, and J. Bergstrom, 83-104. Minneapolis: University of Minnesota Press.

Hill, W. and D. Giler. 1978. "Alien" final shooting script. http://www.dailyscript.com/scripts/alien_shooting.html.

Kavanagh, James H. 1990. Feminism, humanism and science in *Alien*. In *Alien zone: Cultural theory and contemporary science fiction cinema*, ed. A. Kuhn, 73-81, New York: Verso.

Kanevey, R. 2005. *From Alien to The Matrix: Reading science fiction film*. New York: I.B. Tauris.

Knapp, L. F. and A. F. Kulas. 2005. *Ridley Scott interviews*. Jackson: University Press of Mississippi.

Koedt, A., E. Levine, and A. Rapone. 1973. *Radical feminism*. New York: Quadrangle.

McCreadie, M. 1990. *The casting couch and other front row seats; Women in films of the 1970s and 1980s*. New York: Praeger.

McIntee, D. 2005. *Beautiful monsters: The unofficial and unauthorised guide to the* Alien *and* Predator *films*. Tolworth: Telos Publishing, Ltd.

Movie mistakes: Open your eyes. http://www.moviemistakes.com/film37/trivia. (Accessed February 24, 2007).

Newton, J. 1990. Feminism and Anxiety in *Alien*. In *Alien zone: Cultural theory and contemporary science fiction cinema*, ed. A. Kuhn, 82-87. New York: Verso.

O'Bannon, D. and S. Ronald. 1976. Alien script. http://www.dailyscript.com/scripts/alien_early.html

Peary, D. 1984. Playing Ripley in *Alien*: An interview with Sigourney Weaver. In *Screen flights/screen fantasies: The future according to science fiction cinema*, ed. D. Peary, 154-166. New York: Doubleday.

Richardson, D. 1996. "Misguided, dangerous and wrong" on the maligning of radical feminism. In *Radically speaking: Feminism reclaimed*, eds. D. Bell and R. Klein, 143-154. Melbourne: Spinifex Press.

Roth, B. 2004. *Separate roads to feminism: Black, chicana, and white feminist movements in America's Second Wave*. Cambridge: Cambridge University Press.

Rowland, R. and K. Renate. 1996. Radical feminism: History, politics, action. In *Radically speaking: Feminism reclaimed*, eds. D. Bell and R. Klein, 9-36. North Melbourne: Spinifex Press.

Sobchack, V. 1990. The virginity of astronauts: Sex and the science fiction film. In *Alien zone: Cultural theory and contemporary science fiction cinema*, ed. A. Kuhn, 103-115. New York: Verso.

Taubin, A. 1993. The 'Alien' trilogy: From feminism to AIDS. In *Women and film: A sight and sound reader*, eds. P. Cook and P. Dood, 92-100. Philadelphia: Temple University Press.

Tobias, S. 1997. *Faces of feminism: An activist's reflections on the women's movement*. Boulder: Westview Press.

Wandersee, W. D. 1988. *On the move: American women in the 1970s*. Boston: Twane Publishers.

Wood, R. 1985. An introduction to the American horror film. In *Movies and methods II*, ed. B. Nichols, 195-219. Los Angeles: University of California Press.

CHAPTER TWO

REDRESSING RIPLEY:
DISTURBING THE FEMALE HERO

PETER WOOD

That the gendered body is performative suggests that it has no ontological status apart from the various acts which constitute its reality, and if that reality is fabricated as an interior essence, that very interiority is a function of a decidedly public and social discourse, the public regulation of fantasy through the surface politics of the body. (Butler 1990, 336)

Hudson: Hey Vasquez, you ever been mistaken for a man?
Vasquez: No. Have you? (Cameron 1999)

Introduction

For many activists and academics, Judith Butler's conception of gender provides a useful insight into the relationship between the subject's body and the social order through which the subject moves. Gender, according to this model, is both performed by the subject as well as performed upon the subject. As such, gender performance is a series of negotiations, but negotiations that are not necessarily always conducted between equals. When confronted by the regulation of what is deemed natural and proper gender performance, the subject is faced with a serious power imbalance. The "public and social discourse" and "the public regulation of fantasy" are able to refashion a performative act into an ontological status and thereby dictate, or, at the very least regulate, the "natural" state of being female or male (Butler 1990, 336).

For many outside of feminism or various humanities programs at the university level, however, gender remains an ontological fact. Gender is not performance, gender simply is. The difference between performance and ontological status is not merely academic, however, and effects very real political, social, and legal structures that operate upon the bodies of very real individuals. For example, in 2006 attempts were made to enact a near-total ban on abortions in South Dakota and in 2008, twelve states considered near-total abortion ban laws (NARAL 2009). How are these laws related to gender as ontological fact? The South Dakota law reads, in part,

> to fully protect the rights, interests, and health of the pregnant mother, the rights, interest, and life of her unborn child, and the mother's fundamental natural intrinsic right to a relationship with her child, abortions in South Dakota should be prohibited. (Findlaw 2009)

There are several points of interest in this language. First, the woman is defined solely as a mother, even before she gives birth. She is not the pregnant woman, but "the pregnant mother." Furthermore, not only does a pregnant woman become, naturally, a mother, but also she has a "fundamental natural intrinsic right" to a relationship that does not, as yet, exist.

This example of verbal stacking—fundamental and natural and intrinsic and a right—indicates an almost pathological need to reinforce the connection between a woman and motherhood. To properly be a pregnant female is to be, ipso facto, a mother. Furthermore, a pregnant woman's interests are only served by becoming the mother that she was always, fundamentally, naturally, and intrinsically, meant to be. Perhaps there are fundamental, natural, and intrinsic reasons why there are only seventeen women serving on the U.S. Senate or two women serving on the Supreme Court in the fall of 2009 when the population of the United States is estimated to be 53% female (CIA 2009). Maybe there are fundamental, natural, and intrinsic reasons why women in 2008, on average, made 22.9% less than men in median annual income (Institute for Women's Policy Research 2009).

Abortion rights, women's access to higher government offices, and equal pay for equal work are not separate or disparate instances of sexism. Rather, these instances, along with a distressingly large number of others, can be seen as the tangible manifestation of a dominant ideology that still values male superiority and sees gender differences as rooted within intrinsic sexual differences. Judith Butler, along with many other feminists, suggests that the analysis of gender politics, performance, and presentation must be wary of such ontological claims as fundamental, natural, and intrinsic. As she reminds us in the opening quotation, there is an intimate and troubled connection between social discourse, fantasies of the body, and the ways in which the performance of gender is dressed up in the garb of beingness (Butler 1990, 336).

Despite the gains achieved by feminism since the 1970s, and despite the increased agency that female characters exhibit in film and television, the female action hero can provide especially instructive examples of the deep entrenchment of gender norms. Precisely because there are characters like Ellen Ripley from the *Alien* movies and Sarah Connor from the *Terminator* franchise—women who are not only able to fight and kill, but who are also able to outthink many of their male counterparts—the female action hero provides a test case that allows us to examine how popular culture frames issues of gender performance and ontology. She allows a kind of long division that divides what it means to be female by what it means to be an action hero. The remainder of that calculation is often exactly those bits of gender construction that appear in the film as irreducible, natural, and intrinsic. The *Alien* film series is particularly fertile ground upon which to sow these questions because of its unique position in film history: a single female hero spanning four films, four directors (all male), at least six different writers (again, all male), and nearly twenty years. There literally is no other film series like it.

This paper argues that while Ellen Ripley is the undisputed hero of James Cameron's *Aliens*, the film also essentializes Ripley in ways that reinforce the fundamental, natural, and intrinsic connection between being female and having a lower social status than males, as well as the *fact* that being female means being, always already, a mother. Furthermore, the narrative and visual structures of *Aliens* map themselves surprisingly well to the theories of spectatorship that Laura Mulvey outlined in her 1975 essay, "Visual Pleasure and Narrative Cinema." I use the term surprisingly because, for many, Mulvey's initial conceptions are both dated and misconceived. My use of her work is not strictly about theories of spectatorship, and I would agree with those who have concerns about the mythical "male spectator." However, a return to her work is warranted because, despite Ripley's clear position as both protagonist and hero, many of the narrative and visual structures that Mulvey described are apparent within *Aliens*. Even if there is no singular, intrinsic, or uncomplicated male gaze in operation for actual spectators, the very fact that *Aliens* can be mapped so closely to Mulvey's theories indicates that the writing, directing, and editing choices are in service to a particular kind of male spectator.

Before addressing Mulvey, however, I will first examine how the film's fictional world operates to reify gender stereotypes that are all too real in our own. Focusing on several minor details, scenes, and shots, I will argue that the very insignificance of these examples is crucial to understanding how the film destabilises Ripley's heroic status. The choice to combine an ideological analysis with a more psychoanalytic analysis in the essay is deliberate. Both approaches provide various filters that reveal certain aspects of gender performance while obscuring others. By combining approaches I hope to demonstrate that *Aliens* uses a number of strategies to manage Ripley's heroism in such a way that ensures her return to a fundamental, natural role that reinforces a reactionary desire for traditional, heteronormative, and patriarchal social structures.

Secretions

> ... ideology is... an organic part of every social totality. It is as if human societies could not survive without these specific formations, these systems of representations (at various levels), their ideologies. Human societies secrete ideology as the very element and atmosphere indispensable to their historical respiration and life. (Althusser 1969, 232)

> Deitrich: Looks like some sort of secreted resin.
> Hicks: Yeah, but secreted from what? (Cameron 1999)

That ideology is "organic" to social structures is not, in itself, a bad thing, merely a realisation that there is no place from which to stand outside of ideology and, clear of all social influences, see some sort of transcendental *truth*. If the secretion of ideology is indispensable to human history, there is no doubt that certain types of specific ideologies leave very different kinds of resins in the hearts and minds of individual subjects, as well as upon individual bodies. The question "secreted from what," is vitally important when trying to understand cultural artefacts, be they newspapers, films, comic books, sermons, or popular music. *Aliens* is a perfect example of what Jean-Luc Comolli and Jean Narboni see as

> those films which are imbued through and through with the dominant ideology in pure and unadulterated form and give no indication that their makers were even aware of the fact. (1999, 755)

Nearly every scene secretes dominant ideologies about sex and gender disparities and the fundamental, natural, and intrinsic aspects of gender. Certainly, *Aliens* contains ironies and jokes about gender:

> Frost: Hey, sure wouldn't mind getting some more of that Arcturian poontang . . .
> Wierzbowski: The one that you had was a male.
> Frost (grinning): Doesn't matter when its Arcturian. (Cameron 1999)

Yet even in this seemingly gender-bending humour, the connection between phallic power and masculinity is assumed and possessing a poontang ensures a subordinate, if not submissive, position within social power structures. Of course, Ripley is, ultimately, more capable than the men within the film, and she is not submissive in any traditional way. However, as Sarah Lefanu reminds us, "women as protagonists do not necessarily interrogate the social and literary construction of women as gendered subjects" (1989, 24) Ripley, while smart and capable and heroic, is still constructed within a dominant model of gender constructions. The most obvious element of this dominant model is the construction of Ripley as a mother. As Ximena Gallardo C. and C. Jason Smith point out,

> the determined, career-oriented Lieutenant Ripley of *Alien* is shown to be a fake, a failed mother who in reality abandoned her young daughter to an orphan's life. (2004, 66-67)

Such a narrative move seems entirely in step with the culture of the mid-80s, and *Aliens* provides another example of the backlash against feminism during that time period. Presenting compelling evidence of a concerted cultural reaction against the increasing social and economic power of women, Susan Faludi points out that a "backlash against women's rights succeeds to the degree that it appears *not* to be political, that it appears not to be a struggle at all" (1991, xxii; emphasis in original). Thus, backlash, like ideology, operates below the surface, in the background, hidden from conscious view. Others have effectively demonstrated how Ripley's motherhood works to neutralize—or at the very least trouble—her heroism, and indeed, from a particular feminist standpoint, this redressing of Ripley in maternity clothes is a central problem with the film. What I want to examine in this section, however, are those moments of the film that lack the narrative focus of the film's preoccupation with motherhood, moments that blend into the background of the film, and that "appear... not to be a struggle at all." These are the ideological secretions that predispose the viewer of *Aliens* to accept a world in which a female hero is spectacular precisely because such a concept is an aberration.

Beginning with a traditional *Sleeping Beauty* shot, Ripley is revealed at the very beginning of the film as a passive object to be looked at. Her vulnerability is the keystone of this first scene, offering the spectator a comforting, at least in terms of gender structures, entrance to the film. The passivity of the scene is broken by a largely phallic machine that forces a hole in the hull and penetrates the darkness in preparation for the entrance of the salvage team. Of particular note here is that the salvage team is composed entirely of men, as if to indicate that space is both naturally and necessarily a male domain. Some might reply that this is such a short scene, and the salvage team so unimportant to the larger narrative, that assigning ideological content to this particular sequence is academic at best, ideologically motivated at worst. Of course, everything we write or say about a movie, everything a filmmaker writes or does in a movie, is always already within ideology. Therefore, the nature of the salvage team's sex is as ideologically motivated as my questioning of it.

Whereas Ridley Scott's *Alien* attempted to negate gender as a constitutive difference between people, Cameron's *Aliens*, creates a world in which gender divisions and differences appear to be the norm. In Scott's film, Ripley's world is one where a "woman's right to assume authority is not even an issue; authority and power are ceded to persons irrespective of sex" (Kavanagh 1990, 77). Cameron's film, however, creates a world of gender differences. In *Aliens*, women are simply not in positions of authority: Ripley's nurse is a woman, but her doctor is a man; the head of the inquest into Ripley's actions aboard the Nostromo is man; and so is the person in charge of the colony on LV-426. There are women in the Marines, but they do not assume positions of authority. Cameron's film presents a model of sexual disparity from the beginning, offering men more power and agency than women within the normal social order. This normal social order is presented long before Ripley assumes the mantle of "hero," and thus the resin of a particular ideology is allowed to harden and encase the narrative of the film, namely that the division of sexes is natural and intrinsically unequal. Only in extreme circumstances, such as protecting a little girl against a dangerous alien, is Ripley allowed to perform the function of a hero. Yet, because of the gender differences built into the world of *Aliens*, Ripley's status as a hero begins with a kind of gender deficit.

The fundamental difference between men and women that the film posits might explain the off-hand way in which Burke (Paul Reiser)—a stranger and representative of the corporation that is responsible for the events in the first film—refers to Ripley as "kiddo." He uses this diminutive in two early, but significant, scenes. The first is in the hospital when he tells Ripley that it has been fifty-seven years since she was in hypersleep, and Burke informs her that,

> it's really just blind luck that a deep salvage team found you when they did. One in a thousand, really. I think you're damn lucky to be alive, kiddo. (Cameron 1999)

In the second significant scene, Burke and Lieutenant Gorman (William Hope) try to convince Ripley to join the expedition to LV-429:

> Burke: What would you say if I told you I could get you reinstated as a flight officer. The Company has already agreed to pick up your contract.
> Ripley: If I go.
> Burke: If you go. Come on, that's a second chance kiddo. (Cameron 1999)

Less important than Burke's use of words and his condescending attitude—he is, after all, a villain—is the fact that at no point does Ripley become offended or irritated by such a diminutive. In fact, she doesn't seem to register Burke's condescending nature in these scenes, nor, I would suggest, do most viewers. Burke's choice of words can be explained away by the idea that he is being empathetic, trying to put her at ease, or that, as the face of the Wutani Corporation, he is patronising in order to remind Ripley of the power he wields. Again, the problem is less that Burke calls a full-grown, skilled, and capable woman "kiddo," and more that Ripley herself seems entirely oblivious to such a patronising tone. While Ripley's similarities to Rambo have been noted by a number of critics and reviewers—indeed, James Cameron had only recently finished writing *Rambo II*, before working on *Aliens*—can we imagine the character of Colonel Troutman referring to Rambo as "kiddo?" I think not. By what right does a nearly complete stranger have to talk to Ripley as if she were a child?

Burke goes even further with his casual condescension when Ripley refuses Burke and Gorman's request and she becomes agitated and upset. Burke's response is to treat her as a child, saying simply, "ok ... shhh" (Cameron 1999). Here again, Ripley seems to take no note of his attitude toward her. Burke's casual intimacy reinforces notions of inherent male power to *care for* a woman rather than deal with her as an equal. While it is certainly possible to formulate any number of explanations as to how Burke is supposed to be a bit slimy and we are not supposed to trust him, these are simply *ex post facto* excuses. Patronising Ripley is accepted, even to the extent of being ignored, precisely because she is a woman. A male hero is a *hero* first and foremost, but Ripley remains, in Cameron's film, a woman first and foremost.

Perhaps it is her status as a woman that explains why Ripley, unasked and without comment, pours coffee for both Burke and Gorman as they try to convince her to accompany the Marines to LV-426. Here is a representative of the corporation that caused the death of her former crew, that took her pilot license from her, that basically threw her to the docks, and Ripley plays the traditional gender role flawlessly. That she offers sustenance to these men is not at all remarkable, just as a male hero not offering sustenance is equally unremarkable. For instance, there is a similar scene in *The Fifth Element* when Bruce Willis' character is also asked to go on a mission that he does not want to accept by people he does not trust. While he is indeed making coffee, he does not reflexively, one might say "naturally," offer it to his guests.

Later in the film, after Ripley has accepted the position as advisor to the mission investigating LV-426, she approaches Apone (Al Matthews) and Hicks (Michael Biehn) to help with preparations for going down to the planet:

> Ripley: Hi. I feel like a fifth wheel around here. Is there anything I can do?
> Apone: I don't know is there anything you can do?
> Ripley. Well, I can drive that loader. (Cameron 1999)

At this point, Apone and Hicks look at each other dubiously, forcing Ripley to further state that she "has a class 2 license" (Cameron 1999). After Ripley suits up in the powerloader and demonstrates her ability, the two men laugh heartily, as if they had just seen a talking dog or an especially talented child performing some sort of complicated trick. The film shows that Ripley must prove herself capable instead of being accepted as capable. Given that the Marines have a complement of seemingly competent women fighting side by side with the men, it seems odd that Apone and Hicks are so amazed and surprised by Ripley's capability to run loading machinery. Would a male hero elicit such amusement from Apone and Hicks simply because he can do a manual labour job? Only, I would suggest, if the hero was somehow feminized from the start.

The amusement and astonishment on the part of Apone and Hicks demonstrates that *Aliens* secretes a considerably different ideology than the first film. While there are those who see *Alien* as fundamentally flawed in feminist terms, the film's awareness of gender and sexual differences is far deeper and more complex than the sequel. I agree with Constance Penley's assertion that *Alien* is "a film that is (for the most part) stunningly egalitarian," while *Aliens* presents sexual difference as central to character identity (Penley 1990, 125). As I have shown, in scene after scene, ideologies that privilege male authority and that posit fundamental differences between men and women are rife throughout *Aliens*, despite the presence of a female hero as the protagonist.

Finally, before moving on to a more psychoanalytic examination, I want to suggest that the visual construction of the eponymous aliens as a female vagina further contributes to the creation of a world in which gender is naturalised as sexual difference. In both *Alien* and the Special Edition of *Aliens*, the viewer's first exposure to the alien body is in the form of the facehugger: a form that resembles a weird and terrifying mixture of spider and octopus. A disturbing shape to say the least, but one that is not sexualised or gendered in any obvious way. However, the second reveal of the alien is distinctly different in the two movies. In *Alien*, of course, this occurs in the famous chestburster scene when the embryonic and decidedly phallic creature births itself by pushing outwards through the body of Kane (John Hurt). Given how *Aliens* naturalises gender disparities based on sexual differences throughout the rest of the movie, it should come as no surprise that the monsters here are distinctly and decisively made to resemble female sexual organs. While not having the iconic stature of the chestburster scene in the first movie, the scene in the Medlab clearly links aliens with the female form.

In the scene, we see Burke approach one of the glass tanks that contains a chestburster floating in liquid. His mouth is open and his eyes are distant, as if he is at once entranced and repelled. Suddenly, the seemingly quiescent alien splays itself violently against the glass, inches from Burke's startled face. The image presented on the screen at that moment is clearly modelled on the human vagina. *Aliens* introduces the viewer to an alien that is obviously to be read as representative of female sexuality. So obvious is this image that one wonders how Tim Blackmore can claim, in reference to *Aliens*, that "when alien females appear in science fiction they are not immediately read as twisted versions of human women (Blackmore 1996, 220). Perhaps if the viewer's first introduction to the alien body was the alien queen, that argument might hold more weight. However, *Aliens* specifically represents human, female genitalia as a distinct stage in an alien's development. Granted, the image of alien-as-vagina lasts for only a second or two, but my contention throughout this section has been that these small moments, these brief and often unacknowledged sections of the film, secrete a sexist ideology that encases the film, the viewer, and Ripley in a world where biology determines gender and where gender determines social status. Beyond the extreme circumstances that allow Ripley to find her own heroism, the world of *Aliens* is one that offers women two options: lower social status or alien monster.

As Sheri LeFanu argues, feminist analysis depend "not on female characters as simple protagonists; but on the *how* and the *why* and *to what end*" (1989, 25; emphasis in original). To this I would add in what context. Does *Aliens* posit a strong female protagonist—a hero even? Yes. But if "the how and the why and to what end" reflect a deeply reactionary and patriarchal dressing up of Ripley as a bad mother to be redeemed only through reconstituting the nuclear family, the "in what context" forces Ripley's heroism into an ideological framework that continually makes *natural* exactly those social discourses and structures that Butler points to as performative. There is no intrinsic motivation for Ripley to offer coffee to Burke and Gorman, just as there is no natural reason for Hicks and Apone to assume Ripley is incapable. The residue of a patriarchal ideology sustains and permeates the world of *Aliens*, and Ripley's heroism comes out of this world. While the normal rules may be suspended on an alien planet while fighting aliens, Ripley's gender will be reconstituted within the "natural," human world at the end of the film. The relationship between Ripley and the gender politics of the world from which she emerges is just as important to the ideological impact of the film as is the notion of Ripley as the hero of the movie. The small moments I have discussed establish the "normal" relationships between men and women, male and female, subjects and objects. Additionally, by making the very form of the aliens reflect the human vagina, *Aliens* is unambiguously linking the female body with an organism to be feared and destroyed. These relationships create the conditions that encourage viewers to accept Ripley as a hero, but at the same time Ripley remains bounded by the strictures and gender rules of a sexist society, creating an equation that just doesn't add up.

(Dis)Solutions

> ... within our dominant fiction, the phallus/penis equation occupies absolute pride of place. Indeed, that equation is so central... that at those historical moments when the prototypical male subject is unable to recognize "himself" within its conjuration of masculine sufficiency, our society suffers from a profound sense of "ideological fatigue." (Silverman 1992, 16)

Silverman's "ideological fatigue" can be seen in the anti-feminist backlash of the 1980s, out of which, like a chestburster, comes *Aliens*. Often cited by fans as a sequel equal to or better than the original, *Aliens* is without question decidedly different from Ridley Scott's *Alien*. The *mis en scene*, the focus on action instead of horror, and the re-establishment of clear gender divisions—divisions that were, in many ways, dismantled in the first film—all work to provide a visual pleasure that is arguably less challenging, in terms of gender representation, than the first movie. The re-establishment of clear gender divisions based upon certain fundamental assumptions about biological sex is particularly important. Accepting that the "magic of the Hollywood style at its best... arose, not exclusively, but in one important aspect, from its skilled and satisfying manipulation of visual pleasure" and that "[u]nchallenged, mainstream film coded the erotic into the language of the dominant patriarchal order," it is easy to see that visual and narrative structures of *Aliens* reflects many of the mainstream film codes that Mulvey criticised in her essay "Visual Pleasure and Narrative Cinema" (1989, 16). Despite Ripley's presence as a female action hero, the pleasures of the film remain deeply entrenched in dominant patriarchal and sexist strategies that strive to reinforce the phallus/penis equation and that do so in an attempt to create a specific kind of viewing pleasure for a theoretical male spectator.[1]

At the centre of Mulvey's argument is the assertion that:

> The male unconscious has two avenues of escape from ... castration anxiety: preoccupation with the re-enactment of the original trauma (investigating the woman, demystifying her mystery), counterbalanced by the devaluation, punishment or saving of the guilty object... or else complete disavowal of castration by the substitution of a fetish object or turning the represented figure itself into a fetish so that it becomes reassuring rather than dangerous (hence overvaluation, the cult of the female star). (1989, 21)

By showing that *Aliens* does indeed follow these strategies, I suggest that it performs a kind of slight-of-hand: directing our attention to Ripley's heroic actions, but at the same time offering a series of vantage points from which to investigate, punish, and fetishize Ripley. Because the following arguments depend upon certain psychoanalytic concepts, a brief review of the terms phallus and castration anxiety may be helpful before moving on to the three strategies that Mulvey describes.

---

[1] In the years since Mulvey wrote "Visual Pleasure and Narrative Cinema," the concept of a male spectator has, quite deservedly, been questioned and, often, persuasively argued out of existence. In a recent article Clifford Manlove offers an overview of the literature that has taken Mulvey's work to task as well as offering a compelling argument that Mulvey may have fundamentally misunderstood some of the Lacanian theory upon which she based her theories. Despite this issues with Mulvey's work, the pleasures that she describes in "Visual Pleasure and Narrative Cinema" can been seen to exist in any number of mainstream movies. Even if one gives up the notion of a monolithic male spectator, Mulvey's analysis remains a powerful way to understand certain visual and narrative elements of even contemporary movies (Manlove 2007).

Concepts

The concepts of the phallus and of castration anxiety are central to the argument presented in this essay and it is vital to point out that the phallus does not equal, on a fundamentally biological level, the penis. For my purposes, "what concerns psychoanalytic theory is not the male genital organ in its biological reality but the role that this organ plays in fantasy" (Evans 1996, 140). More specifically, the role of the phallus can be seen, according to Jacques Lacan, as a "signifier that is destined to designate meaning effects as a whole" (2004, 275). Certainly, Lacan's formulation of the phallus as destined to do anything is problematic. However, Lacan helps us understand how the phallus structures meaning for a subject in ways far beyond biological anatomy. This is not to say that the penis is meaningless. Indeed, a central warrant to my argument is that

> 'exemplary' male subjectivity cannot be thought apart from ideology, not only because ideology holds out the mirror within which that subjectivity is constructed, but because the latter depends upon a kind of collective make-believe in the commensurability of penis and phallus. (Silverman 1992, 15)

The phallus, then, can be conceived of as both a psychic function as well as an ideological one and in both forms becomes a prop upon which masculinity itself depends. This conception allows us to understand that there is a great deal at stake in representations, both imaginary and ideological, of phallic mastery.

This understanding of the phallus helps clarify that castration anxiety—the anxiety at the heart of Mulvey's arguments—does not solely, or even primarily, "bear upon the penis as a real organ . . ." (Evans 1996, 22). Rather, this anxiety operates upon and through the phallus. If the phallus signifies meaning effects as a whole, and if the penis is misrecognized as the phallus, then castration anxiety represents something far more dangerous than the fear of having one's penis cut off: it represents the undoing of power, perhaps even the undoing of the self if that self is constructed through a masculinity dependant upon phallologocentrism. For Luce Irigaray, the danger to the male psyche lies in the idea that the female "sexual organ represents *the horror of nothing to see*" (1991a, 352; emphasis in original). This "nothing to see" is not simply the unseen, or a blind spot in vision, but represents a much greater threat to male subjectivity. Namely, the threat of nothing to see leads, for the male psyche, to a "defect in [the] systematics of representation and desire . . ." (1991a, 352). In her essay, "Another 'Cause'—Castration," Irigaray expands upon how this nothing represents a

> *hole* in men's signifying economy. A nothing that might cause the ultimate destruction, the splintering, the break in their systems of 'presence,' of 're-presentation' and 'representation.' A nothing threatening ... that *master signifier* whose law of functioning erases, rejects, denies the surging up, the resurgence, the recall of *heterogeneity* capable of reworking the principle of its authority. (1991b, 407; emphasis in original)

Castration anxiety is, in this formulation, inextricably linked to denying any threat to both presence and scopic control, both of which are threatened by the place of ultimate non-individuation and heterogeneity: the womb. The threat posed to a male spectator is the destruction of both the ego "I" and the scopic control of the seeing "eye"— for there can be no controlling gaze, no subjectivity if there is no discreet concept of either the ego or the body. Perhaps this is why Barbara Creed states that the "womb, even if represented negatively, is a greater threat than the mother's phallus" (1990, 139). In other words, the womb demonstrates the lie of the phallus by being a space within which the phallus dissolves. If the phallus means power and the penis means the phallus and male means penis, the dissolution of the phallus can lead to the dissolution of masculinity itself. The female body signifies an abyss that threatens to reveal just how flimsy the phallic prop is that signifies the masculine in a patriarchal ideology. The master signifier of the phallus hides the terrifying secret that its existence is always already staring into an abyss.

The classic film strategies outlined by Mulvey and in operation through *Aliens* are ways of keeping the abyss from staring back. By demonstrating that *Aliens* presents pleasure by investigating, punishing, and fetishizing the female body, I hope to raise questions about how Ripley is dressed up in a hero's clothes, only to be redressed in the costume of a woman who functions as a danger to male subjectivity.[2]

---

[2] These observations are, of course, a reference to Nietzsche's aphorism "Whoever fights monsters should see to it that in the process he does not become a monster. And when you look long into an abyss, the abyss also looks into you" (1989, 89). The definition of abyss as a "... deep, immeasurable space, gulf, or cavity" or "... the primal chaos before Creation," reflect Irigaray's concerns about nothingness and heterogeneity (Dictionary.com 2010).

"investigation"

Aliens presents a number of strategies to investigate and demystify Ripley throughout the film. My focus, however, will be on two particular sequences. The first is the battle that takes place in the processing station, in which the Marines first encounter the aliens as a particularly effective threat to both bodily integrity and scopic control. The second sequence occurs later in the film when Ripley—and the viewer—first encounters the alien queen. During this sequence, *Aliens* enacts a fantasy of phallic control over Irigaray's "nothingness" through the destruction of the queen's womblike nest.

After the Marines land on LV-426, they begin to search for the surviving colonists. As they enter the processing plant, the soldiers move from recognisably human architecture into distinctly alien structures that combine organic and metallic elements. Moving inward, their surroundings become more and more organic, wet, and dark. As noted earlier, Dietrich (Cynthia Dale Scott) comments that the walls covered with a kind of "secreted resin," and the metal walls are quickly replaced with mucous and sinew. Tim Blackmore, in his essay "Is This Going to be Another Bug-hunt," denies that the *mis en scene* signifies a womb, and claims instead that the corridors are only to be read as "an echo of the lethal and intricate tunnel systems established (particularly around Cu Chi) in Vietnam" (1996, 220). Without discounting the Vietnam parallels, it is difficult not to see the almost muscular walls as signifying the ultimate investigation of the woman and creating a fantasy incursion into the womb. Lydia Bundtzen provides a wonderful reading of this sequence when she describes the "band of Marines... with all their fire power and ejaculatory short bursts of guns" as "ineffectual and insignificant male gametes" (1987, 13). Her metaphor is further supported as the Marines come across the first of the colonists. Wedded to the walls by organic fibres and secretions, the woman seems like she is being dissolved within an organic structure. As basic anatomy reminds us, the

> main function of the uterus is to accept a fertilized ovum which becomes implanted into the endometrium... The fertilized ovum becomes an embryo, develops into a fetus and gestates until childbirth. (Wikipedia 2010)

Such a cycle is represented by the tunnels, slick with organic juices keeping the colonists alive as the embryos inside them develop and gestate. The male spectator is given ultimate (if illusory) investigatory powers and allowed inside the womb, thereby bringing the no-thing, the void, the womb into the realm of the eye/I. This void is also a very, very dangerous place. During the first attack by the aliens, the Marines cannot see, cannot fight effectively and the majority are killed. This sequence offers two points of particular note.

First, the Marines are seriously handicapped visually. Scopic control seems denied to them, even as they penetrate into the belly of the beast with any number of high-tech strategies for seeing. The womb, even as it is being investigated, resists the controlling, male gaze. Also of note is that during this sequence only three of the six deaths are explicitly shown to the spectator and two of those are through fire and acid—deaths that signify a melting away of the physical form, the dissolution of a coherent body as it dissolves into the womb of the mother. This first foray is thus a failed investigation, but one that lays the groundwork for the male spectator's control over the threat of castration and dissolution that takes place in the queen's nest.

Later in the film, when Ripley rescues Newt from the alien queen, the male spectator is invited to enact what Irigary sees as the desire "to force entry, to penetrate, to appropriate for himself the mystery of the womb" (1991a, 351). Not only is the structure of the alien queen's nest representative of a womb with its mucous and wet darkness, but the first image of the queen is not of her terrifying predatory and alien nature, but rather of an egg being deposited by a remarkably fallopian structure.[3] The camera then follows this structure slowly until the main body of the queen is revealed, along with her predatory double mouth and her insectoid, matriarchal alien nature. Though horrifying, she is seen and the mystery is solved: the nothing becomes something and that something is constructed as female, mother, and monstrous. The spectator is offered a fantasy of scopic control over the nothing that is signified by woman.

While Mulvey speaks of the voyeuristic impulse to investigate and demystify, *Aliens* goes further and provides a visual fantasy in which the threat of the womb is neutralised by Ripley's destruction of the queen and, more importantly, the queen's womb/nest. As Ripley threatens the eggs in the nest, the queen, as any protective mother might, pulls her forces back and allows Ripley safe passage to retreat. Ripley knows that there is shortly going to be a nuclear explosion that will, in all likelihood, destroy the aliens. Even if it did not, the orbiting spaceship has the capacity to destroy the planet with nuclear weapons. The sensible, intelligent, and

---

[3] This scene might also be read as an example of Freud's primal scene on a level much deeper than merely seeing (or imagining) parental sex. This is a primal scene on a cellular level and allows the spectator to fantasize control over the moment of conception.

tactical thing to do at this moment in the film would be for Ripley to leave the queen's nest with Newt as quickly as possible and with a minimum of conflict. This she does not do. Instead, she stands at the entrance to the nest destroying egg after egg with flames, bullets, and grenades. Not once does she attempt to kill the queen, instead opting to destroy the nest/womb and the queen's eggs in front of the queen, putting both herself and Newt in greater risk. Why is it important to show Ripley making an incredibly stupid tactical and highly emotional decision that will certainly enrage the queen, ensuring even more danger? One answer is that this sequence serves to fulfil the male spectator's ultimate fantasy of control. Thus, the spectator can enact a fantasy destruction of the "nothing" that threatens what Irigary calls "the process of production, reproduction, mastery, and profitability of meaning, dominated by the phallus" (1991b, 407).

Because the film carries out the investigation and destruction of the female by a female, it insulates the male spectator from any possible psychic unease or guilt associated with the investigation/destruction of the womb by having a woman stand in for the male (controlling) gaze. The film visually creates a fantasy of scopic power that allows the male spectator to go, in a sense, where no man has gone before. And then blow it all up.

"the guilty object"

Ripley: How many are there, how many colonists?
Van Leuwen: I don't know, sixty, maybe seventy families.
Ripley: Families. Jesus! (Cameron 1999)

A number of the film's critics have pointed out that the way in which *Aliens* privileges motherhood works against Ripley's heroic status. Gallardo and Smith argue that "Ripley's focus on family" allows her to play the hero, yet remain safely contained within heteronormative and patriarchal ideologies (2004, 97). Additionally, Amy Taubin sees the film as a "family-values picture for the Reagan 80s" as well as "the most politically conservative film of the series" (1993, 94). The importance of Ripley as a mother-figure, however, is also central to what Mulvey describes as the "devaluation, punishment, or saving of the guilty object" (1989, 21). A hero she may be, but Ripley is also constructed as the guilty object in ways that male heroes are rarely, if ever, constructed.

At every turn, *Aliens* works to punish Ripley for being a "bad mommy" while offering redemption in the form of a new family unit composed of Hicks and Newt. If the film's visuals show a fantasy of investigation, the film's narrative plays out a series of punishments for

Ripley's failure as a mother. The Special Edition of the film makes Ripley's role of failed mother explicit:

> Burke: Amanda Ripley Mclaren, married name, I guess. Age sixty-six and that was at the time of her death. Which was two years ago. I'm real sorry.
> Ripley: Amy…
> Burke: She was cremated and interred at West Lake Repository, Little Shoot, Wisconsin. No children.
> Ripley: I promised her I'd be home for her birthday. Her eleventh birthday. (Cameron 1999)

Unfortunately, as a working mother, Ripley didn't return in time for her daughter's birthday, and, in what may be an extreme version of an absentee mother, returns home after her daughter has already died at the age of sixty-six. Ripley's motherhood seems surprising when her character is considered in context of *Alien*. There is no evidence in Scott's film that Ripley had a child. Indeed, the idea flies in the face of scientific common sense. For a person (of either gender) whose job is on a deep range mining vessel and who spends a significant amount of time in cryogenic suspension and flying near the speed of light, it would be highly unlikely, if not impossible, to maintain parental relationships with someone on Earth because of time dilation.   While *Aliens* has been considered "unusually sophisticated in its use of sf [sic] tropes," the nature of space-time seems glaringly absent from the film's handling of story and character (Nicholls 1993, 19). This specific rewriting of Ripley as a working mother who abandoned her daughter makes complete sense as an inciting incident for the punishment of Ripley. Such a strategy enables the film to maintain a pretence of gender equality, but also ensures the right to punish the woman as a necessary and unifying narrative device.[4]

The film pushes the connection between Ripley's failure and the notion of family further when she asks Van Leuwen (Paul Maxwell)—the CEO responsible for the inquest into her destruction of the Nostromo in the first movie—how many colonists are on LV-426. His response is framed in

---

[4] One of the major outcomes of Albert Einstein's work is the understanding that time is not a constant. The faster "A" travels in relationship to "B," the greater the time difference. Both "A" and "B" experience time the same way, but in relation to each other, "A" will age more slowly than "B." The necessity for cryogenic suspension in both *Alien* and *Aliens* indicates that the crews are in space a very long time – possibly even years on each trip. The fact that the nearest star system to ours is 4.5 light years away, and that the Nostromo was obviously further out than that clearly indicates that Ripley and the crew would return to earth many years or even decades after they left.

terms of families rather than the number of people. Why frame the answer in numbers of families? It seems a very imprecise answer to the question. Are they nuclear families? Extended families? What makes the answer so appropriate within the context of *Aliens* is that it again connects Ripley to the role of mother—and a failed one at that. Not only did she fail her daughter and fail to take care of *her* crew, but she also fails, not the men and women, not the people, but specifically the families on the planet LV-426 by not convincing the corporation to take action. Furthermore, the answer of "sixty or seventy" families seems suspect in terms of the film's continuity because the Special Edition reveals that Hadley's Hope, the colony on LV-426, has a population—pre-alien invasion of course—of 170. Simple math demonstrates that this population is highly unlikely to support the number of families that Van Leuwen mentions. Framing the population in terms of families simply makes no sense in terms of realistic dialogue or film continuity. However, it makes perfect sense given the construction of Ripley as a failed maternal figure in need of punishment and redemption.

Immediately after the inquest sequence, the film cuts to the colony itself and reveals a group of children, part of those "sixty or seventy families," as they laugh and play in the corridors of the colonist's command centre. These scenes of happy children highlight Ripley's ineffectuality as a mother because the next scene, Newt's father falling victim to an alien facehugger, promises that all of these children will be killed shortly. If only Ripley had been more effective, the colony might have stood a chance in protecting themselves; however, she has failed to save sixty or seventy families, just as she failed her daughter.

After these scenes in which the spectator knows that most if not all of the colonists will be killed, Ripley is asked to go, as an advisor, with the Marines in order to investigate the planet. She refuses, once again failing as a mother. Ripley's value as a mother (and therefore as a woman) is demonstrated to be lacking because, even as Newt's screams of fear remain fresh in the mind of the spectator, Ripley refuses to help, and tells Burke and Gorman that she's "not going back out there" and that she "wouldn't be any good to them if she did" (Cameron 1999). Seconds later, however, she awakens from a nightmare and agrees to go to LV-426 as an advisor.

The ensuing nightmare of danger and violence constitutes a punishment that stems directly from her role as a working and failed mother. While Mulvey speaks of classic Hollywood texts as punishing or redeeming, *Aliens* uses the punishment as a tool to redeem. *Aliens* does not connect Ripley's punishment and redemption on an overt level, but the film's constant attention to the role of mothering intimates that her redemption is inextricably connected with her ability to assume the role of the *good* mother—which she does by protecting and saving Newt. Newt is roughly the age of Ripley's daughter when Ripley left Earth, and the film explicitly pairs the two as a mother and daughter. From the very beginning, and especially in relation to Newt, the film positions Ripley to be, *a priori*, a mother figure. As Constance Penley states with regard to *Aliens*, "mothers will be mothers, and they will always be women" (1990, 125).

When Newt is first discovered, Corporal Hicks immediately calls Ripley to be the one to try to convince the girl to come out of her hiding place as if he senses Ripley's intrinsic femininity as a precursor to motherhood. Soon, after Newt is treated by a woman medic, she and Ripley begin bonding as mother and daughter. They even share a bedside chat about monsters and where babies come from. Ripley then promises that she will never leave Newt, sealing her promise by stating "cross my heart." Newt finishes the pledge with a small-voiced but determined "and hope to die," as if she knows that Ripley's promises are suspect after leaving behind her biological daughter. Ripley is still under suspicion as a bad mommy and must prove herself capable which is why, narratively speaking, Newt must be brought to the queen's nest. Redemption begins with the rescue of Newt from the other mother in the movie, and ends after the powerloader battle with the queen, when Newt calls out "Mommy!" Ripley has destroyed the armoured, self-sufficient female that threatened to erase the distinctions between male and female, life and death, self and other. In doing so, she has proved herself to be, in the end, a good mother who has learned to honour her promises.

Finally, in the closing scenes, Ripley is putting a cleaned-up and pretty Newt to bed and telling her that it is okay to dream. Newt is not only physically safe, but also emotionally safe because the film leaves no doubt in the spectator's mind that Ripley will continue to be Newt's mother even after they return to Earth. Only by reclaiming her position as a mother in a heteronormative family unit—with Hicks as a mate and Newt as a surrogate daughter—is Ripley saved.[5] Perhaps this is why James Cameron claims that at "the end of [*Aliens*] I think you feel like not only has she survived physically, but she's out of the woods, she's gonna be ok" (Cameron 1999). Indeed, many fans of the film often decry *Aliens*[3] because the nuclear family unit is the first thing to go.

---

[5] While I have not analyzed the relationship between Ripley and Hicks in this essay, the film obviously pairs them as a potential couple.

Action films certainly create gruelling and punishing narratives for their heroes, and *Aliens* is no exception. Indeed, part of the pleasure of an action movie lies in the extreme conflicts and jeopardy that the hero must encounter. However, the male hero is rarely presented as the guilty object. John Rambo may need to return to Vietnam to exorcise his demons, but his demons are never seen as his own fault, whereas Ellen Ripley, from the very beginning, is shown as responsible for the loss of her daughter and implicated, because of her failure at the inquest, in the destruction of the colony. Examining how film assigns blame to a female hero is one way to understand how such a representation can both posit and annul the role of a woman as the maker of meaning.

"fetish"

> When I now disclose that the fetish is a penis-substitute I shall certainly arouse disappointment; so I hasten to add that it is not a substitute for any chance penis, but for a particular quite special penis that had been extremely important in early childhood but was afterwards lost. This is to say: it should normally have been given up, but the purpose of the fetish precisely is to preserve it from being lost. To put it plainly: the fetish is a substitute for the woman's (mother's) phallus ... . (Freud 1997, 205)

> Ripley: Get away from her, you Bitch! (Cameron 1999)

Mulvey's argument regarding the use of fetish as a way to ward off castration anxiety is particularly apt in regards to *Aliens*. In particular, I will argue here that the aliens in general, and the alien queen in particular, become fetish objects. As such, the aliens operate as a double substitute: both for the phallic mother as well as for human females. The latter correspondence is made quite obvious in the previously discussed Medlab scene. The film, so uneasy with the problem of the female hero, uses every strategy that Mulvey outlines for the male spectator to disavow castration anxiety. In addition to presenting the human vagina as a distinct stage of alien development, the alien queen is clearly fetishized as well.[6]

---

[6] Despite the popular culture image of a shoe fetishist fervently worshiping a high-heeled, leather pump, the fetish can operate in a much more complex manner. Freud is worth quoting at length on the duel function of the fetish: "I have to add that there are numerous and very weighty proofs of the double attitude of fetishists to the question of the castration of women. In very subtle cases the fetish itself has become the vehicle both of denying and of asseverating the fact of castration ... Naturally, a fetish of this kind constructed out of two opposing ideas is capable of great tenacity. Sometimes the double attitude shows itself in what the fetishist—

For Mulvey, the fetishized female is exemplified in the films of Josef von Sternberg where the woman "is no longer the bearer of guilt but a perfect product, whose body, stylised and fragmented by close-ups, is the content of the film . . ." (1989, 22). Obviously, the alien queen does not function in quite the same way as Marlene Dietrich in a Sternberg film. However, the queen's visual introduction mirrors what Mulvey sees as the classical Hollywood manner of fetishizing the female body. As previously mentioned, the film reveals the queen in pieces, beginning with the end of a fallopian like structure and then moving slowly and along the queen's body. There is a languorous feel to this shot, and it parallels the manner in which many films have introduced women as objects of desire: the camera reveals shapely legs and then moves slowly up the woman's body, revelling in a slow reveal of each curve. In the case of *Aliens*, the body parts may be different, but the visual language, the languorous and longing gaze upon the body of the Other, is the same. Indeed, if the film were more self-aware of its fetishizing nature, the scene might almost work as parody.

Additionally, both *Alien* and *Aliens* promote the idea that the aliens are perfect killing machines, somehow beyond guilt because they behave only as their fundamental nature dictates. In Scott's *Alien*, Ash states that he "admire[s] its purity" because it is "a survivor unclouded by conscience, remorse or delusions of morality" (Scott 2004). While in Cameron's *Aliens*, Bishop simply remarks that the facehugger is "magnificent." In fact, the very existence of *Aliens* is dependent upon the alien form—especially the H.R. Giger design—operating as a fetish. Certainly there was never a thought about making a sequel focusing on Ripley's life without the alien. In fact, the studio needed to be convinced that bringing Ripley back for the sequel was necessary (Cameron 1999). The black, insectoid body of the alien queen is, on some levels at least, the driving force of desire, the body that displaces castration fear by embodying castration, while also being a body that is open for harassment and can be openly treated as a hostile thing to be destroyed. Of course the fetish might be treated harshly—destroyed even—but there is no question that the fetish is necessary to displace the fear of dissolution and self-loss that

---

either actually or in phantasy—does with the fetish. It is not the whole story to say that he worships it; very often he treats it in a way which is plainly equivalent to castrating it ... Tender and hostile treatment of fetishes is mixed in unequal degrees—like the denial and the recognition of castration—in different cases, so that the one or the other is more evident. Here one gets a sort of glimpse of comprehension, as from a distance, of the behaviour of people who cut off women's plaits of hair; in them the impulse to execute the castration which they deny is what comes to the fore" (Freud 1997, 208-209).

comes from the realisation that the mother's phallus is missing. One missing phallus might lead to more, even if the man still retains his penis because the penis means little without the phallus propping it up. Thus, while the alien queen is destroyed in this film, from a fetishist's point of view, a sequel is necessary and to be expected.

How does the alien queen as fetish undermine Ripley's status as a hero? In large part this is due to *Aliens* welding the two characters together: both are mothers, survivors, and willing to kill for their offspring. The connection between the two is far deeper than a male hero has to his enemies. Rambo may be seen as a mirror of his Vietnamese foes in Rambo II, but he is in no sense the same as them on a fundamental level. Because of the preoccupation with motherhood as fundamental, natural, and intrinsic to the female sex, Ripley and the queen merge into one another, forming a bond based on biological sex. Even more than the alien of the first film, the queen is "coded as a toothed vagina, the monstrous feminine as the cannibalistic mother" (Creed 1990, 140). If the queen serves as a fetish that visually encodes castration fear, as seen in her womb-like nest and the vagina dentata of her extending teeth and jaws, how is Ripley positioned in relation to the *alien other*? When a male hero fights an enemy, quite often he fights against an Other, but because *Aliens* establishes a one-to-one relationship between sex and gender, the male spectator is invited to see the queen and Ripley as mirrors of one another. In other words, the male spectator's Other is Ripley's "same." The connection between Ripley and the queen explains the slippage that Gallardo and Smith point out in the tag line from of *Alien³*: the bitch is back. They note that the term "bitch" signifies at first the alien queen, then Ripley, and then the queen once more (2004, 120). This collapsing of identities and the dissolution of the boundaries between hero and enemy may be intrinsic to the functioning of *Alien³*, but it is prepared for by *Aliens*. The deeply rooted sameness between Ripley and the queen makes Ripley's status as a hero, at the very least, suspect—no matter how many aliens she kills or rescues she attempts.

Jeffrey Brown, in his essay "Gender and the Action Heroine: Hardbodies and the Point of No Return" comments on Mulvey's essay "Visual Pleasure and Narrative Cinema" by stating that for Mulvey, "the sexual difference demarcated by the active/passive split marks the cinematic gaze as a masculine look that objectifies women as spectacles to be looked at," and that the "masculine gaze of the camera forces female viewers to adopt either a narcissistic over-identification with women on the screen or a masochistic male point of view" (1996, 56). For Brown:

the modern action heroine is far from passive. She fights, she shoots, she kills, she solves the mysteries, and she rescues herself and others from dangerous situations. In short, she is in full command of the narrative, carrying the action in ways that have normally been reserved for male protagonists. (1996, 56)

While I agree with Brown that that there are "revelatory possibilities [in] women assuming these roles" (1996, 63), the visual and narrative strategies of *Aliens* never quite manage to achieve escape velocity from the gravity-well of a viewing pleasure that is rooted in the desire to protect the phallus as a prop for male subjectivity and power. Ripley is certainly active, certainly heroic. Yet, the real question becomes, is she the film's maker of meaning, or an elaborately disguised bearer of meaning? I suggest that the film's denial of castration anxiety through the strategies of investigation, punishment, and fetishism bar Ripley from becoming the maker of meaning in ways that are reserved for male heroes.

Conclusions

Cameron's *Aliens* re-establishes sexual difference in both the human and alien spheres. Although the dialogue implies that the aliens are as indiscriminate as ever in their choice of hosts, on screen it's a female human who suffers the involuntary Caesarean birth. Similarly, it's the alien queen who, guarded by her warriors, lays the eggs (Taubin 1993, 95).

Jeffrey Brown argues that there is no functional difference between Ripley as a female hero and how a male hero might function for viewers. He goes on to say that because male viewers "accept Ripley in a heroic role regardless of her biology" they also choose to identify with her "*in the same way*" as they might identify with, for example, Rambo (1996, 69; emphasis in original). However, as Amy Taubin points out, gender difference in *Aliens* is not magically erased simply because Ripley is the film's protagonist. Indeed, as I have demonstrated *Aliens* continually links gender performance with biological sex, and the voyeuristic male gaze is thus encouraged by a great many of the film's visual and narrative tactics. Accepting Ripley, or any other female action protagonist, as a hero is a different proposition than the claim that male viewers would identify "in the same way" (Brown 1996, 69). As evidence of this, the following remarks from viewers clearly demonstrate that Ripley remains a source of voyeuristic pleasure:

The conflict between Ripley and the queen near the end is certainly a highlight. Nice to see two overzealous females trying to kick the crap out of each other. What kind of action is better, honestly? (Huxtable 2006)

I loved the team that Ripley and Newt made (I love it when I see girlpower, being a female lover). (Alex K. 2006)

Great sequel, more action, aliens, deaths, and Sigourney in her panties again, nice. (Brodyman 2006)

Aliens contains one of my favorite "cat fights" in any film. (Sponseller 2006)

As these statements demonstrate, the intersections of gender, action, viewer identification, and sexual objectification are far more complex than Brown suggests, and it is difficult to imagine male action heroes being talked about in ways that seem, to some, quite natural when talking about female action heroes.

My point here is not to enter into a detailed reader-response analysis of *Aliens* but to suggest that *Aliens* offers, at best, a conflicted vision of what it means to be a female action hero.[7] The cognitive dissonance of a statement like "Ripley gets ample occasion to act heroically and, as usual, to run around in her underwear" (Foskin 2006), does not usually appear in discussions of male heroes. Apparent in Foskin's statement is a tension between identifying Ripley as a hero and Ripley as a sexual object, particularly because she certainly does not spend the film running around in her underwear. The popularity of *Aliens* demonstrates that the fans accept Ripley as a heroic figure, but this acceptance is marked, not only by the sexual rhetoric as seen above, but paternalistic comments like Wesley Mill's observation that Ripley's "decisiveness is what makes her character so endearing" (2006). Are the characters played by Bruce Willis, Sylvester Stallone, and Arnold Schwarzenegger "endearing" because of their decisiveness? The very question seems, somehow, incorrect when applied to male action heroes. This incorrectness is exactly my point: Ripley may be heroic, but her heroism is defined by and through her status as a

---

[7] There seems to me a great deal of work to be done on the analytic possibilities that sites such as Amazon.com, Netflix, IMDB.com and other internet discussion groups offer. Those in the humanities might look to sociology and statistical analysis for ways to theorize the pleasure of film and television as experienced by actual viewers. Such an analysis is beyond the scope of this paper, but for an example of dealing with fan comments and reviews, see "A Superhero for Gays?: Gay Masculinity and Green Lantern" (Palmer-Mehta and Hay 2005).

woman. She is not only a hero, but also, and at the same time, a sexual object.

Male viewers are not necessarily identifying with Ripley in the same way as they would a male hero. Such transgender identification is, of course, possible. However, such an identification is certainly not part of the textual or visual strategies found in *Aliens*. While Ripley certainly offers a spectator the opportunity to identify with a strong, heroic female character, an examination of the ideological secretions and psychoanalytic strategies of the film reveals the deeply contradictory nature of Ripley's representation in *Aliens* as well as deeply entrenched notions about gender.

Like an electron that, through an influx of energy, is kicked up into a higher orbit around a nucleus, Ripley's environment kicks her into the role of the hero. As the energy expends itself, however, Ripley's orbit is returned to that of a traditional, heteronormative family. She has herself a new boyfriend and a new daughter, so now she won't have to work, either as a space pilot or a dock-worker. If, as the film suggests, Ripley and Newt can now safely dream, what is it that they will dream? Perhaps, just perhaps, Ripley will dream of a culture that does not misconstrue the performative as the ontological, or misunderstand gender as biological sex; perhaps she will dream of a culture that does not represent women as guilty objects to be punished, or as fetishes to be admired and/or destroyed. Might Newt dream of joining a deep-space salvage team or becoming the head of a vast corporate empire or a doctor or a military leader, or are those dreams not available to little girls? There is no question that *Aliens* helped the character of Ellen Ripley to become one of the best know female action heroes in film history. There is no question that Sigourney Weaver's performance in all of the films brings an intelligence and strength to the character of Ripley that is an inspiration for some viewers. Yet, despite the positive aspects of the film, *Aliens* secretes a resin of patriarchal ideology and threatened male subjectivity that continually disrupts—even if it fails to destroy entirely—Ripley's performance as a female action hero.

References

Alex K. 2006. "The aliens series just went up a notch!" Amazon.com.
    http://www.amazon.com/gp/cdp/member-reviews/A2T2MYZEB81N
    OQ/002-4099377-7946448?ie=UTF8&display=public&page=12
Althusser, L. 1969. *For Marx*. London: Allen Lane.

Blackmore, T. 1996. 'Is this going to be another bug-hunt?': s-f tradition versus biology-as-destiny in James Cameron's *Aliens*. *Journal of popular culture* 29 (4): 211-226.

Brodyman. 2006. Comments. Amazon.com. http://www.amazon.com/gp/product/customer-reviews/B00012FXAE/ ref=cm_cr_dp_2_1/104-0201144-1420721?%5Fencoding=UTF8&customer-reviews.sort%5Fby=-SubmissionDate&n=130.

Brown, J. 1996. Gender and the action heroine: Hardbodies and the 'point of no return.' Cinema Journal 35 (3): 52-71.

Bundtzen, L. K. 1987. Monstrous mothers: Medusa, grendel, and now alien. *Film Quarterly* 40 (3): 11-17.

Butler, J. 1990. Gender trouble, feminist theory, and psychoanalytic discourse. In *Feminism/Postmodernism*, ed. Linda J. Nicholson, 324-340. New York: Routledge.

Cameron, J. 1999. *Aliens, special edition DVD*. Twentieth Century Fox.

CIA. 2010. "North America, United States." https://www.cia.gov/library/publications/the-world-factbook/geos/us.html

Comolli, J. and J. Narboni. 1999. Cinema/ideology/criticism. In *Film theory and criticism: Introductory readings, 5th edition*, ed. L. Braudy and M. Cohen, 752-759. New York: Oxford University Press.

Creed, B. Alien and the monstrous feminine. In *Alien zone: Cultural theory and contemporary science fiction cinema*, ed. A. Kuhn, 128-141. New York: Verso.

Dictionary.com. 2010. Abyss. Random House, Inc. http://dictionary.reference.com/browse/abyss.

Evans, D. 1996. *An introductory dictionary of Lacanian psychoanalysis*. New York: Routledge.

Faludi, S. 1991. *Backlash: the undeclared war against American women*. New York: Crown Publishers, Inc.

FindLaw. 2010. South Dakota women's health and human life protection act (HB 1215). http://news.findlaw.com/nytimes/docs/abortion/sdabortionlaw06.html

Foskin, D. 2006. One of the best sci-fi movie sets around. Amazon.com. http://www.amazon.com/gp/cdp/member-reviews/A3GKOMCQTTWPUI?ie=UTF8&display=public&page=20

Freud, S. 1997. Fetishism (1927). In *Sexuality and the psychology of love*, 204-209. New York: Touchstone.

Gallardo C., X. and C. J. Smith. 2004. *Alien woman: the making of Lt. Ripley*. New York: Continuum.

Huxtable, B. 2006. One of the greatest sci-fi actions ever created. Amazon.com. http://www.amazon.com/gp/cdp/member-reviews/AF3R MNRNRSG7W/002-4099377-7946448?ie=UTF8&display=public&page=3

Institute for Women's Policy Research. 2010. The gender wage gap: 2008. http://www.iwpr.org/pdf/C350.pdf.

Irigaray, L. 1991a. This sex which is not one. In *Feminisms: An anthology of literary theory and criticism*, ed. R. Warhol and D. Price Herndl, 350-356. New Brunswick: Rutgers University Press.

—. 1991b. Another 'cause'—castration. In *Feminisms: An anthology of literary theory and criticism*, ed. R. Warhol and D. Price Herndl, 404-12. New Brunswick: Rutgers University Press.

Kavanagh, J. 1990. Feminism, humanism and science in *Alien*. In *Alien Zone: Cultural theory and contemporary science fiction cinema*, ed. A. Kuhn, 73-81. New York: Verso.

Lacan, J. 2004. *Ecrits: A selection*. Translated by Bruce Fink. New York: W.W. Norton & Company.

Lefanu, S. 1989. *Feminism and science fiction*. Bloomington: Indiana University Press.

Manlove, C. 2007. Visual 'drive' and the cinematic narrative: Reading gaze theory in Lacan, Hitchcock, and Mulvey. *Cinema journal* 46 (3), 84-90.

Mills, W. 2006. Review. Netflix.com. http://www.netflix.com/MovieDisplay?dmode=CUSTOMERREVIEW &lnkctr=mdpGlanceMemRev&movieid=60029358&trkid=6243&pageNum=2

Mulvey, L. 1989a. Visual pleasure and narrative cinema. In *Visual and other pleasures*, 14-28. Bloomington: Indiana University Press.

—. 1989b. Changes: Thoughts on myth, narrative and historical experience. In *Visual and other pleasures*, 159-176. Bloomington: Indiana University Press.

NARAL: Prochoice America. 2010. Abortion bans. Pro-Choice America, http://www.prochoiceamerica.org/issues/abortion/abortion-bans/.

Nicholls, P. 1993. "Aliens." In *The encyclopedia of science fiction*, ed. J. Clute and P. Nicholls, 19. New York: St. Martin's Griffin.

Nietzsche, F. 1989. *Beyond good and evil*. New York: Vintage Books.

Palmer-Mehta, V. and K. Hay. 2005. A superhero for gays?: Gay masculinity and *Green Lantern*. *The journal of American culture* 28 (4): 390-404.

Penley, C. 1990. Time travel, primal scene and the critical dystopia. In *Alien Zone: Cultural theory and contemporary science fiction cinema*, ed. A. Kuhn, 116-127. New York: Verso.

Scott, R. 2004. *Alien* (the Director's Cut). Twentieth Century Fox.

Silverman, K. 1992. *Male subjectivity at the margins*. New York: Routledge.

Sponseller, B. Comments. IMDB Website. http://www.imdb.com/title/tt0090605/usercomments.

Taubin, A. 1993. The 'alien' trilogy: From feminism to aids. In *Women and film: A sight and sound reader*, ed. P. Cook and P. Dodd, 93-100. Philadelphia: Temple University Press.

Wikipedia. 2010. Uterus. http://en.wikipedia.org/wiki/Uterus.

CHAPTER THREE

PARADOX AND TRANSCENDENCE IN *ALIEN³*: RIPLEY THROUGH THE EYES OF SIMONE DE BEAUVOIR

EVA DADLEZ

> The womb, that warm, peaceful, and safe retreat, becomes... a dark, contractile gulf, where dwells a serpent that insatiably swallows up the strength of the male.
> —Simone de Beauvoir, *The Second Sex*

Introduction

Noel Carroll, in writing of the philosophy of horror, has proposed that the genre depends for its impact on category violations. Carroll speaks mainly of the kinds of incompatible properties ascribed to fictional monsters and their fantastic biologies, cases of "interstitiality and categorical contradictoriness" that involve "conflict between two or more standing cultural categories" (Carroll 1990, 43). There is a sense in which claims such as these apply to the human heroine of the *Alien* films as well as their titular monster, especially when we consider the third cinematic occasion on which Ellen Ripley puts on an appearance. That the character is virtually a model for the violation of standard gender roles and gender expectations, and thus a violator of preestablished categories on this looser interpretation (which employs Carroll's analysis to help us understand heroines as well as monsters), is something that has been addressed in nearly all of the literature concerning the series, most unmistakably that concerning the third film. Ilsa Bick writes of the manner in which *Alien³* challenges traditional ideas concerning masculine and feminine power (Bick 1994). Several critics address the relationship of monstrosity to gender and maternity (Herman 1997, Moore and Miles 1992). Others focus on *Alien³*'s religious imagery as it relates to the violation of dogma and of prescribed roles (Schemanske 1996, Murphy 1992). Louise Speed investigates the third film's dissolution of gender roles and thereby its violation of action picture conventions (Speed 1998). Indeed, some interpretations of *Alien³* cast Ripley as the Typhoid Mary of an AIDS allegory with apocalyptic overtones, playing on the tension between immunity and infection (Gibson 2001, Young 1994). All of these projects cast a practiced eye on the kinds of paradoxes and conflicts presented in *Alien³* in the person of its protagonist. All present interpretations and resolutions, many of which are at least apparently at odds and, in fact, may even create new paradoxes as theses of equal plausibility, compete for our attention. My own proposal is to resolve at least a few of these tensions by considering *Alien³* from a particular philosophical perspective that in itself sheds a good deal of light on the paradoxes inherent in conceptions of woman. This is the perspective provided by Simone de Beauvoir in *The Second Sex*.

I will contend that the film *Alien³* cinematically embodies many of the insights in de Beauvoir's "myth of the feminine." It is assumed here that fiction can, and frequently does, convey philosophical insights by means both of its symbolic representations and of the conflicts, tensions, and contrasts that it invites us to entertain. This particular fiction does so, first, by affiliating its heroine Ripley with the alien, a true *Other* insofar as it represents the ultimate biological deviation from the norm, and then by stressing the difference and alienness of Ripley's sex in presenting her against the backdrop of the almost exclusively masculine world of Fury 161. Next, it does so by presenting Ripley in paradoxically incompatible roles of destroyer and preserver, monster and saviour, roles with both religious and political overtones that vividly reflect conceptions of woman as *Other*. Finally, the film conveys de Beauvoir's insights by showing us Ripley's transcendence, her refusal to be subjected to given conditions, her choice of an authentic, albeit brief, existence.

My introduction will close with a necessary technical note. This paper will for the most part concern itself only with the most recent release of *Alien³*, the 2003 restored work print.[1] This version of the film represents the closest approximation to the composite, if not collaborative, vision of two people. The first of these is director David Fincher. The second is former director and storyline contributor Vincent Ward, who directed another dark and compelling film with monastic overtones called *The Navigator*. In an effort to create a blockbuster suited to the attention span of the lowest common denominator, Fox cut back what had been a longer

---

[1] Throughout this paper, "assembly cut" and "restored work print" are used to refer to the Special Edition from the 2003 Collector's Edition.

film, sacrificing plot coherence and character development to non-stop gore and action sequences. The theatrical release was severely criticized for its failure to make us care about the characters or understand their motivations and for offering little more than a "grisly game of monster tag" with no real plot development (Hinson 1992). The restored work print rectifies most, if not all, of these liabilities. *Alien³* rejoices in an extraordinary and talented cast—more talented, perhaps, than that of any other film in the series. The additional thirty minutes or so of footage rescued from the cutting room floor is more than enough for such performers to establish their characters as unique and convincing people rather than fodder for the alien. Abandoned plot elements which left some very frustrating loose ends in the theatrical release are reintegrated to create a tighter and more coherent plot, and a more compelling emergence and evolution of events from those preceding them. So this paper will focus only on the 2003 work print, simply because it is by far the better film, one more likely to capture what its director and writers may have wished to express (Howe 1992, Canby 1992, Burns 2004).

Simone de Beauvoir: Woman as *Other*

It is the assumption of this paper that *Alien³* shows us a vision of woman as she is thought and said to be by cultural and religious forces. This is a kind of double vision, as inaccurate as it is pervasive, at once characterizing woman as dangerous and as nurturing, as destructively disruptive and as self-sacrificing. She is simultaneously to be shunned and to be used. Her nature is at once debilitating and supportive. There is an interdependence between these two conceptions of woman, especially insofar as both are underwritten by the same attitudes and agendas. No one has described these interdependent conceptions of the feminine better than Simone de Beauvoir in *The Second Sex* in the course of her description of woman's relegation to the category of the *Other*. The film under consideration does not endorse this (dual) conception of woman any more than does de Beauvoir. Rather, it may well constitute the same kind of indictment of cultural, psychological and religious conceptions as that which is offered in *The Second Sex*. It will be argued that *Alien³* can be considered as a kind of dramatic illustration of the conception of the feminine foisted upon us by "legislators, priests, philosophers, writers, and scientists" who, in the words of de Beauvoir, "have striven to show that the subordinate position of woman is willed in heaven and advantageous on earth" (de Beauvoir [1952] 1970, xxii).

It should be clear at the outset that what de Beauvoir offers us is primarily a conceptual analysis. Our thoughts and perceptions are organized by a conceptual scheme, a way of seeing the world. Concepts are the instruments by means of which we think. It is de Beauvoir's contention that the relegation of woman to the status of the *Other*, a relegation that is conceptual in nature, is implicated in the oppression of women. de Beauvoir regards otherness as a "fundamental category of human thought," but one whose relativity is, in other circumstances, made manifest as "groups realize the reciprocity of their relations" in the course of interacting (de Beauvoir [1952] 1970, xvii). This reciprocity has not been recognized between the sexes, however:

> The terms masculine and feminine are used symmetrically only as a matter of form, as on legal papers. In actuality the relation of the two sexes is not quite like that of two electrical poles, for man represents both the positive and the neutral, as is indicated by the common use of man to designate human beings in general; whereas woman represents only the negative, defined by limiting criteria, without reciprocity. (de Beauvoir [1952] 1970, xv)

In other words, man is the norm and woman is the deviation. More than one philosopher has given voice to just such a conception. A woman is, according to Aristotle, "an infertile male" – a female is a female "in virtue of a particular deficiency" (Aristotle 1942). The concept is reflected again in religious thought. Eve is, after all, a byproduct of Adam. In the words of Aquinas,

> in a secondary sense, the image of God is found in man and not in woman, for man is the beginning and end of woman, just as God is the beginning and end of every creature. So when the Apostle had said that *man is the image and glory of God, but woman is the glory of man,* he adds his reason for saying this: *For man is not of woman, but woman of man; and man was not created for woman, but woman for man.* (Aquinas 1994, 60)

We should not forget psychology. Freud tells us that "masochism is truly feminine," though it is believed to be so because of the "suppression of women's aggressiveness which is prescribed for them constitutionally and imposed on them socially," suggesting that masochism may not be thought an inherent trait. Psychoanalysis, he claims, "does not try to explain what a woman is" but only asks how she comes into being. The fruits of this inquiry, however, present the clitoris as a mere (undersized) "penis-equivalent" and penis-envy, a peculiarly feminine castration complex, as a fundamental developmental experience. That is, part of how a woman "comes into being" involves her awareness of *not* possessing a male body part, of not – in effect – being male (Freud 1994, 227-8, 233-41). Again, femininity is conceived as a deviation from the norm, a kind of deficiency.

To be *Other* in the senses described above, the senses that de Beauvoir points out to us, involves one in a loss of identity, both personal and social. Woman is never defined in herself, but relative to man. When we consider what de Beauvoir calls "the myth of the eternal feminine," the conception of woman embodies contradictions which confront women with an ideal – if that is what it is – which is *literally* impossible to achieve. (Perhaps this is why we must turn to science fiction for a truly compelling illustration, since it sets empirical possibility at a distance.)

> The myth is so various, so contradictory, that at first its unity is not discerned: Delilah and Judith, Aspasia and Lucretia, Pandora and Athena– woman is at once Eve and the Virgin Mary. She is an idol, a servant, the source of life, a power of darkness.... And her ambiguity is just that of the concept of the Other: it is that of the human situation insofar as it is defined in its relation with the Other. (de Beauvoir [1952] 1970, 133)

The concept of woman is fundamentally unstable:

> through her is made unceasingly the passage from... good to evil, from evil to good. Under whatever aspect we may consider her, it is this ambivalence that strikes us first. (de Beauvoir [1952] 1970, 133)

De Beauvoir asks us to consider how man seeks in woman the *Other* as Nature and then reminds us of

> what ambivalent feelings nature inspires in man. He exploits her, but she crushes him...she is the source of his being and the realm that he subjugates to his will. (de Beauvoir [1952] 1970, 133)

Woman is *for* man, yet he cannot count on it, and so there is something to be feared. A refusal to be used can be characterized as an intentional deprivation, an aggressive act, a betrayal of justified expectations. A free woman who will not be used, someone who is a fellow being and not just the *Other*, seems dangerous:

> In place of the myth of the laborious honeybee or the mother hen is substituted the myth of the devouring female insect: the praying mantis, the spider. No longer is the female she who nurses the little ones, but rather she who eats the male.... The same dialectic makes the erotic object into a

wielder of black magic, the servant into a traitress, Cinderella into an ogress, and changes all women into enemies: it is the payment man makes for having in bad faith set himself up as the sole essential. (de Beauvoir [1952] 1970, 179)

It is de Beauvoir's well-known contention that one is not born, but rather *becomes* a woman, that femininity as it is culturally defined is a matter of indoctrination rather than of inherent or essential traits. The emphasis on woman's difference from man (especially an emphasis on allegedly inborn differences), whether that emphasis makes of her a saviour or a monster, inevitably hinders her transcendence, because that transcendence depends on seeing woman *in herself* and not merely in relation to man. To transcend is to take responsibility for oneself and for the world and, thereby, to choose one's own freedom. It will be argued in the following sections that the film *Alien³* provides a superb, even a nuanced, depiction of what de Beauvoir means by the "myth of the feminine." It not only illustrates de Beauvoir's ideas in this regard, but goes on to depict the role such conceptualizations play and the attitudes they reflect in the social, religious, and corporate world. Finally, although the film elaborates these conceptions of woman in the person of Lieutenant Ellen Ripley, it also shows us an individual who has achieved liberty and transcendence by refusing to submit to given conditions, refusing, that is, to be stabilized as an object and doomed to immanence and a limited, uncreative life. Indeed, the first words uttered in the film, uttered moreover by the only female voice we hear in the course of the movie other than that of Ripley (that of the computer) are: "stasis interrupted."

Marooned in Testosterone Paradise

The almost exclusively masculine environment into which Ripley is cast at the beginning of the film makes her status as *Other* immediately apparent. *Alien³* begins by stripping Ripley of the nuclear family so obligingly provided by James Cameron in *Aliens* and stranding her on Fury 161, on the doorstep of a Double-Y Chromosome Work-Correctional Facility. Deprived of Hicks and Newt and Bishop (whose role in the aforesaid nuclear family could only have been that of a vastly overqualified *au pair*), Ripley is thrust into an entirely patriarchal, purely male environment, the purity of which has apparently not been sullied even by a stray X chromosome, at least in a human being. Until the advent of Ripley and the alien queen she unknowingly harbours, the only female on Fury 161 is Babe the ox (the Rottweiler with which some viewers will be familiar appeared only in the Theatrical Release), who plays host to the alien and dies almost immediately. In fact, all the females in this film start out or wind up dead. The norm, the standard or backdrop against which everything else is measured, is entirely male and not, one finds, very hospitable to anything *Other*.

Ripley's otherness is reinforced by the film's patriarchal religious overtones which make her presence both a disruption of the established masculine order, an order perceived as *natural*, and a sin or transgression in the making. That is, Ripley is, in this environment, *unnatural* in every sense, a descriptor that is always loaded with religious connotations. The prison setting is surprisingly monastic. At one point there is even faint chanting in the background which bears some resemblance to religious music. The prison has the air of a grim, almost medieval fortress, with few modern amenities: "we got no entertainment centres, no climate control, no video system, no surveillance, no freezers, no fucking ice cream, no rubbers, no women, no guns," an inmate tells Ripley. Torches and candles often replace other light sources. Dim, arched passageways abound. Heavy coats and heads shaved to discourage lice from taking up residence give the impression of cowl and tonsure from a distance. And, of course, this is a predominantly religious community of celibate males.

Images of descent and hellfire are also common, facilitating conceptions of Ripley as both devil and saviour. Recall that the serene and saintlike Ripley of the cryotube (referred to at one point as *Snow White* by a cynical Marine in *Aliens*) is sullied and blackened once a fire which begins in the subflooring hurtles her back into time and down to the waking world. The first attempt to destroy the alien goes badly wrong and sends walls of flame rushing through the passages of the prison, devouring the lives of inmates indiscriminately, as if in one of those Bosch paintings of unpleasant features of the afterlife. The principal direction of movement in this film flows in a downward direction. The fire in the Sulaco begins in the subflooring, and Ripley falls from the heavens. The alien is, according to Ripley, "just down there, in the basement." In the end, Ripley *falls into* the white hot fire of the open furnace.

Note also that, at the very outset of the film, we are presented with a set of contrasting images of precisely the kind that de Beauvoir attributes to the myth of the feminine. Our first glimpse of Ripley is in her pristine cryogenic compartment, looking, as some writers have pointed out, like a "saint in her glass reliquary" (Gallardo and Smith 2004, 123). Everything is white, frosted, peaceful, until "stasis [is] interrupted." Fire is detected in the cryogenic compartment, the emergency evacuation vehicle is jettisoned, and Ripley plummets down into the black, oily ocean of Fury

161. She is washed ashore in a desolate industrial wasteland, her body coated with black slime. This is about as much of a contrast as it is possible to achieve: black rather than white, dirty rather than clean, exposed to the elements rather than protected, cast forth rather than retained, down in the mud rather than up among the stars, free rather than confined. In fact, the sun sets soon after Ripley arrives. Later in the film, we are told (when inmates consider leaving the facility to escape the alien) that the night she has ushered in will last for another week, with temperatures at forty degrees below zero. Stasis has indeed been interrupted. It has certainly been interrupted in the prison colony, where Ripley's very femininity is a deviation and an invitation to transgression.

Ripley the Destroyer: A Negative Deviation from the Male

There is a clear sense in which Ripley's role in the film embodies the darker, more monstrous conception of the *Other* that de Beauvoir describes. de Beauvoir has shown us that, once women attempt to take on the role of fellow beings,

> the egg is no longer a storehouse of abundance, but rather a trap of inert matter in which the spermatozoon is castrated and drowned. The womb, that warm, peaceful, and safe retreat, becomes a pulp of humors, a carnivorous plant, a dark, contractile gulf, where dwells a serpent that insatiably swallows up the strength of the male. (de Beauvoir [1952] 1970, 179)

Indeed, the "dark contractile gulf" bears some resemblance to the dank, claustrophobic, unlit passageways through which the inmates hunt, and are hunted by, the alien. Ripley is the bringer of evil, the bringer of the beast, the destroyer of mankind—just as de Beauvoir says that Eve is the mediatrix of damnation (de Beauvoir [1952] 1970, 159).

Even before it becomes apparent that Ripley has brought unwelcome visitors with her, it is clear that Ripley's is a disruptive, chaos-creating presence, not because of what she does but because of what she is or, rather, because of what she is not. She is not male. Therefore, she is trouble. Her very presence disrupts the status quo, something that is evident in the complaints of the Superintendent: "I don't want to disturb the order.... I don't want a woman walking around and giving...[the inmates] ideas." Dillon, the spiritual leader of the "apocalyptic millenarian Christian fundamentalist" sect which the prisoners have formed, sees Ripley as a threat, "as a violation of the harmony, a potential break in the spiritual unity." Until Ripley came, says Dillon, there was "no temptation."

She is a threat to the religious vows of the now-celibate prison population of murderers and rapists, the majority of whom have given up sex for a shot at salvation.

She is a threat, not because of what she will do, but because of what *they* will do, for which they will then blame her. "I just want to say," the prisoner Morse indicates with some asperity,

> that I've taken a vow of celibacy. That also includes women. We've all taken a vow.... I, for one, do not appreciate Company policy allowing her to freely intermingle with inmates.

Note that women are incidental even to such vows. Analogously, Dillon says to Ripley, "You don't want to know me lady. I am a murderer and a rapist. Of women." As with Morse, the objects toward which the conduct is directed, whether that conduct involves rape or restraint, call for additional specification. The *Other* is never a given. "It amounts to this," says de Beauvoir,

> just as for the ancients there was an absolute vertical with reference to which the oblique was defined, so there is an absolute human type, the masculine. (de Beauvoir [1952] 1970, xv)

A woman is always a deviation from the norm.

Perhaps it is Ripley's freedom that constitutes a problem beyond her otherness. De Beauvoir tells us that a free woman who shakes off the preconceptions of others is perceived as a threat. Certainly, Superintendent Andrews seems to think so. He immediately takes steps to restrict Ripley's movements to the infirmary, a prime location for biological deviations from the norm. Indeed, in this context Ripley's femininity is a clear liability, a kind of infirmity. "It's in everybody's best interests if the woman doesn't come out of the infirmary," says the superintendent, "and certainly not without an escort." Later he tells her, "You're fucked. [And she has been, at least insofar as she has been violated while asleep in her cryotube.] Confined to the infirmary. Quarantined." His conviction of Ripley's disruptive influence is made evident when he blames her for the death of inmate Murphy, the first victim of the newly hatched alien. Even though Murphy's death is at first thought accidental, since he is shredded by a ventilation fan which obliterates evidence of the alien's attack, Superintendent Andrews immediately convicts Ripley, but not for anything she has *done*: "This accident with Murphy is what happens when one of these dumb sons of bitches walks around with a hard on." Ripley, initially and quite ironically, acknowledges that Andrews' restrictions are "for my own good," without any intention of submitting to them. Indeed, Andrews spends most of the remainder of his life striving and failing to keep Ripley cloistered and watched and quarantined. Before he is finally dispatched by an alien in which he does not believe, his last words are, "get that foolish woman back to the infirmary!" Ripley constitutes a threat to the two prison administrators, who foresee her female presence as instigating unrest and violence among the inmates, as well as possible trouble with the Company. She will later become a threat to Weyland-Yutani, the corporation which controls so much in Ripley's world, since they know she seeks to foil their plans to acquire a specimen for their bioweapons division.

And, of course, Ripley really *is* a threat, a destroyer of order, and a bringer of chaos. She is, in the words of Dillon, "intolerable." Part of the thesis of this paper is, after all, that the film shows us how women are perceived, what they are thought really to be like. This paper therefore assumes that Ripley is clearly a monster by association. An alien egg has fallen with her out of the sky and what lurked within it has made use of the only other female, a beast of burden, as incubator. Ripley herself is literally *fallen*. Moreover, she is host to an alien queen which, when mature, will produce enough eggs to annihilate the human race. That Ripley, perforce, identifies with the aliens is demonstrated when she says to the rampaging alien she attempts to lure into killing her, "Don't be afraid. I'm part of the family." As Ripley says to Dillon in the April 1991 draft of the script, though not, unfortunately, in the film: "I get to be the mother of the mother of the apocalypse."

Of course, Ripley's arrival in the double-Y chromosome paradise of Fury 161 is fraught with religious symbolism. She is Eve, affiliated with a perfectly unmistakable serpent. She is the bringer of the *beast*, a term which is used on several occasions to refer to the alien and which is replete with biblical and apocalyptic associations. Her arrival, in fact, brings with it the threat of doom for all humanity. The apocalyptic imagery is pervasive. It is an *apocalyptic* Christian fundamentalist sect which inhabits the facility. Murphy, the first inmate to be killed by the newly emerged alien, is singing "In the Year 2525" just before the fatal encounter, a song which contains the line "guess it's time for judgment day" and which further suggests that God may "tear...everything down and start again." After the Superintendent is snatched by the alien and the inmates realize Ripley's warnings are to be taken seriously, Dillon too refers to the apocalypse: "We give you thanks, oh Lord. Your wrath has come and the time is near for us to be judged. The apocalypse is upon us. Let us be ready." In fact, the apocalypse is what Dillon has been waiting for all along. During his first conversation with Ripley, he describes the prison as a good place to wait—"for God to return and raise his servants to redemption." Ripley, as the repository of the beast in this anticipated apocalypse, represents the forces of chaos, destruction, and disruption. Paradoxically, it is the role of saviour and redeemer just as much as the role of destroyer that is reflected in what de Beauvoir calls the myth of the feminine and in the images of Ripley the film affords.

Ripley the Saviour: A Positive Deviation from the Male

"The Church," de Beauvoir indicates,

> expresses and serves a patriarchal civilization in which it is meet and proper for woman to remain appended to man. It is through being his docile servant that she will also be a blessed saint. And thus at the heart of the middle ages arises the most highly perfect image of woman propitious to man.... She is the inverse aspect of Eve the sinner; she crushes the serpent underfoot; she is the mediatrix of salvation. (de Beauvoir [1952] 1970, 159)

And, surprisingly, this image fits Ripley as well. She descends from on high to rescue mankind. She doesn't so much crush the first alien underfoot as cause it to explode, but one ought not to quibble when salvation is on the line.

Let us begin with the ways in which woman can be regarded as a servant. She is a nurturer, there to serve the needs of others and to be fulfilled in the act of fulfilling. It is her function, her purpose to take care of people, to provide for them. And in *Alien³* most of the players want to use Ripley. The alien clearly wants to use her as an incubator. And use is famously tied to protection—the protection of the resource that one exploits. The alien protects Ripley to ensure that she continues to play host to the queen. Not only does the full-grown alien refrain from harming her, but it even allows itself to be trapped, something that eventually leads to its destruction, in an effort to protect her when Dillon pretends to take Ripley hostage. Weyland-Yutani wants to use Ripley and the alien she is incubating for its bioweapons division. They too wish to *protect* Ripley. Andrews tells Clemens about the almost unheard-of high-level transmission he has received from Weyland-Yutani: "They want her looked after. They consider her very high priority." The inmates want to use Ripley for sex and four of them attempt to rape her. In a particularly disturbing scene, two prisoners discuss possible pickup lines they intend to try on Ripley, while hoisting the body of the dead, alien-infested ox (the only female in the film besides Ripley, the dead Newt, and the voice of the computer) aloft on a chain in the abattoir. "Treat a queen like a whore and a whore like a queen. Can't go wrong," says Frank to Murphy as the carcass swings back and forth on the heavy chains. Eve and the queen of heaven are but two sides of the same coin in the inmates' conception, just as de Beauvoir has indicated. Each has its uses, as Ripley is useful to all concerned.

Although Ripley is aided in her escape and thus protected from the would-be rapists by their spiritual leader Dillon, she is saved only to be useful in another way – to save *them* and the rest of the human race from the alien. Ripley is, of course, the only individual who has any experience of the alien or any experience in fighting it. It is she who warns the inhabitants of Fury 161, and who later organizes them and guides them in devising a plan to trap the alien. As the men panic when they finally realize the trouble they're in, Dillon turns to Ripley: "Hey sister – What about you? How about showing us a little leadership?" He, the most intelligent of the men who are left alive, knows that she is their only hope. (There is a certain resistance on the part of some other prisoners, as might be expected: "She's the one that brought the fucker. Why don't we just get her head and shove it through the fucking wall?" It is soon quelled, however.)

As Ripley, at first unknowingly and then with increasing suspicion, nurtures the alien queen, she also provides aid and comfort to former assailants as she helps them formulate a battle plan. Ripley races to help a prisoner when the quinitricetyline is inadvertently set alight, causing flames to explode through the passageways. That prisoner was the primary assailant in the attempted rape. Indeed, her attempts to destroy the alien are clearly actions that will save even the power-hungry corporate moguls of Weyland-Yutani from their own miscalculations. When she becomes certain that she is harbouring an alien, she attempts to convince both the full-grown alien and (later) Dillon to kill her. "Now do something for me," she pleads with the alien, "Just... Just do what you do." The alien is uncooperative. It refuses because, as Ripley puts it, "it knows I'm carrying its future." She then begs Dillon to end her life: "I don't have much time and can't do what I should. I need you to help me. I need you to kill me." Dillon refuses for the same reason the alien did. She is of much greater use alive: "I want to get this thing," Dillon says, "I need you to do it. If it won't kill you then maybe that helps us fight it." As the *Other*, Ripley has become a potential saviour and preserver. All hopes are ultimately pinned on someone unknown and alien to fight and defeat something equally unknown and alien.

Even Ripley's final, almost biblical, temptation brings out images of the nurturer, the caretaker. Ironically, given that she is host to the foetal queen, Ripley is offered a different kind of motherhood as an inducement to surrender herself to Weyland-Yutani. Bishop – the human prototype rather than the android – tries to convince Ripley to turn herself over to the Company. "We want to kill it and take you home, we want to take that thing out of you," Bishop says. He promises a surgical rescue from the alien, quick and painless: "You can still have a life. Children. And most important, you'll know it's dead." As with other gestures of protection and helpfulness that Ripley has enjoyed, this one also involves her being regarded as an exploitable resource. The offer of children is obviously calculated, since it ought to be particularly significant for Ripley. A child would replace the daughter who died at the age of 66 while Ripley was in hyper-sleep (as per the director's cut of James Cameron's *Aliens*). It would replace Newt, from whose loss Ripley may not as yet have recovered. Finally, it would replace the gestating alien queen, trading good for evil.

Hardly an idiot, Ripley does not believe Bishop. She slams a gate closed between them, preventing the Company from interfering in her final plans and symbolically cutting herself off from its influence. It is only when he realizes he has lost that Bishop reveals his true colours. In the very words of Golic, the madman who freed the alien after Ripley and the inmates first trapped it in the toxic waste storage area, Bishop refers to the alien as "magnificent."[2] As the serpent did to Eve, Bishop also tries to tempt Ripley with knowledge: "Think of all that we could learn from it. It's the chance of a lifetime. You must let me have it. It's a magnificent specimen." Ripley's last words to Bishop are "you're crazy." He is merely a more powerful and dangerous version of the mad Golic.

It is at this juncture that Ripley becomes the saviour of mankind, sacrificing herself in order to effect the salvation of the human race. The vision of the *Other* as a saviour and nurturer, as one who can be counted on to sacrifice herself for others, is brought to its ultimate and inevitable *denouement.* Morse, though wounded, opens the furnace in which Newt and Hicks were cremated. Cruciform, arms extended, obviously Christlike, Ripley falls backwards into the light. It is significant, I think, that the alien queen does *not* make a belated appearance in the assembly cut, as it assuredly does in the theatrical release. In the latter, the alien

---

[2] It should come as no surprise that a merciless, perfectly efficient exploiter of all possible resources interested only in its own survival should appeal to the Company. There is room in the literature for further discussion of the alien as a symbol of capitalist expansion.

eerily reminds the viewer of the Immaculate Heart of Mary and the Sacred Heart of Christ, with the Alien queen-embryo taking the place of the symbolic, exposed heart. (Gallardo and Smith 2004, 151)

In the assembly cut, Ripley is on her own. Not someone's host. Not someone's mother. Not a vessel.

Ripley Transcends

In refusing to be used by the alien and by Weyland-Yutani, in rejecting passivity and rejecting offers of care, Ripley achieves transcendence, and does so despite hindrances of epic proportions. For de Beauvoir, a subject

achieves liberty only through a continual reaching out towards other liberties. There is no justification for present existence other than its expansion into an indefinitely open future. Every time transcendence falls back into immanence, stagnation, there is a degradation of existence into the '*en-soi*' – the brutish life of subjection to given conditions – and of liberty into constraint and contingence. This downfall represents a moral fault if the subject consents to it; if it is inflicted upon him, it spells frustration and oppression. In both cases it is an absolute evil. (de Beauvoir [1952] 1970, xxviii)

Ripley's external situation has, of course, been thrust upon her. Circumstances have conspired to maroon her on Fury 161 with uncongenial companions and even less congenial predators. Circumstances have turned her into an unwilling host for the alien queen, since she has been violated while in stasis. Circumstances have created a situation in which Ripley stands between the human race and its annihilation. None of these states of affairs were chosen, none were voluntary, and none were consciously submitted to. Ripley is trapped in a situation not at all of her own making, like nothing she could have wished for or imagined, and certainly like nothing she would have chosen.

At times, she wants to submit, to be passive, to resign responsibility for her own existence. Twice, she asks to be killed, literally putting her existence in the power of another. Ripley invites the alien to kill her, but it won't cooperate. Then she turns to Dillon: "I need you to help me.... I'm dead anyway. I can't survive it." As has already been indicated, Dillon still needs Ripley's help and so refuses to kill her until they have exterminated the first alien. Ripley must live with her self-revulsion, infected with the potential to destroy humanity. Dillon has refused to "take care of her," at least for the moment. More is expected from her before she is done.

Finally, Ripley chooses to fight. She does not consent to be subjected to the conditions into which she has been thrust. She does not submit to what appears inevitable. She rejects spurious offers of rescue.

As de Beavoir tells us,

> every individual concerned to justify his existence feels that his existence involves an undefined need to transcend himself, to engage in freely chosen projects. (de Beauvoir [1952] 1970, xxviii)

Ripley chooses to resist, even though for her this is neither the most attractive nor the easiest option. Her death at the moments she wishes for it most would guarantee the company's capture of the alien, something that might well pose a threat to all humanity. So she joins forces with her fellow prisoners of circumstances on Fury 161. In choosing to act rather than submit, in taking on a challenge rather than passively allowing circumstances to shape her destiny and that of humanity, Ripley is liberated. In becoming free, a woman becomes a fellow-being rather than a deviation from the norm. In taking charge of the battle for humanity, Ripley joins humanity, becomes its avatar. "To gain the supreme victory," de Beauvoir maintains in the final sentence of *The Second Sex*, "it is necessary...that by and through their natural differentiation men and women unequivocally affirm their brotherhood" (de Beauvoir [1952] 1970, 689). By transcending limitations imposed by circumstances and taking responsibility for her own fate, Ripley becomes responsible for the fate of humanity. No longer *Other*, she is simply human.

Alien³ provides not only depictions of woman as *Other*, as has been discussed at length, but simultaneously an image of woman as a liberated fellow being, not merely a deviation, but a person in her own right. Dillon, Ripley's closest collaborator, who finally sacrifices himself to further Ripley's plan of action, refers to her from the beginning as "sister." It is also interesting to note that Ripley herself is, in most aspects of appearance, indeed a fellow being. Her head is shaved and she is dressed like the inmates. She is as physically tough as the men and much more competent than most of them. Even the rape attempt, given Ripley's appearance (just another bald prisoner in baggy clothes) and the fact that she is approached from behind, suggests male-on-male sodomy. Her connection with Clemens, the only man with whom she voluntarily sexually interacts, is neither coy, nor passive, nor romantic. "You're very direct," says Clemens. And he isn't complaining.

To sacrifice, as Ripley has done, coyness and charm and the usual artillery of feminine attractions and passivities does not seem so dreadful to de Beauvoir, "if these treasures cost blood or misery." She urges us not to forget that "our lack of imagination always depopulates the future." We can only consider that future abstractly, deploring – in our secret souls – the fact that we don't inhabit it, and regretting the loss to evolution of present advantages and pleasures. "But the humanity of tomorrow will be living in its flesh and in its conscious liberty," de Beauvoir says. For this humanity,

> that time will be its present and it will in turn prefer it. New relations of flesh and sentiment of which we have no conception will arise between the sexes; already, indeed, there have appeared between men and women friendships, rivalries, complicities, comradeships – chaste and sensual – which past centuries could not have conceived. (de Beauvoir [1952] 1970, 687-688)

Likewise, Ripley has sacrificed inessentials. She has burned away all but that which makes us human.

Ripley's final free action, her plunge into the fire, signals her refusal to be subjected to given conditions – a refusal to allow herself to be used or to accept protection at a price. "Man-the-sovereign will provide woman-the-liege with material protection and will undertake the moral justification of her existence," writes de Beauvoir,

> thus she can evade at once both economic risk and the metaphysical risk of a liberty in which ends and aims must be contrived without assistance. Indeed, along with the ethical urge of each individual to affirm his subjective existence, there is also the temptation to forgo liberty and become a thing. (de Beauvoir [1952] 1970, xxi)

Ripley not only refuses, ultimately, to be subjected to given conditions herself, but earlier rallies the remaining inmates. She contrives her ends and aims with little assistance and considerable opposition. The survivors of the alien's ravages would prefer to sit passively and await rescue by the company: "I'm smart enough to wait for some fire power to show up before we go out to fight the thing," says Aaron, known as "85" by the inmates once they discover his IQ in the company records.

Ripley shocks the inmates back to reality by offering them the truth. Like Eve, her encounters with the serpent-like alien have given her knowledge, knowledge which she proceeds to impart to her masculine counterparts. She tells the men that they are expendable, that they are being used, that sitting quietly and awaiting rescue will bring their destruction. She fills them in on the true motives of the Company, its total lack of concern for their well-being:

When they first heard about this thing, it was crew expendable. The next time they sent in Marines—they were expendable too. What makes you think they're gonna care about a bunch of lifers who found God at the ass end of space? Do you really think they're gonna let you interfere with their plans for this thing? They think we're crud. They don't give a fuck about one friend of yours that's died. Not one. (Ripley)

And Dillon adds, "We're all gonna die. Only question is when.... Only question is how you check out. Do you want it on your feet or on your fucking knees?"

It is clear even in the closing scenes that Ripley could have allowed herself to trust the company and to hope for rescue. However, de Beauvoir believes that

this is an inauspicious road, for he who takes it – passive, lost, ruined – becomes henceforth the creature of another's will, frustrated in his transcendence and deprived of every value. But it is an easy road; on it one avoids the strain involved in undertaking an authentic existence. (de Beauvoir [1952] 1970, xx-xxi)

Even in the surreal and melodramatic context of science fiction, it is evident that Ripley rejects the apparently safe and less painful path, choosing instead an authentic existence in choosing to exist no longer. If she finally chooses to die, her death has become a personal decision. Her action is her own and not, as first seemed possible and all too easy, someone or something else's.

Despite the ontologically outrageous trappings of science fiction, *Alien³* manages to convey more than a little of de Beauvoir's vision, not by reporting what that vision is, but by letting us share it. Its vivid, impossible scenarios reflect real distortions in conceptions of the feminine, the alienness that is conceptually imposed upon women, just as the alien queen invades and imposes herself on Ripley's body. Recollect that all the feminine personae in this film are either entirely monstrous, as is the alien queen, or entirely inanimate, as are Newt, the ox, and the computer. Only Ripley is active; only she escapes from passivity and subjection, as de Beauvoir says that women can and must do. Only Ripley "aspire[s] to full membership in the human race" (de Beauvoir [1952] 1970, xxix) and only she becomes its embodiment in resisting its annihilation.

References

Aquinas, T. 1994. On the first man; Question XCIII Fourth Article: Whether the image of God is found in every man? In *The philosophy of woman: An anthology of classic to current concepts*, ed. M. Briody Mahowald, 54-62. Indianapolis: Hackett.

Aristotle. 1942. *Generation of animals*. Translated by A.L. Peck. Cambridge: Harvard University Press.

Bick, I. J. 1994. Well, I guess I must make you nervous. *PostScript: essays in film and the humanities* 14: 45-53.

Burns, S. 2004. Restoration Hardware. *Philadelphia Weekly,* 28 January.

Canby, V. 1992. Alien 3; HAL, if you're still out there, here's a computer-friendly sequel. *New York Times*, 22 May.

Carroll, Noel. 1990. *The philosophy of horror, or paradoxes of the heart*. New York: Routledge.

de Beauvoir, S. [1952] 1970. *The second sex*. Translated by H.M. Parshley. Reprint, New York: Alfred A. Knopf.

Freud, S. 1994. Femininity. In *The philosophy of woman: An anthology of classic to current concepts*, ed. M. Briody Mahowald, 224-241. Indianapolis: Hackett.

Gallardo C., X. and C. J. Smith. 2004. *Alien woman: The making of Lt. Ellen Ripley*. New York: Continuum.

Gibson, P. Church. 2001. You've been in my life so long I can't remember anything else: Into the labyrinth with Ripley and the alien. In *Keyframes: Popular cinema and cultural studies*, eds. M. Tinkcom and A. Villarejo, 35-51. London: Routledge.

Herman, C. 1997. Some horrible dream about (s)mothering: sexuality, gender and family in the *Alien* trilogy. *PostScript: essays in film and the humanities* 16: 36-50.

Hinson, H. 1992. Alien 3. *Washington Post*, 22 May.

Howe, D. 1992. Alien 3. *Washington Post,* 22 May.

Moore, C. and G. Miles. 1992. Explorations, prosthetics and sacrifice: Phantasies of the maternal body in the *Alien* triology. *Cineaction!* 30: 54-62.

Murphy, K. 1992. The last temptation of Sigourney Weaver. *Film comment* 28: 17-20.

Schemanske, M. 1996. Working for the company: Patriarchal legislation of the maternal in *Alien 3*. In *Authority and transgression in literature and film*, eds. B. Braendlin and H. Braendlin, 127-135. Gainesville: University Press of Florida.

Speed, L. 1998. *Alien 3*: A postmodern encounter with the abject. *Arizona quarterly* 54: 125-151.
Young, R. M. 1994. Alien 3. *Free associations* 4: 447-53.

CHAPTER FOUR

GETTING OFF THE BOAT:
HYBRIDITY AND SEXUAL AGENCY
IN THE *ALIEN* FILMS

SARAH BACH AND JESSICA LANGER

In *Alien: Resurrection* (1997)[1], Ellen Ripley has been awakened by the United Systems Military from the peace of her self-sacrificing death in *Alien*[3]. Their scientists on the vessel Auriga have recreated Ripley as a genetically hybrid woman-alien, and she, yet again, must fight the acid-blooded aliens for the sake of people who attempt to use her for their own purposes. At one point in the film, whilst she and the crew of the Auriga explore the human-cargo vessel The Betty—a vessel carrying cryogenically frozen humans which are being used by the military as experimental hosts for alien larvae—an alien attacks; with the superhuman strength imparted by her hybridity, she rips its penile tongue out of its mouth. In the aftermath of the battle, as the crew stare at her, she spits sarcastically, "So, who do I have to fuck to get off this boat?" This is a symbolic moment in which Ripley, the central character played by Sigourney Weaver, simultaneously acknowledges the system she has been fighting throughout the series—patriarchal control by way of sexual power—and dismisses it entirely. Of course, she has no intention of *fucking* anyone or anything in order to gain her freedom. She no longer needs to take part in heterosexual sexual exchange in order to succeed within the system of patriarchy, but instead this line foreshadows her breaking of the system itself, utilizing her newfound human-alien hybridity to place herself outside the system and bring it down from without. This chapter will trace the development of Ripley's sexual agency throughout the *Alien* films in

---

[1] In citing each film in the *Alien Quadrilogy*, we refer to the Theatrical Release versions. The Special Editions are often substantively different, as we mention later in this chapter, and so it is necessary to specify the versions we have used in the preparation of this chapter.

her relationships with aliens and with other humans – and, ultimately, within her own hybridity and that of the aliens. In using the term "hybridity" we mean to suggest two inflections. First, we refer to the Bhabhaian idea that hybridity is activated by the resistance of the colonized to the colonizer. The aliens can be read as subjects of human exploration and attempted colonialism, and Ripley's body can be conceptualized as a site of repeated attempts at both human patriarchal and alien colonization, especially in *Alien: Resurrection*, when it is explicitly the site of both.[2] Second, we refer to an Irigarayan model of identity formation in which the subject is inherently unstable and in which this instability is not rejected but rather is productively incorporated into the identity of the subject.[3]

There is significant work being done on the films, by Patricia Melzer, Pamela C. Gibson and others,[4] that uses the paradigm of queer studies to conduct analyses which consider Ripley's sexuality beyond the boundaries of heterosexuality; a queer reading of Ripley's sexuality may be particularly apropos in relation to her relationship with Call in *Alien Resurrection*. Our analysis, however, focuses on Ripley's sexual agency in a heterosexual context. While a queer reading of the films presents one way in which Ripley may flout the patriarchal/patriarchy-analogous structures she encounters, it is also possible to read Ripley's sexual and sexually metaphorical situations in a heterosexual context, and her human-alien hybridity as a breaking of patriarchy as much as lesbianism would be.

Patriarchy, Sex and the Body

Patriarchy, of course, "is not a single or simple concept but has a whole variety of different meanings" even within the context of feminism (Beechey 1979, 66). In the context of the *Alien* films, however, the most significant aspect of patriarchy is that of *control over the body*, especially but not exclusively the female body. Abigail Bray and Claire Colbrook, drawing on Deleuze's positive bodily ethics, suggest that in the tradition of Western philosophical "phallocentrism, women's bodies are positioned

---

[2] See especially Bhabha (2004).
[3] See, for instance, Berg (1991). We are also indebted to Constable for the notion of using Irigaray in this context.
[4] For further reading on this topic, see, for example: Gallardo and Smith (2004), Gibson (2001), Melzer (2006), Picart (2004), and Stacey (2003). Our thanks to Elizabeth Graham for her assistance in compiling these references.

as prerepresentational, silent, negated and violently objectified by an active male reason" (1998, 37). Women have also, paradoxically, been seen as radically embodied to the exclusion of reason, which is reserved for men whose bodies are not the focus of their existence as women's are. Thomas Doherty, in his essay on the first three films, identifies this concept at work within the discourse of science fiction specifically. He writes, for instance, that intelligent machines are "far more threatening to the male (defined by his ability to reason) than the female (defined by her body) (1996, 183)." The corollary to this dichotomy would seem to be that mutated and changed bodies are more threatening to the female than to the male; however, because patriarchal ideology includes male control over the female body, any uncontrollable physicality—either female or alien, as the two often overlap symbolically—would produce both the science-fictional effect of extrapolation and the horror effect of the threat of the *Other*, effects that these films both use and subvert. This is not to say that male bodies are insignificant or are left alone in these films; however, male bodies are most significant to this analysis when they perform functions, such as birthing young or being penetrated, that are typically performed by female bodies.

This focus on the body as site of power struggle, in turn, is related to two main aspects of *sexual power*: First, the existence and persistence of sexual violence predicated on power; and second, the concept of control over the means of reproduction. In the *Alien* films, however, because there are not two dichotomous actors as there are in human patriarchal society (men and women) but rather three (men, women and aliens), the power structure of patriarchy is disrupted and therefore modified. There is no singular patriarchal structure even within the human aspect of the film: the Company, the military, the crew, the convicts, even the gendered androids all represent slightly different interactions with patriarchy. The two aforementioned aspects of patriarchy therefore function differently at different times within the quadrilogy. As well, the aliens take on the powers normally reserved for men in a patriarchal system, which further distorts the system itself. They displace sexual power from within patriarchy to outside it as they cannot be conceptualised along the lines of human social structures. This displacement is especially significant, as we will show, where human men are the victims of penetrative sexual violence and of forced gestation and *birth*. Therefore, patriarchy in the context of this essay refers to a general male-dominated structure in which power is predicated on gender and women are conceptualised as objects rather than subjects, but the specifics of each iteration depend on context, and the concept itself becomes blurred in the context of the aliens, whose gender and social structures are non-human.

Following this line of thought, attempts to control Ripley are generally manifested in the films as attacks against her ability to control what happens to her own body, both in terms of sexual violence and attempts to control her means of reproduction. As we will show throughout this chapter, sexual violation—both in the traditional human sense and in other, less familiar contexts—occurs in these films with stunning and frightening regularity; various individuals and groups attempt to gain control over the situations in which they find themselves by taking power through violent sexual acts. In defiance of these violations, Ripley, over the course of the quadrilogy, develops a sense of herself as separate from the patriarchal society of her origin, first through her refusal to follow its dictates and then through her acceptance of physical hybridity between herself and an alien.

Although this human-alien hybridity does not come to fruition until the fourth film, Ripley's hybridity is a work in progress from the beginning of the quadrilogy, beginning with the ambiguity of her gender presentation. She is presented with both masculine and feminine identifiers. The actress Sigourney Weaver has a strong beauty, with a straight nose, a well-defined jawline and a boyishly slim body. Over the course of the films, her hair is sometimes lush and sometimes shaven, and she is dressed sometimes in unisex jumpsuits and sometimes in what looks like leather fetish-wear: this characterization creates mutability in terms of her gender identity. Doherty considers Ripley's bodily ambiguity and identifies it as androgyny, conceiving of it as her undoing. In the third film, for instance, he sees a condemnation of Ripley's liminal position, and suggests that Ripley's death is symbolic of the impossibility of successfully transgressing the boundaries of gender and enabling a hybrid identity that allows for and includes otherness (1996, 198). (Of course, the fourth film contradicts this idea – but it had not yet been released at the time of Doherty's writing.) We concur to a certain extent with Doherty's characterization of Ripley's gender presentation, but we suggest that she is not so much androgynous as *ambiguous* and changeable. The Ripley of *Alien: Resurrection* is hybrid not only in terms of socially- and discursively-constructed gender roles but also in terms of physicality: she is first invaded by the alien, and then cloned and combined with it to create a "neo-Ripley" whose physicality and subjectivity are related to but not the same as that of the original human being. "Ripley's identity," Constable writes, "is thus set up as an intersection point between two distinct characters" (2000, 191). We aim to expand on Constable's suggestion. Ripley functions here as a site of intersection not only between the specific characters of Ripley and the alien queen but also between alien identity and a rigid human patriarchal paradigm.

Alien, *Aliens* and the Aliens

Soon after *Alien* (1979) opens, there is a journey down a sterile white "birth canal" to a clean, glowing, particularly inorganic "womb" where the crew of the Nostromo, a celestial tugboat carrying minerals for use on Earth, are waking up from cryosleep.[5] "Mother", the ship's computer, has awakened them to listen to an unknown transmission coming from the planetoid LV-426. The crew are obligated to respond to any systematized transmission of possible intelligent origin, and crewmembers Kane, Lambert, and Captain Dallas disembark to investigate. They return carrying Kane, whose face is engulfed by an alien parasite. Over Ripley's objections, the android science officer, Ash, breaks quarantine to allow the three in, a decision that the entire crew will come to regret.

The point in *Alien* at which Ripley first becomes a victim of sexual violence occurs shortly after the alien has killed Captain Dallas. As the next in charge due to second-in-command Kane's death, Ripley takes command of the Nostromo and gains access to "Mother." Ash, who has previously overridden her well-founded misgivings about the planetoid and its inhabitants, attempts to stop her, but she confronts him, cornering him until he responds with violence and knocks her down. He then rolls up a pornographic magazine and attempts to suffocate Ripley by forcing it into her mouth. The effect of this act is triply symbolic. First, of course, it is a physical violation that resembles forced oral sex. Second, the act of forcing her to *eat* the magazine suggests that he is forcing her to consume and therefore internalize the content. The content itself suggests a third meaning, associated with the second. Pornography may be read as a patriarchal society's apparatus for the proliferation of images of women that are oppressive and limiting in their stereotypical and highly stylized sexual nature;[6] significantly, these images exalt an image of femininity to which Ripley herself does not conform as she is not subordinate and powerless but rather authoritative and powerful. In forcing the magazine into her mouth, both as food-proxy and penis-proxy, Ash attempts to force Ripley into the subject-position of a woman subordinate to patriarchy.

---

[5] Constable writes at great length and in great detail regarding this scene and its maternal implications (2000, 173-177). Creed also mentions the scene (1993, 18).
[6] See especially MacKinnon (1989, 314-346).

Ripley, however, refuses to accept either the physical or ideological assault, and fights against this positioning. She struggles with Ash and attempts to free herself from his grip. Although her need of a male crewmate's help emphasizes the strength of the patriarchal constrictions against which she is fighting—this necessity can be read as another patriarchal trope, hemming her in on all sides by male-dominated convention—her resistance to Ash's act signifies her struggle for autonomous sexual agency. He punishes Ripley not only for intruding on the Company's directive to bring the alien back to Earth, but also for intruding on and interrupting the proper patriarchal order; in using pseudo-sexual force in this punishment, Ash is using a particularly patriarchal form of violence to attempt to force capitulation to its rigid norms.

The extent to which patriarchal power is coded in terms of sexual power in the film is also wryly demonstrated by the fact that the two beings that collude in the alien's attack on the crew, Ash and Mother, are beings without sexual subjectivities: they are *gendered* but not *sexed*. Ash is an android, what Lynda Zwinger calls "the most abject object in the film" (1992, 75), and Mother, who "births" her crew into known danger and sacrifices them to the ends of the company, is

a mother so gothic she will collude with evil capitalists and aliens in the murder of her children. (74)

It is not that Ash wants sex; rather, he uses the oppressive power of patriarchal sexual ideology to subdue Ripley. Both Ash and Mother are aligned with the patriarchal Company, and both Ash's sexually-inflected attack on Ripley and the sterility and disembodiedness of the Nostromo's parody of birth indicate that the Company is a patriarchal institution and is interested in upholding patriarchal power structures.

The alien's power structure is not as clear as that of the Company and its agents, however. At times it seems aligned with the penetration-driven patriarchal system of the Company, while at other times it seems a maternal, creative force, and it never fits perfectly into either of these humanity-based moulds. The alien is deliberately, specifically *Other*, and is presented, therefore, as hybrid in its use of power. A frequently discussed demonstration of this dynamic is the case of Kane, who, near the beginning of *Alien*, trespasses with Dallas and Lambert on the alien's nest, investigating the birthing "pods" of the creatures. As Kane takes a look, a pod cracks open and a facehugger jumps out at him, covering his helmeted head, obscuring his face and implanting him with the larva that will become an alien. The facehugger is a grotesque combination of vagina and phallus. Here, as well as in far greater visual detail in the second film, *Aliens*, we see the monstrous embodiment of the maternal vagina and the violence of the phallus, combined in a hybrid form that represents both the sexualized violence of the facehugger's penetration and the corrupt *motherhood* that such penetration bestows on its victims. Creed sees the alien pod as a maternal womb and the contents as a figure that seeks to force Kane to return to a pre-Oedipal state connected to and absorbed by the mother (1993, 18-19). Constable (2000, 181) expands on Creed's analysis and links the horror of this scene to Julia Kristeva's account of abjection, which involves the demarcation of boundaries to exclude the abject. We would suggest a third reading: that the Alien is neither exclusively monstrous innards-figure nor subjectivity-obliterating force, but is rather both and is *also* a penetrative impregnator which utilizes the sexual violence of forced reproduction. It is a thing that, as Creed suggests, has a "womb" that "impregnates" Kane (1993, 19). Therefore, the horror of this sequence of scenes—the attack on Kane, the "birth" of the Alien from his chest, and his subsequent death—stems not only from the spectacle of the monstrous, fleshy mother, as Constable suggests, nor only from the erasure of fully-formed Freudian subjectivity, as Creed writes, but also from the violation of the patriarchal order in which women are the victims, not perpetrators, of sexual violence, and are the only ones to be impregnated and give birth. Kane's death represents the patriarchal inability to adapt to the gender hybridity represented by the alien; he, a man aligned with the patriarchal Company, is not able to withstand this fracturing of the system of patriarchy, which demands a hierarchical and dichotomous rather than hybrid construction of gender.

While the alien's danger to Kane is carried out through forced reproduction, in the cases of Lambert and Ripley this threat is carried out through sexual violence. Navigation Officer Lambert is the only other woman on the Nostromo, and she and Ripley are often implicitly contrasted. Lambert is fair and blue-eyed while Ripley has darker colouring, and Ripley's body is boyish while Lambert's is curvier, superficial differences that nevertheless set up a visual contrast between them from the outset. Their interactions are often antagonistic as well: for instance, when Ripley asserts that she would have left Lambert, Kane and Dallas outside the ship due to quarantine regulations if Ash had not overridden her decision, Lambert slaps her, and when the two argue over the best course of action to take once the alien gets loose, Lambert is tearful while Ripley is angry. Their reactions to the events of the film are usually opposite. Lambert becomes extremely upset when Captain Dallas is killed, which contrasts with Ripley's more matter-of-fact approach. Lambert's panicked insistence that Ripley break quarantine rules when Kane is attacked, and her aforementioned anger and physical violence towards Ripley suggest that Lambert is presented as the over-emotional, explicitly feminine foil to Ripley's more ambiguous gender presentation. As described earlier in this chapter, Ripley's body oscillates between conforming to the ideals of femininity and flouting them, sometimes at the same time, as when her beautiful curly hair crowns her slim-hipped, jumpsuit-clad body. Her actions fluctuate in the same way between an assertiveness identified in a patriarchal system with masculinity and the feminine necessity of fighting back against figurative sexual assault. Throughout the film, Ripley subverts the expectations of femininity in this way, whereas Lambert is identified as explicitly feminine.

Lambert's encounter with the alien is, therefore, significant in its sexual violence. The alien rises before her, its shadow falling over her, a menacing presence that leaves her paralysed with fear. Instead of a shot of the alien biting into Lambert's head, as we have seen during Parker's death only moments before, there is a perversely languorous, intimate shot of the alien's tail curling around Lambert's leg, rising to her thigh. The moment is drawn out and brutally slow, focusing on how the alien touches Lambert. The next shot is a close-up of Lambert's face: she is sobbing, her eyes closed. The alien's killing of Lambert is coded in terms of patriarchal sexual violence, as it is implicitly a rape-murder; because she is a woman who is herself coded in feminine terms, the sexual violence against her is portrayed as a violation that resembles the work of human patriarchy. This scene contrasts with the ambiguity of the alien's sex presentation earlier in the film and with the alien's gender presentation in later films, setting up the alien as a gender-hybrid who is capable of various gender presentations including explicit patriarchal maleness and exclusive maternal femaleness.

The moment at which Ripley herself becomes the object of sexual violence by the alien occurs at the end of *Alien*. The alien reveals its presence in the shuttle, violating what Ripley had thought would be a safe space that would ensure her survival. As Ripley undresses, the camera moves around the shuttle; it is unclear whose point of view the shot represents. This question is answered when the alien reaches out to Ripley from its hiding place, dripping slime from long fingers that resemble bones ripped from living flesh. Again we have a doubled symbolic representation of the alien. It is both so radically embodied that reason—and in this case, sentience—is nonexistent, a state usually identified as feminine in Western patriarchal philosophy as Bray and

Colbrook (1998) suggest, and violently, menacingly phallic, implicitly threatening by its presence and posturing to penetrate Ripley's body as it penetrated Lambert's. This is especially significant in that Ripley is explicitly sexualized in this scene, an "erotic spectacle," with the camera's focus on her near-nude body and with voyeuristic shifts in point-of-view (Torry 1994, 348). Weaver herself, speaking about the scene in an interview, has said: "I think it's kind of provocative—you're almost seeing me through the alien's eyes" (Peary 1984, 162).

The alien does not attack immediately, but lingers instead in this moment: its power over Ripley's life and death seems coded in terms of sexual power. Weaver holds that the alien is not evil but is "following its natural instincts to reproduce through whatever living things are around it," a reading that would suggest that the alien sees Ripley, like all humans, as sexual prey (Peary 1984, 162). The alien draws out this experience of power as a precursor to the sexualised attack that, if Lambert's experience is any indication, will follow. When the alien does make itself known to Ripley in a show of aggression, she is defenceless and explicitly female, forced into the feminine position of actee rather than actor, and stripped of her clothing and, therefore, whatever power she has derived from the jumpsuit's ability to hide her body and thus her femaleness. Her solution is to retreat into a space suit, significant in that it is the armour of the patriarchal, colonial Company. The suit hides her body from both the camera and the alien, signifying her reappropriation of her own sexual autonomy which at this point in the quadrilogy can only occur within the framework of patriarchal constructions of sex and power. In a patriarchal system, the power of the explicitly female body is that of passive sexual attractiveness, not active sexual agency, and she must hide her body and take on the outer guise of masculinity in order to achieve that agency. Robert Torry touches on this: he writes that in this scene, Ripley shifts her position from object of the sexual gaze to "that of armed and armoured phallic warrior" (1994, 348). But can agency that is allowed to exist only in tandem with conformity to an oppressive system be considered true agency? That Ripley must conform to at least one aspect of patriarchal ideology in order to defeat the alien suggests that, although she has escaped with her life, she has not yet escaped the confines of a patriarchal system.

Near the beginning of the second film in the quadrilogy, *Aliens* (1986), is Ripley's horrific dream of giving birth to an alien; therefore, at its very outset the film raises the spectre of vulnerability to alien sexual violence in terms both of forcible penetration and of forcible birth. After she wakes up in terror, a representative of the Company, Burke, tells her that the Company has recently lost contact with a colony they had attempted to establish on LV-426 (Hadley's Hope), and they fear that it has been overtaken by the aliens. He then manages to convince Ripley to accompany a Marine mission to rescue any surviving colonists.

Once on LV-426, however, Burke uses captive alien facehuggers as embodiments of sexual violence against Ripley and Newt, the young sole survivor of the colony of Hadley's Hope who functions in the narrative and ideological structure of the film as Ripley's surrogate child. Burke, an agent of the patriarchal Company, sets two facehuggers free in the room where Ripley and Newt are sleeping. He does not seem to want to assault Ripley or Newt himself; rather, he wishes to impregnate them with the alien larvae, an act that is sexual by proxy. The violation that this act represents is doubled in that Ripley is not only a potential victim of the alien's sexual violence, but she is also Burke's intended victim. He uses the alien as a proxy for his own desire to control Ripley, lending credence to the assertion, indicated by Ash's conduct as well, that such violence is less about sexual desire than it is about control. Burke knows that he cannot control Ripley directly without risking himself in a physical fight, nor can he convince her to keep the alien for the Company instead of destroying it. His attempt to impregnate her with the alien, an attempt to force Ripley to follow his plans, is motivated by the desire to control her in the interest of his capitalist ambitions—in a sense, he wishes to control the means of alien production by controlling the means of Ripley's reproduction.

Though Ripley's reproductive agency is first challenged by patriarchy through Burke's attempt to *impregnate* her with an alien larva, it is challenged in a different way by the alien queen at the climax of the film. This battle has been read as a fight between two "generative powers," each mother trying to destroy the other's children. Constable writes that

[t]he battle between the two species types places them in an oppositional relation while drawing attention to the similarity between the two protagonists. Both are parthenogenetic mother figures who are tropes for the perpetuation of their respective species. The conflicts between them take the form of attempting to destroy each other's generative powers. (2000, 189)

In this context, sexual power is bound up with motherhood: Ripley's protection of Newt, her adopted child, is the signifier of her status as a functional mother. This particular function of sexual agency is especially significant because of the way in which it is subverted by Ripley here. Control of childbearing, the biological path to motherhood, is a method of sexual control in a patriarchal system, and forced childbearing, of which we have seen a perversion in the chestburster aliens, is a form of sexual violence. However, Ripley's *motherhood* of Newt is *unconnected* to the process of childbearing as Newt is her surrogate but not her biological, daughter. Therefore, a site of sexual agency can be located in the non-biological nature of Ripley's relationship with Newt. The relationship represents a fracturing of the normatively sexual mode of motherhood, in her emotional connection to Newt *despite* her lack of biological connection rather than *because of* the biological connection between a mother and a daughter. It is an active and chosen connection rather than a passive biological connection and functions as a site of Ripley's power. The fact that Ripley has not given birth to Newt makes her no less a mother, but it divorces the sheer physicality of childbirth, with its potential to be the apotheosis of a sexually violent act, from the longer-term, more emotionally oriented act of motherhood. Ironically, by attacking Ripley's adopted child *because* she is Ripley's child, as Constable suggests, the alien queen implicitly acknowledges the reality of the chosen familial bond between Ripley and Newt—a bond that is outside of the patriarchal ideal of the biological, nuclear family as primary unit of society. Therefore, the queen attacks from a place outside of patriarchy, not within it, and reinforces the alien disruption of human patriarchy.

Death and the Alien

At the end of *Aliens*, although Ripley, the Marine Hicks, and Newt escape alive, only Ripley will survive to fight again. By the opening of *Alien³* (1992), rape has already taken place; Ripley's fear in the opening sequence of *Aliens* is actualized here, and she is unknowingly *pregnant* with an alien. Over the course of the film, Ripley comes to terms with the fact that she has become a victim of exactly that thing—sexual violation and the resultant loss of reproductive agency—which she has fought so hard against. Ripley's challenge in this film is to move beyond victimhood in order to regain agency. The ship has crash-landed on a planet inhabited exclusively by a penal colony of male rapists and murderers, Ripley is carrying within her an alien larva that will kill her when it reaches maturity, and the Company is coming to retrieve the alien regardless of the consequence to Ripley. The only avenue of escape open to her is death.

Ripley's arrival on the prison planet Fury 161 is met with hostility on the part of the inmates; they fear primarily that her presence will prompt them to break their vows of celibacy. Because of this, Doctor Clemens suggests that Ripley should remain in the infirmary for her own safety when, upon waking up, her first concern is to get back to her shuttle and check for the presence of the alien. She refuses to be cowed, however, and threatens to go without clothes unless he provides her with some which he does. Although she is aware of the threat inherent in being the sole woman on a prison planet inhabited by sexually violent men, Ripley does not acknowledge this, refusing to surrender her agency to the implicit threat of sexual violence. The prison superintendent, however, is not pleased to hear that Ripley has left the infirmary and sneers that she has been "parading around" in front of inmates, "giving them ideas." In speaking about Ripley this way, the superintendent explicitly allies himself with patriarchal sexual violence. This destructive conception of women's sexuality, in which women are considered responsible not only for their own sexuality but for men's as well, is particular to patriarchy; in this paradigm, a woman is considered to be sexually aggressive if she is not actively demure. Ripley represents a threat to this construction. Ironically, she intimidates the superintendent both in her refusal to conform to patriarchal ideals of demure, subordinate femininity and simultaneously in her refusal to hide her femaleness.

Later, when Ripley joins the inmates for a meal, she thanks Dillon, the inmate who has taken on the role of the prison planet's spiritual leader, for speaking at the funeral for Newt and Hicks. Dillon does not accept her thanks, asserting instead that he is a man who rapes and murders women, two acts that represent the ultimate extreme of patriarchal misogyny. Ripley responds with: "Really... Well, I guess I must make you nervous." As Ilsa Bick writes, Ripley's statement demonstrates her refusal to accept the prisoners' power structures:

> By that one utterance, Ripley takes the traditional notion of male, phallic power in its unquestioned prerogative of aggressive penetration – and turns it on its bald head. (1994, 45)

By inverting the structure of patriarchal power, in which men are sexual aggressors and women must fear that aggression, Ripley seizes a measure of power.

A similar moment occurs in the next scene, when Ripley interrupts Clemens' questions about the need to cremate Newt and Hicks and initiates sex with him by asking, "Are you attracted to me?" The immediate effect of this interpolation is that Ripley avoids telling him about the possible alien larvae within the bodies. This is also, however, the first time in the quadrilogy that we see Ripley take the initiating role in sexual activity. Although there was sexual tension with Hicks in *Aliens*, it remained implicit, evident only in prolonged looks and an exchange of first names prior to Ripley going off in search of Newt. With Clemens, Ripley finally has the opportunity for consensual sex, and she takes advantage of that opportunity as soon as it seems reasonable. She acknowledges the desires of her body and fulfills them; in exerting initiative, she exerts power, converting herself in this instance from sexual object to sexual actor.

Later in the film, Ripley is attacked by a group of inmates who intend to rape her. The superintendent had warned Ripley that her female presence would have a dangerous effect on the men—that is, that patriarchal sexual power structures were paramount on the planet. This attempted rape can be read as a symbolic punishment for her refusal to show fear of, or even demonstrate acknowledgment of, this threat, her refusal to be controlled by the inmates' uncontrolled urges. Certainly, these urges are primarily of power, not lust, as is the case with rape in the patriarchal system: as Ximena Gallardo C. and C. Jason Smith argue, although Ripley is female and they are male,

> the film deconstructs their impulse by refusing to show Ripley as the feminine. The scene is not about lust or reproduction: it is about defining masculine power through the subjection of the female body. (2004, 139)

Although she fights back, Ripley is not strong enough to fend off her would-be rapists; she cannot escape until Dillon intervenes. This scene echoes the magazine scene in the first film: despite her refusal to capitulate to sexual aggression, she is physically too weak to fight off the several men and one android threatening her; symbolically, she is still bound by patriarchy.

Once Ripley and the audience see an ultrasound of Ripley's chest, which reveals an alien queen embryo growing inside her, the threat of being sexually assaulted by the prisoners is relegated to the background; a more lethal rape has already been committed. Ripley spends the rest of the film coming to terms with her impending death and working to make sure that humanity is safe before she chooses to die. In the final scenes of the Theatrical Release, Ripley gives birth to the alien as she throws herself into the furnace, her hopes for escape realized in the finality of death. It is worth noting that in the Special Edition, this scene is substantially changed. Most significantly, Ripley falls into the flames without the alien bursting forth from her chest, and her arms remain outstretched in the crucifixion position instead of stroking the newborn chestburster until it stops squealing. The change suggests a major shift in connotation. The Theatrical Release version can be read as more emotionally ambiguous, with Ripley demonstrating a maternal instinct towards the alien even as she kills them both, while the Special Edition suggests Ripley as a more straightforward Christ-figure. We prefer the Theatrical Release version as we believe it is truer to Ripley's character, and it also makes more sense in light of Ripley's maternal feelings towards the aliens and her self-description as the "monster's mother" in the fourth film.

The meaning of Ripley's suicide itself is also contested. As we mentioned earlier, Doherty (1996) sees her death as symbolic of the pragmatic impossibility of what he considers her gender ambiguity. She cannot exist within male-dominated contexts because she is a woman, and she cannot succeed as a mother because she is too masculine (198). According to Doherty, in the end, Ripley dies because no gender in a binary-patriarchal system can contain her; there is nothing left for her but the Alien and then the furnace (198). Kathleen Murphy positions the scene as a religious self-martyrdom, and Ripley's assertion of sexual agency in her encounter with Clemens as one step towards it. Murphy writes that

> it is as though, in satisfying the flesh's appetite for primal connection, she is assenting to that final crucifixion, the moment when she will take leave of the physical home she has defended so long. (1992, 20)

Gallardo and Smith (2004) complicate this religious contention. They write that "the Company is the nastiest rapist of all" (150), and because "there is no God but the Company to submit to... Ripley rejects that option" (152). We would build upon their argument. In a situation with few choices, and no good ones, Ripley's very activation of her agency, her decision to die in a way of her own choosing, is in a sense a cry of victory. Caught between two rapists, the alien rapist who has impregnated her and the Company that objectifies her and values her only as a vessel of capital, she chooses to live and to die by the hand of neither, but rather by her own. The fact is that death is inevitable, and her decision actively to choose the manner of her death is her triumph. In a sense, in doing so, Ripley regains as much control over her own body as is possible. This eventuality is a modification of the ending of *Alien*, in which Ripley was able to protect herself and expel the alien from the shuttle only by suiting up in the armour of the patriarchal Company: instead of capitulating to patriarchy to save herself, she rejects it entirely and accepts the fatal consequences. Although her resurrection by government scientists in *Alien: Resurrection* represents a beyond-death trump card, her choice, nevertheless, signifies her ultimate agency, and She carries this power into the fourth film.

Monsters, Mothers and Hybridity

Ripley returns in *Alien: Resurrection* as a very different person, created through genetic engineering by the United Systems Military out of a combination of her own genes and those of the Alien. Adam Roberts writes that the film is "fascinated with monstrous hybridity and revolting mutation" (2006, 284), and the film does function as the apotheosis of the monstrosity, and the hybridity, of Ripley and the aliens both.

Of great significance in this film is Ripley's relationship with the *female* android, Call. Call demands to be taken seriously but instead is treated by most of the crew in an exaggeratedly objectified manner, literal objectification of the android amplified by patriarchal objectification of the female. This treatment is complex and oscillating. At first Call is treated as a sexual object, then as a mechanical non-person after her android status is revealed and sometimes both at once. Captains Elgyn and Perez call her a "little girl," and Elgyn says she is "severely fuckable," laying out the patriarchal expectations of femininity, the demand for simultaneous innocence and sexual availability. Johner harasses her constantly and ambiguously, hooting at her like a monkey. Later, once she is revealed as an android, the cold-sleep survivor Purvis, kidnapped by the mercenaries on the Betty and brought to the United Systems Military ship Auriga as a host for alien offspring, calls her a "toaster," literally objectifying her. Like Ash of *Alien*, she is the "most abject object in the film" (Zwinger 1992, 75).

Both Ripley and Call are hybrid, and both are "constructs," as Call puts it. Ripley is a literal human-alien hybrid, and Call may be read as a hybrid of literal (as android) and ideological (as woman) objectification under patriarchy, a position that makes her hybridity more complex than was Ash's or Bishop's. The relationship between Call and Ripley begins tumultuously, however. After Call witnesses Ripley's rebuff of Johner's sexual advances in the gymnasium as well as a truly stunning feat of athleticism in which Ripley sinks a basket over her shoulder from a full court away, Call enters Ripley's room, hoping that she can kill Ripley before the scientists retrieve the alien. When she sees that it is too late, Call offers Ripley freedom through death, from her apparent destiny as tool of the United Systems Military using the liberating power of a deadly knife. Ripley, however, takes the weapon and impales her own hand upon it. This act symbolizes Ripley's metaphorical disregard for the threat of sexual violence that once held power over her. Instead, Ripley herself is damaging to the knife, which sizzles and smokes when it comes into contact with her acidic blood. Metaphorically, as well as in actuality, she can now defend herself against any phallus or phallus-proxy, whether man, woman or alien. It is her hybridity, the fact that her physical as well as discursive identity is now defined not by its position within the boundaries of a patriarchal system, but by its transgression of the same, that enables this success.

The struggle for agency, as we have seen, has been central to Ripley's character throughout the series, and she finds in Call a counterpart in this struggle. Ripley's relationship with Call is built on similarity and overlapping of experiences, highlighting both characters' attempts to resist patriarchal oppression, and it is fraught for the same reason: they each see in the other an experiential mirror. For instance, when Call says to Ripley, "You're a thing, a construct, they grew you in a fucking lab," she could as easily be talking about herself. This dynamic leads both to their initial conflict and to their reconciliation later in the film.

There is another mirroring in the film, albeit an uneven one, between Ripley and the alien queen, the latter grown in the former's chest; each is a hybrid of human and alien. As Ripley has been infused with alien genetic material, so has the queen been given human aspects through its gestation within Ripley, aspects that are even more in evidence in her offspring. After her search, Ripley finally finds the queen in her nest; several of the crew are there with her, cocooned in slime. Among them is the scientist Gediman, who engineered the Ripley-clone and the queen within her and who says exultantly despite his captivity,

> At first, everything was normal. The Queen laid her eggs. But then she started to change. She added a second cycle cell. So, this time there is no host. There are no eggs. There is only her womb, and the creature inside. That is Ripley's gift to her: a human reproductive system. She is giving birth for you, Ripley, and now she is perfect!

This time, even the alien queen herself is being used by the Company in the service of forced reproduction. In becoming part-human, the alien has become subject to human patriarchy because she has become susceptible to human male control of her reproduction. This mirroring is uneven, as suggested above, because the mirroring of the characters' hybridity does not extend to mutual success in surviving their use as subjects of patriarchal power: although Ripley "get[s] off the boat," the alien queen is killed by her own child. The child turns to Ripley rather than the alien queen as a mother figure. In this act we see two simultaneous inversions:

the queen, like a human, has become a victim of its chestbursting progeny, and Ripley, like an alien, has become a primarily biological generative power. Ripley and the queen have, in a way, become each other; however, Ripley breaks free in the end from both human and alien power.

The child, a hybrid of human and alien like its mother the queen, mirrors Ripley as its mother does, and it is in her victory over the alien child where Ripley's victory is at its most complete. Ripley's reactions to the child are complex and ambiguous at first, but resolve at the end into an action that becomes the apotheosis of her journey towards sexual agency. When Ripley witnesses the birth of the alien child and its subsequent killing of both the queen and Gediman, she appears frightened, but instead of killing the child, she leaves the room and rejoins the crew of the Betty. This withdrawal from action, alongside Ripley's welcoming of the child's demonstration of affection towards her in the form of puppylike face-licking, suggests that there is tension between Ripley's biological maternal bond with the child and her instinct to save herself and the crew from destruction. However, when the child intrudes into the Betty and threatens Call, Ripley steps in and kills it. As we discussed earlier, Ripley's purpose in developing full sexual agency is to be free from sexual violence and to control her own reproduction; the child represents reproduction that was forced upon her, despite her maternal attachment to it. In this reading of the film, we would identify the child's threatening of Call as a significant tipping point because when Ripley defeats the child and thus saves Call, she defeats patriarchy in both senses. She kills the result of its agents' final attempt to use her reproductive capacity for their own gain, and she rescues Call—as a female android, the "most abject object" of patriarchy in the film—from said violence. In protecting Call at all costs, including the sacrifice of her grotesque but pitiable progeny, Ripley gains her greatest victory over patriarchy.

Conclusion: An Ambiguous Victory

The final scene of *Alien: Resurrection* is a homecoming of sorts. Ripley and Call look out the window of the Betty, awed, as the golden-lit surface of Earth moves beneath them. After a time, as they reach the surface, Call asks, "What do we do now?" Ripley, seeming almost surprised at the question, thinks for a moment and replies, "I don't know. I'm a stranger here myself." Ripley is, indeed, a stranger to the world. She has changed into something outside of human experience and human conception, hybrid of body and mind, both physically and metaphorically triumphant over the sexual violence and reproductive control imposed by patriarchy on the films' human civilization.

The process of shedding patriarchal control over her sexual agency has been fourfold: she has progressed from using patriarchy at the end of the first film, to fighting it in the second, to sacrificing her life in defiance of it in the third, and finally to defeating it in the fourth. In a sense, this process has been one of alienation or, rather, *Alien*ation. In becoming a hybrid of human and the aliens she has fought for so long, in accepting the alien *Other* into herself, Ripley has managed to break out of a system that subordinates its own Other. Her hybridity is patriarchy's paradoxical gift to her: the ability to defy the system that made her and to overcome its hold on her. In her strangeness, her alien-ness, lies Ripley's greatest strength.

However, there remains one fly in the ointment. The patriarchy itself has not been defeated; it has shown that it is willing and able to cheat even death, that most reliable of conditions, to use Ripley's body to accomplish its goals. Even her final victory over patriarchy in the end is metaphor rather than metonym. She has killed the child, the result of Gediman's experimentation, she has rescued Call, the avatar of female objectification, and she has won freedom for herself. However, she has not defeated the United Systems Military and she has not destroyed patriarchy itself. Her victories are indirect, displaced onto the victims of patriarchy such as the child and Call rather than the men who perpetrate it, and the series has set up with its cloning-from-death storyline an open-ended, permanent route for the United Systems Military to take control again. Whilst Ripley's is a story of personal triumph, it is not one of systemic victory: the patriarchal militaries, companies, scientists, and crews are still out there, waiting to be fought some more by more strong women, or even again by Ripley herself. In a sequel, perhaps.

References

Alien, DVD. Directed by Ridley Scott. Twentieth Century Fox: Los Angeles, CA, 1979.

Aliens, DVD. Directed by James Cameron. Twentieth Century Fox: Los Angeles, CA, 1986.

Alien^3, DVD. Directed by David Fincher. Twentieth Century Fox: Los Angeles, CA, 1992.

Alien: Resurrection, DVD. Directed by Jean-Pierre Jeunet. Twentieth Century Fox: Los Angeles, CA, 1997.

Battersby, C. 1998. *The phenomenal woman: Feminist metaphysics and the patterns of identity.* Cambridge: Polity Press.

Beechey, V. 1979. On patriarchy. *Feminist review* 3: 66-82.

Berg, M. 1991. Luce Irigaray's 'Contradictions': Poststructuralism and feminism. *Signs* 17(1): 50-70.

Bhabha, H. K. 2004. *The location of culture.* London: Routledge.

Bick, I. 1994. Well, I guess I must make you nervous: Woman and the space of *Alien³*. *PostScript* 14(1-2): 45-58.

Bray, A. and C. Colbrook. 1998. The haunted flesh: Corporeal feminism and the politics of (dis)embodiment. *Signs* 24(1): 35-67

Constable, C. 2000. Becoming the monster's mother: Morphologies of identity in the *Alien* series. In *Alien zone II: The spaces of science fiction cinema,* ed. A. Kuhn, 173-201. London: Verso.

Creed, B. 1993. *The monstrous feminine: Film, feminism, psychoanalysis.* London: Routledge.

Doherty, T. 1996. Genre, gender and the *Aliens* trilogy. In *The dread of difference: Gender and the horror film,* ed. B.K.

Grant, 181-99. Austin: University of Texas Press.

Gallardo C., Ximena and Smith, C. Jason. 2004. *Alien Woman: The Making of Lt. Ellen Ripley.* New York: Continuum.

Gibson. P. C. 2001. "You've been in my life so long I can't remember anything else": Into the labyrinth with Ripley and the alien. In *Keyframes: Popular cinema and cultural studies,* ed. M. Tinkcom and A. Villarejo, 35-51. London: Routledge.

MacKinnon, C. 1989. Sexuality, pornography, and method: Pleasure under patriarchy. *Ethics* 99(2): 314-346.

Melzer, P. 2006. Technoscience's stepdaughter: The feminist cyborg. In *Alien constructions: Science fiction and feminist thought,* 108-148. Austin: University of Texas Press.

Murphy, K. 1992. The last temptation of Sigourney Weaver. *Film comment* 28(4): 17-20.

Peary, D. 1984. Playing Ripley in *Alien*: An interview with Sigourney Weaver. *Omni's screen flights/screen fantasies: The future according to science fiction cinema,* ed. D. Peary, 154-166. New York: Doubleday.

Picard, C. J. S. 2004. The third shadow and hybrid genres: Horror, humor, gender, and race. In *Alien Resurrection. Communication and critical/ cultural studies* 1(4): 335-354.

Roberts, A. 2006. *The history of science fiction.* London: Palgrave.

Stacey, J. 2003. She is not herself: The deviant relations of *Alien Resurrection. Screen* 44(3): 251-276.

Torry, R. 1994. Awakening to the other: Feminism and the ego-ideal in *Alien. Women's studies: An interdisciplinary journal* 23(4): 343-63.

Zwinger, L. 1992. Blood relations: Feminist theory meets the uncanny alien bug mother. *Hypatia* 7(2): 74-90.

CHAPTER FIVE

ALIEN'S ELLEN RIPLEY: AMBIGUOUS INTERPRETATIONS AND HER AUTONOMY

ELIZABETH GRAHAM

...motion pictures are a genuine educational institution... in the truer sense of actually introducing [a person] to and acquainting him with a type of life which has immediate, practical, and momentous significance....

Because motion pictures are educational in this sense, they may conflict with other educational institutions. They may challenge what other institutions take for granted. The schemes of conduct which they present may not only fill gaps left by the school, by the home, and by the church, but they may also cut athwart the standards and values which these latter institutions seek to inculcate.
—Herbert Blumer, *Movies and Conduct* [1933] 1970, 196-197

Introduction

Over the past four decades, a number of female protagonists have appeared in science fiction, horror, action films and television shows: the *Bionic Woman, Wonder Woman, Xena: Warrior Princess, Buffy the Vampire Slayer,* Max in *Dark Angel, Laura Croft: Tomb Rader,* Sarah Connor in the *Terminator* films, and Selene in *Underworld,* and many more. However, none of these stands out in our minds like Sigourney Weaver's Ellen Ripley in the *Alien* films. Ripley "offers a prototype for a new female lead that differs profoundly from the typical science fiction and fantasy film heroine" (Bell-Metereau 1985, 10). She was the first female protagonist in the science fiction/action/horror film genre to receive public acclaim and, therefore, she represents a turning point for female roles.[1]

Since the release of *Alien* in 1979, Ellen Ripley has received a great deal of attention. A quick search on Google points to over 870,000 Web sources to explore. Film critics, academics, and members of the general public have pondered the meaning of Ripley and her place within the hybrid film genre of science fiction, action, and horror. Their insights and interpretations vary significantly and often appear to contradict each other. However, regardless of the specific focus of the comments on Ripley, in many there is an underlying reliance on traditional gender role dichotomies.[2]

While much recent feminist film criticism has taken up the theoretical position of intersectionality, and I agree that such a position offers important insights, I will not engage with this literature. Like Rismen, I believe

> that gender must be understood within the context of the intersecting domains of inequality [gender, social class, race/ethnicity, sexuality, nationality, etc.].... I do not agree, however, with an operational strategy for scholarship that suggests the appropriate analytic solution is to only work within an intersectionality framework.... To focus all investigations into the complexity or subjective experience of interlocking oppressions would have us lose access to how the mechanisms for different kinds of inequality are produced. (2004, 442-3)

There remains a great deal to learn about each of these mechanisms and it is only through exploration of each individually *and* collectively that a comprehensive understanding can be achieved.

Consistent with that position, the purpose of this chapter is to further our understanding of the ways in which the concept of gender has functioned as an ideological foundation for three varied interpretations of Ellen Ripley. In addition, accepting that feminist scholars need "to also study change and equality when it occurs rather than only documenting inequality" (Risman 2004, 435), I also offer an alternative interpretation of Ripley that reflects positive societal changes related to gender.

---

[1] The *Alien* films to which I refer throughout this chapter are the 2003 Director's Cuts and Special Editions versions of the films. I have chosen these because they include footage not seen in the original Theatrical Releases.

[2] Throughout this chapter, traditional gender role dichotomies refers to early to mid 20th century Western views regarding appropriate gendered behaviour with the often illustrated beliefs about the distinctiveness of the categories feminine and masculine.

I begin the chapter by presenting three common and varied interpretations of Ripley found in the literature. These interpretations are *definitions of the situation*[3] that reflect principal aspects of the Western socio-cultural context in relation to women prior to and during the release of the *Alien Quadrilogy*. The specific aspects discussed in this chapter are the dominant ideological views and structural arrangements regarding gender, the emergence and establishment of Second Wave Feminism and the backlash against feminist ideals. The varied interpretations of Ripley are presented as resulting from that context and are reflective of Symbolic Interactionists' assumption that we attach meaning to people, objects, and situations according to the use they have for us at the time which rests on how well they fit our assumptions about similar situations that are based on prior interactions with others. Continuing from a Symbolic Interactionist framework, the latter part of this chapter is devoted to an alternative interpretation of Ripley that identifies her as reflective of the positive changes women have experienced in society over the past few decades. She is an example of an autonomous character that does not fit the false dichotomy of masculine versus feminine.

Divergent Interpretations of Ripley

Three common interpretations of Ripley are Ripley as the monstrous feminine, Ripley as the woman in man's clothes, and Ripley as the traditional woman and mother.[4] My intention for this section is not to focus on the specific details of any one critic or theorist. Rather, I am focusing on these basic concepts that are commonly applied in interpretations of Ripley. I should also point out that I am not claiming these three concepts are the only lenses through which Ripley has been interpreted. In fact, some of the critics whom I cite in this chapter do not necessarily focus on these concepts but aspects of their work reflect one or more of them. Each of these interpretations offers a very distinct picture of Ripley that at first glance appears to contradict the others. However, we

---

[3] *Definition of the situation* is a person's interpretation of a situation and the objects in it. It is an agreement among persons about who they are, what actions are appropriate in the setting, and what the behaviours mean. To establish the definition of the situation, people must decide on the type of social occasion that is occurring (including rules and conventions); the identities claimed by participants; and the identities participants will be granted in the interaction (Charon 2004).

[4] Traditional woman and mother and traditional gender roles throughout this chapter refer to the popular 1950s views of women and gender in Western societies.

see that one interpretation is no more accurate than the others and that they all assume that gender is a dichotomous concept.

Monstrous feminine

"[T]he concept of the monstrous feminine... is related intimately to the problems of sexual difference and castration" (Creed 1996, 36). Creed, perhaps the most commonly cited theorist in discussions of this concept, explains the monstrous feminine in relation to Kristeva's discussion of abjection—"that which does not 'respect borders, positions, rules,' that which 'disturbs identity, system, order'" (Creed 1996, 36). She claims that "the function of the monstrous [is to]... bring about an encounter between the symbolic order and that which threatens its stability" (1993, 11). While Creed, herself, does not describe Ripley as an example of the monstrous feminine, some adopt this position, and others point to a parallel between Ripley and the alien which is identified as the monstrous feminine. At a very basic level, this identification of Ripley as the monstrous feminine is understandable given that "signs of sexual differences are a form of abjection which Kristeva delineates" (Speed 1998, 133). Woman's difference, or in this case Ripley's difference, in relation to the *male* norm is explained in terms of the manifestation of men's fears of the female – the vagina dentata, witch, or Medusa. Her actions have the potential to destroy the established patriarchal order.

There is no doubt that Ripley as the monstrous feminine can be seen in numerous scenes in the *Alien Quadrilogy*. Whether through her mere presence or her actions, she often challenges or threatens existing power structures in her world. In the first film she challenges the authority of her captain and the science officer and ultimately disobeys the Company by destroying its ship and cargo. For example, in *Alien*, when Dallas and Lambert return to the Nostromo with Kane, after he has been attacked by a face-hugger, Ripley insists that they must follow "quarantine procedures." After Ash, the science officer, lets the three crewmembers in, Dallas is in the infirmary with Ash who is examining Kane and the face-hugger that is attached to him. Dallas yells at Ripley, who is outside the infirmary watching through a window,

> "Ripley when I give an order I expect it to be obeyed."
> Ripley yells, "Even when it is against the law!"
> Dallas sharply replies, "You're God damn right!!"

From this exchange it appears that following the orders of a superior officer is paramount. By refusing to allow the crew entry, Ripley is threatening the power of her Captain and challenging the existing structural arrangements within the Company that employs the crew.

Similar instances of Ripley's potential destructive power are also present in the three other films in the series. In *Aliens*, Ripley's condemnation of the Company continues and is seen in her verbal attack of the Board members. She also undermines the military's hierarchy and purpose by disempowering the Lieutenant and encouraging the troops to ignore Company orders by destroying the aliens. In these interactions, Ripley mirrors the monstrous feminine—the alien. They share a "similar status as potential threats to a vulnerable male power" (Berenstein 1990, 65)[5]—threats that the Company wanted to control and harness.

In the third film, *Alien³*, Ripley is seen to be more like the alien. They are both outsiders who jeopardize the established order by possessing a power, real or imagined by those around them, that men cannot control. Early in the film, the men make clear that they fear what Ripley's presence might make them do. They are instantly uncomfortable and anxious. Ripley's femaleness threatens the vow of celibacy they have taken: In "comes woman, that old root of all evil, bringing with her the serpent that means the death of humankind" (Billy 1995, 230). Her awareness that she threatens the social order is evident when she talks with Dillon shortly after the cremation of Hicks and Newt. When Dillon says, "You don't want to know me, lady. I'm a murderer and rapist," rather than a response indicating Ripley's revulsion of him, she replies, "Well, I guess I must make you nervous."

And, in *Alien Resurrection*, Ripley is synonymous with the monstrous feminine. She is part human and part alien, but as a clone she is not a member of either society. She "disturbs identity" (Creed 1996, 36) by being beyond and outside recognized labels. She does not respect or abide by the roles of human or alien society, and in recognizing the alien aspect of herself, Ripley ultimately admits and embraces her power. We see this in such scenes as the one in which Ripley explains to Purvis (the sole surviving alien host), with some degree of pleasure, "I'm the monster's mother."

The Woman in Man's Clothing

In opposition to interpretations of Ripley as a female threat to male power, others prefer to explain her behaviour as reinforcement of traditional Western perceptions and expectations of appropriate

---

[5] See also Constable 1999.

maleness. Rather than viewing Ripley as outside the normative patriarchal structure and threatening it, she and similar female characters are described "as 'pseudo males' or as being not 'really' women" (Hills 1999, 38).

Gallardo and Smith claim that "interpretation of Ripley as a *woman in man's clothing* coincide with Clover's definition of the Final Girl as male surrogate, masculinized" (2004, 21-22; my emphasis). Hermann (1997), Kavanagh (1990), and Tremonte (1989) are illustrative of this interpretation, drawing comparisons between Ripley and the classic American western hero in statements like she is

> ready to go one-on-one against the alien in a scene which reconstructs the classic American cultural image of the gunfight. In the space western of the future the sheriff is replaced by a woman, while what is important for ideological humanism is preserved – a tough gal, rather than a tough guy. (Kavanagh 1990, 80)

Whether specifically compared to a western character like *Shane* (Tremonte 1989) or a more general idea like the sheriff of the future (Kavanagh 1990), the fundamental argument is that Ripley is "[u]surping the role of the father and warrior... she becomes figuratively and symbolically, a male-coded character" (Hermann 1997, 44).

As in the case of the monstrous feminine, there are easily identifiable scenes from each film, although fewer in the first film, that can serve as examples of the woman in man's clothing. Ripley's battles with the aliens throughout the four films can be interpreted as reconstructions of the classic western gunfight and more generally as indicative of the behaviour of the traditional masculine hero. In *Alien*, her ingenuity and resourcefulness in battling the alien and her rational leadership style in relation to the crew of the Nostromo are indicative of the characteristics audiences value in their male heroes. Her *Rambo* image with ammunition belts criss-crossing her chest and machine guns in each hand supported by a backdrop of Marines in *Aliens* adds the element of machismo to the hero image in the first film. With a strong element of rationality and a sense of responsibility that is characteristically associated with traditional male characters such as *Shane*, Ripley leads the troops and battles the alien. Even in the battle with the alien queen, which so many others have described as two mothers fighting to protect their children, she can also be viewed as not merely taking on the role of a man but as giving up her femaleness.

In the third film, Ripley is homogenized with the male inmates, not just in terms of her shaved head and prison clothing, but also in terms of her "we're fucked" pronouncements and assertive initiation of sex with

Dr. Clemens. Again we can see Ripley as reminiscent of the western genre male hero; however, I believe that in this film she more closely resembles the bad guy with a heart of gold like Clint Eastwood's Preacher in the 1985 film, *Pale Rider*, who comes to lead and defend the community that initially views him as an outsider. Her physical confrontations with the prisoners as well as the alien support such an analogy. She is the self-confident aggressor who is willing to do battle with whomever or whatever menace she faces.

In the final film, *Alien Resurrection*, Ripley also exhibits some elements of a character like Preacher; however, her dominant traits seem to be more closely aligned with the futuristic character of Arnold Schwarzenegger's terminator in the 1991 *Terminator 2: Judgement Day*. Ripley has the confidence and steadiness of the hero; however, there are additional elements of distrustfulness and cold objectivity of someone who is not just on the margins of society, but an outsider who is unfamiliar with the habits of humanity. She does not flinch and is willing to endure even self-inflicted pain and injury if it means that she can accomplish her objective.

The Traditional Woman and Mother

Interpretations of Ripley as the traditional Western version of woman and mother are composed in one of two ways. First, there are constructions highlighting what makes her *feminine* while downplaying or dismissing characteristics and behaviours generally identified as *masculine*. These interpretations often focus on Ripley's physical appearance or expressions of *maternal* emotions. Second, there are constructions that involve redefining traditionally masculine behaviours as appropriate feminine behaviours which, interestingly, also rely on expressions of maternal emotions.

Some film reviewers and theorists highlight Ripley's femininity through attention to her physical appearance. David Ansen, for example, refers to the Ripley in *Alien* as a "'tough astronette' (rather than 'tough astronaut')" (in Gallardo and Smith 2004, 20). Similarly some film theorists describe this Ripley as having a "body [that] is pleasurable and reassuring to look at. She signifies the 'acceptable' form and shape of woman" (Creed 1996, 62). These interpretations are frequently seen in relation to Ripley's striptease near the end of *Alien*. Others appear to want Ripley to be a traditional woman when they criticize her bald, macho image in *Alien*[3] and imply that there is a contradiction between this image and that of a sexually attractive female, and perhaps more specifically, the sexually attractive Ripley of *Aliens*. Alluding to this, Doherty comments that "*Alien*[3] can't decide whether it wants to eroticize or de-sex her" (Doherty 1996, 196).

A number of other theorists also highlight Ripley's femininity by focusing on maternal bonding. This focus is particularly common in work related to *Aliens*; however, instances in the other films, such as Ripley's concern for the cat in *Alien*, also support the maternal interpretation of Ripley. The work focusing on the Ripley in *Aliens* claims that her "feminization is completed by the discovery of Newt... She is now positioned as a surrogate mother to the civilian child" (Constable 1999, 185). Clough goes so far as to state that Ripley

> has been "fixed up," fixed into femininity. This fixing is even more pronounced in *Aliens*, in which the femininity of the "new" woman is finally refitted into a reconstructed family. (1992, 65)

In criticizing *Alien*[3]'s move away from Ripley's femininity, Doherty maintains that viewers of *Aliens* were "deeply invested" in the bond between Ripley and Newt, and the elimination of that relationship is commensurate with destroying "the whole meaning of the previous, beloved film" (1996, 184). Hermann makes similar claims in statements such as, "Ripley's maternal instincts are the quiet engine that drive her and the narrative forward" (1997, 41-2).

The second construction, redefining the traditional masculine behaviours of Ripley as acceptable feminine behaviours, also takes up the notion of maternal bonding, justifying Ripley's violence under the pretence of a mother protecting her child. This is evident in the attention to the fight scenes between Ripley and the alien queen in *Aliens*: "In the dual scenes between Ripley and the alien mother, the visual parallel is unmistakable: two queens fighting for their respective offspring" (Doherty 1996, 195). Hermann (1997), Clough (1992), Bundtzen (1987), and others also present the image of two battling mothers (Ripley and the alien queen) in *Aliens*. In addition, Ripley as the maternal aggressor can also be seen in the other films. Ripley's loss of Newt at the beginning of *Alien*[3] can be interpreted as the fuel for a mother's rage against the aliens as well as her intense confrontations with the violent offenders of Fury 161. Similarly, in *Alien Resurrection*, Ripley's violent outburst when she discovers other Ripley clones in the lab and her compassionately motivated destruction of the deformed Ripley that she found alive reflect a maternal desire to end the suffering of the weak and vulnerable and prevent the powerful Company's ability to use and abuse the weak.

Divergent Interpretations of Ripley in Context

That such different interpretations as the monstrous feminine, the woman in man's clothing, and the traditional woman and mother can emerge from one socio-cultural context should not be surprising. It is always the case that people come to any situation, including the viewing of a film, with their own stock of knowledge that influences their interpretations of what they observe thus allowing for differing definitions of the situation (see also Davis 1989 and Nardi 1984). However, the socio-cultural context from which these three interpretations emerged amplified the potential for their existence because of the context's inconsistency regarding gender. Prior to and during the release of the *Alien Quadrilogy* the inconsistent views regarding gender can be summed up as a power struggle between competing ideologies. The Western ideology of masculinity and femininity as discrete, dichotomous gender categories coexisted with and struggled against the counter ideology posited by Second Wave Feminism, and both influenced the organization of society.

The ideology of rigid gender categories was clearly the dominant view during the 20th century within the Western world and was reflected in film criticism. As Jennings points out, "according to film theorists of the late 1970s... how we see and look is governed by the binary constructs of masculinity and femininity in a patriarchal society" (1995, 197). Similarly, Hills claims that within patriarchal society there is an assumption that "notions of femininity and masculinity are completely stable... [There is] no allowance for any negotiation as to how we may place ourselves in relation to these notions, in life or as spectators of film" (1999, 198). However, in the midst of that perspective's dominance there was the emergence of a challenge to it in the form of Second Wave Feminism. In conjunction with the rise of this challenge, changes occurred in ideas, behaviours, and structural and legal arrangements that affected everyday life, and especially the lives of women. Byers identifies this time as a "period of reaction to historical events... that threatened male hegemony by loosening traditional restraints on women" (1989, 78). In response to the feminist challenge, those advocating adherence to the masculine-feminine dichotomy retaliated.

Consider the changes we have seen in Western society since the 1950s; some support the traditional Western view of gender while others support a cornerstone of feminism, gender equality. In the 1950s, people were adapting to the post-war era—Rosie the Riveter was being persuaded to revert back to June Cleaver in order to make jobs available to the men who had returned from war. Television shows like *Leave it to Beaver* and

Father Knows Best with images of women in aprons with children all around them were dominant in mainstream Western culture. During this time, people were also exposed to the writings of militant feminists who were determined that society, and women in particular, recognize the oppressive, patriarchal inequality that controlled women's lives, thoughts and feelings. They encouraged women to reject patriarchy's mandated gender roles and argued for changes not only in terms of social structures and policies but also in terms of ideology.

Amidst this changing imagery of women, de Beauvoir was finding an audience for her now classic book *The Second Sex* in which she argues for women's financial independence because "a woman supported by a man... is not emancipated" ([1952]1989, 679). Only a decade later, Betty Friedan called for women to reject derogatory patriarchal views of women, describing that prevailing view as:

> They're not interested in the broad public issues of the day. They are not interested in national or international affairs. They are only interested in the family and the home. They aren't interested in politics, unless it's related to an immediate need in the home, like the price of coffee. (1963, 37)

Such beliefs were common in the 1950s and 1960s; however, at least in part because of women like de Beauvior and Friedan, contrary images of women were entering mainstream society, especially the media, and changes were beginning to happen in the structural and legal areas of society. For example, while in the entertainment media we had images of Twiggy and the Bond Girls, we also began to see in the news media images of women protesting social injustice who were more concerned about actions than their physical appearance.

In the following decades, additional changes occurred in many Western countries. In the United States in the early 1970s, the Equal Rights Amendment was in the Senate and the U.S. Supreme Court had ruled on *Roe v. Wade* (Gallardo and Smith 2004, 17-18). In Canada, beginning in 1976 there were significant increases in the number of women under 30 who were never married, held university degrees, and were members of the work force (Lindsay and Almey 2004).

Despite these changes affecting women's lives, one belief about women remained largely unchanged—motherhood. While the patriarchal meaning of motherhood is a very prominent image in Western society and generally functions to reinforce the belief in dichotomous gender roles as natural, in the mid 1970s feminists like Adrianne Rich claimed that "many women are *even now* thinking in ways which traditional intellection denies, decries, or is unable to grasp" (1976, 284).

Mary Daly, like Rich, rejected the legitimacy of the dominant patriarchal ideology. However, she did not limit her concern to motherhood:

> Patriarchy appears to be "everywhere".... As a rule, even the more imaginative science-fiction writers... cannot/will not create a space and time in which women get far beyond the role of space stewardess. (1978, 2)

Throughout the 1970s and 1980s there were other changes that benefited women in Western societies, but there were also attempts to reverse or deny those benefits. Canada removed abortion from its Criminal Code. In the United Kingdom the percentage of undergraduate degrees awarded to women increased from 8% to 45% (Hicks and Allen 1999). Anti-sex discrimination and pay equity policies were also introduced (Women and Equality Unit 2006). However, in Western media and politics there was a renewed emphasis on patriarchal, traditional gender roles. Movies like *Baby Boom* and *Rambo* reinforced and glorified the traditional view of feminine and masculine as dichotomous. Ronald Reagan ran for President of the United States and won on a platform that included *Family Values*, privileging the breadwinner-housewife family structure. After leaving office he wrote an article that favoured the overturn of *Roe v. Wade* (Reagan 1983).

Conflicting views of gender co-existed; however, the way in which these conflicting views could be discussed remained restricted by established language. While the concepts of feminine and masculine and the ways in which they were applied to people were being challenged, available language was limited, thus illustrating the dominant belief that gender is composed of two discrete categories. Consequently, the meanings attached to gender, as well as examples of fluidity or violation of the established categories varied but remained constrained by the boundaries of a limited language. Hills criticism of what she refers to as a "binaristic logic" illustrates the consequence of such a linguistic limitation:

> action heroines cannot be easily contained or productively explained, within a theoretical model which denies the possibility of female subjectivity as active or full... some new mode of understanding has to be developed to take account of the new and changing representations of women in the action cinema. (1999, 39)

The Ripley in *Alien* (1979) reflects the contradiction that existed in society at that time, and the three common interpretations of her reflect the language constraints. While Ripley will never be forgotten for the infamous bikini scene at the end of the film which exemplifies the traditional patriarchal image of woman, she also challenges male authority, wears a gender neutral uniform throughout most of the film, and in the end is the *last wo-man standing*.

The depictions of Ripley in the sequels to *Alien* mirror the continued societal inconsistency regarding gender roles. The 1982 *Aliens* introduced audiences to Ripley as a mother—both biological and surrogate—with romantic sparks aimed at Hicks, consistent with the Reaganites' Family Values. However, she is also in charge and accepted as such among the macho Marines. In *Alien³* Ripley is again depicted as mother—mother mourning the death of Newt, mother of the alien growing inside her chest, and symbolic mother of humanity—and also sexual[6] but simultaneously butch, tough, with a shaved head, and able to stand up to the intimidation tactics of the male prisoners. The Ripley of *Alien Resurrection* is literally a constructed being who repeatedly reinforces and also fractures the "binaristic logic" of traditional gender roles.

When we look at these decades, the 1950s through the 1990s, leading up to and during the release of the *Alien* films, there is no doubt that those were times of contradiction, flux and uncertainty, and the interpretations of Ripley during that time function as reflections of that situation. However, the fact that Ripley is viewed as the monstrous feminine, the woman in man's clothing, and the traditional woman and mother indicates the need to move beyond the traditional Western view of the dichotomous nature of gender to one that makes room for diversity, one that encourages "thinking in ways which traditional intellection denies, decries, or is unable to grasp" (Rich 1976, 284).

Ripley's Autonomy and Divergent Interpretations

I have suggested that the conflict and inconsistency of the earlier socio-cultural context and the simultaneous limitation of language regarding gender made it difficult to see Ripley as someone who exists outside the false dichotomy of feminine and masculine. The socio-cultural inconsistency that began in the 1950s has continued into the present and become the norm, opening up an opportunity for us to view gender

---

[6] This is the only time in the four films in which Ripley engages in sexual relations.

differently and consequently to view Ripley as not simply a woman who is or is not feminine or masculine or some total of fractional elements of the two but as "an example of the ways in which a fluid identity can be constructed" (Jennings 1995, 204), as an example of an autonomous individual.

According to Govier, one can be thought to have autonomy if

> one is capable of controlling one's own life; this requires competence in discovering one's talents, feelings, beliefs, and values; defining who one is... understanding oneself; and directing one's life.... The autonomous person is capable of introspection, autobiographical retrospection, critical reflection and deliberation, and the reconciliation of conflicting desires; she is faithful to herself. (Govier 1993, 103)

Benson (2006) and Burrow (2007) explain that autonomy requires a sense of self-worth which is contingent upon self-confidence, competence, and self-trust. Autonomous individuals "must have a certain sense of their own worthiness to act" (Benson 2006, 650). They must act according to what they deem appropriate in spite of the demands or expectations others may have of them in a particular context and believe that they are capable of answering for those actions (Benson 2006, Burrow 2007). These individuals are not socially isolated, nor are their thought-behaviour patterns static. They are aware and sensitive to the attitudes of others, and they engage in reflexive thought regarding the things they need, want, and value which means that they have the ability to correct themselves when they come to incorrect conclusions (Govier 1993, 111).

When audiences were first introduced to Ripley, she did not initially stand out as a strong female character let alone as an autonomous individual. There is no doubt that there are multiple examples in the *Alien Quadrilogy* of Ripley's lack of autonomy, and many of the examples of Ripley as the "traditional woman and mother" essentially imply such a lack of autonomy. In the early scenes of *Alien* she was just another mid-level officer working for the Company and taking orders from a male captain. However, we should not think in terms of absolute autonomy. According to Burrow, and Govier (1993) agrees,

> [E]ven persons lacking self-determination in many aspects of their lives may not thereby lack autonomy, not if they act autonomously within certain pockets of their lives. (2007, 2)

I would argue that Burrow (2007) is, at least indirectly, acknowledging that social interactions are complex, and the context in which they occur as well as the complexity of individuals as whole beings must be taken into consideration. When we consider Ripley's character development across the quadrilogy, a strong argument can be made that she fits the criteria of an autonomous individual as described by Burrow (2007), Benson (2006), and Govier (1993) despite instances of her lack of autonomy. I shall return to this point below.

Another issue that arises in exploring Ripley's autonomy is that while claims of Ripley as autonomous can be found in the literature, they remain undeveloped. Typically, the term is used as nothing more than a one-time descriptive label. For example, Kavanagh describes the Ripley of *Alien* as a "strong woman who must mobilize all her *autonomous* intellectual and emotional strength" (1990, 77; my emphasis). In referring to Kavanagh's statement, Neale concludes that "[t]his is what differentiates her from the rest of the human crew" (1989, 215). While attaching the label of autonomous to Ripley, neither Kavanagh nor Neale offer the reader any explanation or justification for that label. Their use of the term seems to be based on the belief that Ripley is a strong woman. However, Byers explains that strength alone is insufficient justification for such a label. Presenting an autonomous woman in film

> is not merely a matter of presenting a strong female image as a model; rather it broaches the possibility of significantly repositioning women within the narrative and visual structures of classic cinema. (Byers 1989, 84-85)

Ripley's character development across the four films does appear to reflect this criterion of repositioning identified by Byers (1989). Further, her autonomy becomes more apparent and recognizable as a fundamental component of her character as she moves through each film. This is particularly the case in relation to Ripley's sense of her own worthiness to act:

> It is not simply that there is a change in Ripley's context, but rather it is her response to it which transforms her from a cog in the company structure and opens the possibility for her subjected body to become something quite different. (Hills 1999, 48)

Indeed it is largely her response to the context in which she finds herself, her ability to take action as opposed to simply reacting throughout the quadrilogy, that has given rise to our fascination with her for so many years, as the following chronological overview illustrates.

Ripley's Growing Autonomy

In 1979 Ellen Ripley was a communications officer on a deep space commercial towing vehicle, the Nostromo. As was the case with the other crewmembers, audiences knew nothing and learned very little of Ripley's past, her beliefs and values, or her relationships with the other crewmembers. Ripley, like the others, appeared to be "a cog in the company structure" (Hills 1999, 48). It was not until the context changed that Ripley became interesting, even though at that stage it was difficult to conclude whether she was merely *re*acting to circumstances or acting as an autonomous individual. This lack of clarity is evident from the differing interpretations of Ripley I have presented above. However, if we consider her in terms of the four films, we can reject the idea that her behaviours are mere *re*actions and see that she is an autonomous protagonist.

Once established as the leader in *Alien*, Ripley does not blindly or obediently accept the hierarchy of authority within the Company or the orders that trickle down within that structure, nor does she challenge or disobey that structure as a matter of course. At the same time, she does not hesitate to fall back on the hierarchy of authority when it suits her needs, as illustrated when she uses her position to force Parker and Brett to comply with her orders. She acts according to her beliefs even when other crewmembers challenge or attempt to stop her. Whether she is refusing to allow Kane aboard the Nostromo after the facehugger has attacked him, standing up to Burke and Dallas, fighting the alien, or disobeying Company orders and destroying the Nostromo she is expressing her autonomy by taking actions that reflect her belief that the Company is wrong to treat human life, in this case the lives of the crew, as expendable. Lastly, we also see Ripley's autonomy at the end of the film when she records her Final Report as acting commander, illustrating that she is capable and willing to answer for her actions by reporting to the Company and returning to earth.

Ripley, the Company, the alien, and her antagonistic relationship with both are the only things that survive *Alien* to reappear in *Aliens*. Early in that reappearance audiences are provided with some context—information about Ripley's past, beliefs and values, and relationships. She is a mother whose child died while she was lost in space; she is overwhelmed with guilt and fear, and based on her experience she feels nothing but distrust and animosity for the Company. In addition, Ripley's autonomy is evident from the beginning of the film. She is true to herself. In the hospital, while talking to Burke, she forcefully redirects the conversation to the topic of her choosing – her daughter. In her review hearing with officials from the Company, Ripley is insistent, defiant and confrontational in an attempt to make the officials understand what she is telling them about the aliens. She is not an egotist, but she knows that she is the only one who understands what the aliens are capable of doing to humanity. In this film, Ripley also acknowledges her conflicting desires—self-preservation versus destruction of the alien—and ultimately takes action that is consistent with her beliefs. She accepts the responsibility that accompanies the knowledge she possesses and is confident in that stock of knowledge. She agrees to go with the Company's Marines on a mission that Burke has told her is to find and destroy the aliens. Ripley also takes action that is consistent with her beliefs when she learns of the Company's true intentions (to capture and harness the power of the aliens) and pushes aside Lieutenant Gorman, taking control of the vehicle in order to save the Marines who are inside Hadley's Hope, the terra-forming colony. She is not simply engaging in the mental activity of thinking about what should be done; she takes action and does so despite the resistance of others. Hills describes her as having the

> ability to adapt to the new: to negotiate change. Ripley illustrates the importance of critical thinking in response to new signs which occur in her environment, a willingness to experiment with new modes of being and the ability to transform herself in the process. (1999, 40)

By the end of this film, Ripley possesses a self-competency that was generally sporadic in the first film. She is more easily able to act on her thoughts and embodies a confidence that encourages the Marines to follow her orders. For example, in the Director's Cut she orders Bishop: "I want these specimens destroyed as soon as you're done with them. Is that clear?" Officially, she has no authority, but he and the Marines, like Ripley herself, have come to respect and trust her abilities. It is largely because of these abilities that audiences see Ripley with Newt and Hicks flying into space rather than Ripley as the sole survivor as she had been in our first encounter with her.

When Ripley awakens on the prison planet, Fury 161, in *Alien³* she is informed that Newt and Hicks are dead. Whether unfortunate as Doherty (1996) claims or not, she is alone again. However, her accumulated experiences have fortified her self-confidence, self-trust, and sense of self-worth. From the beginning, she interacts with the male inhabitants of Fury 161 exemplifying those traits despite the fact that others question and challenge her autonomy at every turn simply because she is a woman, the only woman. For example, Superintendent Andrews orders Ripley to remain in the infirmary for her own safety, and he is dismissive of her warnings about the alien. However, her self-trust and confidence do not wane. She knows that action must be taken because *re*action will come too late. She knows the necessity of discovering whether there is an alien presence in the prison and that she must be on the offensive if, in fact, there is an alien present. Without hesitation and against the orders of the Superintendent, she begins to take the necessary steps.

Many of Ripley's encounters with the men of Fury 161 also reveal her autonomy. Like Jennings, I believe that "Ripley's initiative in the sexual encounter [with Dr. Clemens]... reinforces the idea of an active female sexuality" (Jennings 1995, 202). However, I further contend that it illustrates her self-confidence and sense of self-worth, especially in light of the fact that her shaved head and gender neutral prison clothing are often interpreted as incompatible with a woman's sexual attractiveness as indicated by some who like Doherty (1996, 196) speculate that the film was "de-sex[ing] her." Also, as we saw in *Aliens*, Ripley reconciles her conflicting desires, this time in relation to the men who attempted to rape her. Despite her anger toward them, she acts in accordance with her values and labours to save them from the aliens. Her most notable autonomous act though, is her self-destruction at the end of the film. At that point she is in control of her life (and death). She is taking action that is consistent with her beliefs and values, denying the Company the opportunity to use her.

Finally, in *Alien Resurrection*, we see Ripley, now a human-alien hybrid clone, who is an example of a character with a great deal of autonomy, despite being a creation of the Company for its own purposes. She speaks straight forwardly and takes action without allowing others to manipulate her. We see this throughout the film including the scene in which she sarcastically asks the crew of the Betty, "So, who do I have to fuck to get off this boat?" We see similar indications of Ripley's autonomy when she stands up to Johner's sexual intimidation tactics, and when piercing her own hand with a knife, she shows Call that her control over herself cannot be taken away even with the threat of death. Ripley also acts to destroy the other clones despite the judgmental reactions of Johner and Christy. While having an awareness of others' thoughts and attitudes, Ripley does not in any way let them alter what she thinks needs to be done.

It is this Ripley of *Alien Resurrection* that has been least subjected to the limitations of traditional femininity and masculinity as they are presented in language by those interpreting her character. Perhaps it is easier to see her without the blinders of traditional gender role constructions because she has been significantly removed from reality; she is a human-alien hybrid clone, and we are encouraged to see her as not really human. General Perez refers to her as a "meat by-product," and Call claims that she is a thing, "a construct" created in a lab. This encouragement helps to free the audience's imagination and, as a consequence, our interpretations of this Ripley as well as her previous incarnations are not as restricted by our expectations of what it is to be human, or more specifically a man or a woman as they were in the past decades.

Even this placement of Ripley on the margins of humanity would not, by itself, encourage us to see her as an autonomous individual. Considering her as autonomous also requires that we alter our understandings of gender. Through the challenges, conflicts, and turmoil surrounding gender during most of the 20th century, we have reached a point at which there is no clear consensus about gender. That is to say, there are still those who adhere to the traditional dichotomous view of gender, some who argue the existence of as many as five genders, and others who suggest that gender is altogether an obsolete concept. And, it is because of this lack of consensus in conjunction with the final incarnation of Ripley that we are now able to see her as an autonomous individual who exists outside the boundaries of a dichotomous concept of gender

Ripley's Autonomy: A Gender Issue

The difficulty with identifying Ripley as an autonomous individual is rooted in the problem of dichotomous gender roles. In essence, indicators of individual autonomy have been constructed as masculine while indicators of a lack of autonomy have been constructed as feminine. Thus, if Ripley is seen first and foremost in relation to traditional Western femininity, she cannot be seen as autonomous. Burrow helps us understand this by explaining that the body is "a site for suffering *constraints* on autonomy" (Burrow 2007, 2). That is, there remain those who continue to have expectations of individuals based on their sex. This is particularly important when we are concerned with women and issues related to femininity as has been the case in many of the interpretations of Ripley. Burrow identifies three ways in which "social norms and ideals of femininity can restrict autonomy through the body." First, there is the traditional Western view that women should be dainty and occupy minimal physical space. She explains that this view restricts self-expression and implies that a woman values herself only minimally. Second, women who attempt to acquire the ideal female body image as advocated in Western society may experience "depleted bodily energy" thus limiting their capacity to act physically. Third, in a culture that accepts or excuses violence against women, women are encouraged to be passive rather active in their social interactions (Burrow 2007, 2-3).

With Burrow's points in mind, it seems reasonable to assume that an analysis of women's behaviour that is located within that traditional gender role framework would have to conclude that women are not able to act in an autonomous manner which seems to be the logical extension of the three interpretations of Ripley that I discussed in this chapter.

If Ripley is seen as the monstrous feminine, for example, she is seen as a threat to traditional gender roles. The idea is that what she threatens is more important than what Ripley is. Because we are encouraged to focus on the threatening nature of her presence, it is easy to see her as deserving both the verbal and physical violence that is inflicted on her, or, at a minimum, we are not surprised by it. Captain Dallas' verbal assault on Ripley when she challenges his authority in *Alien* is something almost to be expected in the context. In *Aliens*, Ripley encounters a similar form of violence that is not unexpected when the Company revokes her licence, effectively destroying her ability to earn a living because she had the nerve to stand up to the Board. The attempted rape in *Alien³* also seems to be almost expected—Ripley's femaleness alone was sufficient temptation for the male prisoners. Within the context of the film this attack is her punishment for disobeying the order of the Superintendent that she remain in the Infirmary. And, in *Alien Resurrection*, the film in which Ripley is most synonymous with the monstrous feminine, Johner's attempts at sexual intimidation, although they ultimately fail, send the clear message that threats to or disruption of the established gender order will not be tolerated.

If Ripley is conceptualized for us as the woman in man's clothing as Hills (1999) claims Clover does with her concept of the Final Girl, it seems that we are being asked to accept the idea that women cannot be autonomous unless they overcome femininity and adopt a masculine persona. As I laid out in the previous section, Ripley's autonomy clearly increases as we move from the first to the last film. It is not a huge leap to argue that there is an inverse relationship between Ripley's autonomy and femininity across the films. Particularly in the first three films, changes in Ripley's physical appearance exemplify this idea of femininity being incongruent with autonomy which is depicted as masculine. While Ripley occasionally engages in behaviours that can be identified as autonomous (and has been identified as masculine) and while her clothes are basically gender neutral in *Alien*, her soft shoulder length curly hair and her bikini attire at the end of the film tend to overpower the viewer's imagination, leaving a lingering image of femininity. In *Aliens*, Ripley is presented to audiences as a mother and romantic interest, but her flowing curls are cut short, and she is draped in the masculine armour of ammunition belts and the transformer style loader she uses to fight the alien queen. The Ripley in *Alien*[3] is "homogenized" with the men of Fury 161 (Vaughn 1995)—she is given prison issue clothing and her head is shaved. While we see this masculinised transformation of Ripley's physical appearance in the first three films, the final film completes the transformation by presenting audiences with a Ripley that behaves and seems to think in a masculinised manner.

Finally, descriptions of Ripley as the traditional woman and mother inevitably seem to call our attention to aspects of the character and her behaviour that are consistent with the traditional feminine gender role and often function to constrain her autonomy. The extensive attention given to the final bikini scene at the end of *Alien* is one example. Similarly, the fight scene between Ripley and the alien queen has been identified by many as an example of the supposed maternal bond between Ripley and Newt in *Aliens*. This interpretation, unlike the gunfight analogy I discussed above, highlights Ripley's femininity and implies a mother's *re*action rather than her action. That is inconsistent with the idea of autonomy and the rational male sheriff of the Wild West. When Ripley is among the male prisoners of Fury 161 in *Alien*[3], by virtue of being the only woman she is subjected to the male gaze;[7] she becomes the sexual object in the fantasies of the men around her despite her homogenization. *Alien Resurrection*, while offering audiences a very different Ripley who is the least restricted by a traditional feminine ideal and the most autonomous, still does not completely escape the inverse relationship of femininity and autonomy. It seems that Johner is right when he says to Christy, after watching Ripley destroy the clone lab and earlier versions of herself, it "must be a chick thing" or at least a gender thing.

Conclusion

Many of us rarely stop to think about the relationship between who we are as individuals and the type of society in which we live. However, there is no doubt that what individuals think and how we behave is significantly influenced by the social context in which we find ourselves; how we are labelled in one aspect of our lives can affect how we are labelled in another aspect. This examination of Ellen Ripley and the ways in which

---

[7] For a discussion of the male gaze, see Mulvey 1989.

she has been interpreted over the years was an opportunity for me to explore that relationship.

All the interpretations of Ripley that I have discussed are products of the socio-cultural context from which they emerged—monstrous feminine, woman in man's clothing, traditional woman and mother, and autonomous woman. The first three of these definitions of the situation rest on the assumption that behaviours should be interpreted according to their paramount relationship with gender based on essentialist views of feminine and masculine roles. Given the status of femininity within such a patriarchal framework, I believe it is impossible to accept the fourth possibility of a woman as an autonomy individual. Only by moving beyond the restrictions of a dichotomous model of gender and recognizing that women's identities are composed of much more than a patriarchal view of femininity can the autonomy of women even be considered.

Burrow calls our attention to "the body as a site for suffering *constraints* on autonomy," but she goes on to explain that "autonomy... requires competencies of resistance and resolution" (2007, 2-3). While I am uncomfortable with the use of the term resistance because in discussions about women it is too often paired with compliance to create a false dichotomy and a simplistic explanation of women's behaviours, I agree with her general view and believe that women are rejecting the "*constraints* on autonomy" much more today than in the past, the relationship between the individual and society is changing. This rejection is a consequence of the struggle between a well-entrenched patriarchal system and feminist ideals. Like many societal struggles, this struggle spread over many years, and resulted in the co-existence of conflicting views about women that are reflected in films like the *Alien Quadrilogy* and interpretations of them. However, women are not simply conforming to or resisting social norms; they are making choices within contexts. Choices that are examined without consideration of the contexts in which they occur may easily be interpreted as compliance or resistance to traditional Western gender roles. However, if those choices are examined in relation to the contexts, a more fluid and autonomous individual reveals herself.

References

Alien Quadrilogy, DVD. 2003. Includes *Alien, Aliens, Alien^3, Alien Resurrection*. Los Angeles: Twentieth-Century Fox Home Entertainment.

Bell-Metereau, R. 1985. Woman: The other alien in *Alien*. In *Women worldwalkers: New dimensions of science fiction and fantasy*, ed. J. B. Wheedan, 9-24. Lubbock, Texas: Texas Tech Press.

Benson, P. 1994. Free agency and self worth. *Journal of philosophy* 91 (12): 650-668.

Berenstein, R. 1990. Mommie dearest: *Alien, Rosemary's baby* and mothering. *Journal of popular culture* 24 (2): 55 – 73.

Billy, T. 1995. "This whole place is a basement": The gnostic/existentialist vision of *Alien³*. *Journal of evolutionary psychology* 16 (3 – 4): 229 – 235.

Blumer, H. [1933]1970. *Movies and conduct*. New York: Arno Press.

Bundtzen, L. 1987. Monstrous mothers: Medusa, grendel, and now *Alien*. *Film quarterly* 40 (3): 11 – 17.

Burrow, S. 2007. Body limits to autonomy: Emotion, attitude, and self-defence. In *Agency and embodiment*, ed. S. Sherwin, S. Campbell, and L. Meynell, 126 – 144. Philadelphia, PA: University of Pennsylvania Press.

Byers, T. 1989. Kissing Becky: Masculine fears and misogynist moments in science fiction films. *Arizona quarterly* 45 (3): 77 – 95.

Charon, J. 2004. *Symbolic interactionism* (8th edition). New Jersey: Pearson, Prentice Hall.

Clough, P. T. 1992. "The Final Girl" in the fictions of science and culture. *Stanford humanities review* 2 (2 – 3): 57 – 69.

Collins, R. 1994. *Four sociological traditions*. Oxford: Oxford University Press.

Constable, C. 1999. Becoming the monster's mother: Morphologies of identity in the *Alien* series. In *Alien zone II: The spaces of science fiction cinema*, ed. by Kuhn, 173 – 202. London: Verso.

Creed, B. 1996. Horror and the monstrous feminine: An imaginary abjection, In *The dread of difference: Gender and the horror film*, ed. Keith and Grant, 35-65. Austin: University of Texas Press.

Daly, M. 1978. *Gyn/Ecology: The metaethics of radical feminism*. Boston: Beacon Press.

Davis, E. 1989. Viewers' interpretations of films about alcohol. *Studies in symbolic interaction* 10: 199 – 212.

de Beauvior, S. [1952] 1989. *The second sex*. (Translated and edited by H. M. Parshley). New York : Knopf.

Doherty, T. 1996. Genre, gender, and the *Aliens* trilogy. In *The dread of difference: Gender and the horror film*, ed. B. K. Grant, 181-199. Austin: University of Texas Press.

Edmonds, L. 2004. Here there be monsters: Ellen Ripley redefines the science fiction hero(ine). In *The image of the hero in literature, media, and society*, eds. Wright and Kaplan, 126 - 130. Pueblo, CO: Colorado State University.

Friedan, B. [1963] 1983. *The feminine mystique*. New York: Dell Publishing.

Frye, M. 1983. *The politics of reality: Essays in feminist theory*. Trumanburg, NY: Crossing Press.

Gallardo C., X. and C.J. Smith. 2004. *Alien woman: The making of Lt. Ellen Ripley*. NY: Continuum.

Govier, T. 1993. Self-trust, autonomy and self-esteem. *Hypatia* 8 (1): 99-120.

Greer, G. [1971] 1981. *The female eunuch*. London: Paladin Books.

Hermann, C. 1997. Some horrible dream about (s)mothering sexuality, gender, and family in the *Alien* triology. *PostScript: Essays in film and the humanities* 16 (3): 36 – 50.

Hills, E. 1999. From 'figurative males' to action heroines: further thoughts on active women in the cinema. *Screen* 40 (1): 38 – 50.

Jennings, R. 1995. Desire and design – Ripley undressed. In *Immortal, invisible: Lesbians and the moving image*, ed. Wilton, 193 - 206. NY: Routledge.

Kavanagh, J. 1990. Feminism, humanism and science in *Alien*. In *Alien zone: Culture, theory and contemporary science fiction cinema*, ed. Kuhn, 73 – 81. London: Verso.

Lindsay, C. and M. Almey. 2004. A quarter century of change: young women in Canada in the 1970's and today. Ottawa: Status of Women Canada.

Marshment, M. 1989. Substantial women. In *The female gaze: Women as viewers of popular culture*, eds. Gamman and Marshment, 27 – 43. London: The Women's Press.

Mead, G. H. 1934. *Mind, self and society*, ed. Morris. Chicago: University of Chicago Press.

Melzer, P. 2006. *Alien constructions: Science fiction and feminist thought*. Austin: University of Texas Press.

Mulvey, L. 1989. Visual pleasure and narrative cinema. In *Visual and other pleasures*, 14-28. Bloomington: Indiana University Press.

Nardi, P. 1984. Toward a social psychology of entertainment magic (conjuring). *Symbolic interaction* 7 (10): 25 – 42.

Neale, S. 1989. Issues of difference: *Alien* and *Blade Runner*. In *Fantasy and the cinema*, ed. Donald, 213 – 223. [S. I]: British Film Institute.

Newton, J. 1990. Feminism and anxiety in *Alien*. In *Alien zone: Culture, theory and contemporary science fiction cinema*, ed. A. Kuhn. London: Verso.

Reagan, R. 1983. Abortion and the conscience of the nation http://www.nationalreview.com/document/reagan200406101030.asp

Rich, A. 1976. *Of woman born*. New York: W.W. Norton & Company, Inc.

Risman, B. 2004. Gender as a social structure: Theory wrestling with activism. *Gender & society* 18 (4): 429 – 450.

Speed, L. 1998. *Alien3*: A postmodern encounter with the abject. *Arizona quarterly* 54 (1): 125 – 151.

Stryker, S. 1980. *Symbolic interactionism*. Menlo Park, Calif.: Benjamin-Cummings Publishing Co.

Tremonte, C. 1989. Recasting the western hero: Ethos in high-tech science fiction. *JASAT* 20: 94 – 100.

Vaughn, T. 1995. Voices of sexual distortion: Rape, birth, and self-annihilation metaphors in the *Alien* trilogy. *The quarterly journal of speech* 81 (4): 423-435.

Wolf, N. 1991. *The beauty myth*. New York: William Morrow and Company, Inc.

AFTERWORD

ELIZABETH GRAHAM

It has now been more than three decades since audiences first encountered Ellen Ripley in *Alien* and more than one decade since her last appearance in *Alien Resurrection*. While the ending of *Alien Resurrection* left open the possibility for Ripley to return in a fifth *Alien* film, Hollywood shifted its interest away from her and humans in general within the *Alien* series. In *Alien vs Predator* (2004) and *Alien vs Predator: Requiem* (2007), the focus was on the extraterrestrials in the form of a space hunt on earth where humans are the insignificant creatures caught in the cross-fire. For a fuller discussion of this, see Appendix E. That we see continued fascination with the *Alien Quadrilogy* and Ripley, and that numerous scholars continue to explore the *Meanings of Ripley*, despite Hollywood's shift, is a testament to the influence Ripley and the quadrilogy have had in society. In addition, both of the non-Ripley films have been declared box office and critical failures, and that leaves little doubt about the importance of Ripley to the franchise.

Now there is talk of two more films in the near future under the creative control of Ridley Scott the director who started it all with *Alien* in 1979. The rumour is that these films will be prequels to that first film. Moving the franchise back in time like that would make it virtually impossible for Sigourney Weaver's Ripley to reappear for another battle with the aliens. However, since Scott will be at the helm, the possibility exists that we may see another female character with the depth and complexity that has caused so much popular and academic discussion for the past 30 years.

While nothing may ever come of hoping for a Ripley-like character in future *Alien* films, there have been a number of other strong, female protagonists appearing as central characters in science fiction/action/horror films in recent years. As of yet, none seem to stand out at first in the minds of audiences as Ripley does, but it is worth noting that she did not stand out at first either; it was nearly all about the alien. The release of films such as the *Underworld* films, the *Resident Evil* films, *Serenity*, *Aeon Flux*, and *Ultraviolet* with characters who share many of Ripley's traits hold out the potential for critical explorations and discussions of female protagonists similar to those in this collection. In most of these films, the central character is clearly a woman who battles against the odds, usually entering the final battle alone, or as a reluctant leader, but managing to prevail. She is often conflicted, vulnerable but strong, self-contradictory, sexual but not passive, and self-sacrificing.

This collection focuses only on the first iconic female protagonist of science fiction/action/horror—Ellen Ripley. The contributors grapple with a number of the issues associated with gender relations in twentieth century, Western society. They direct the reader's attention to issues of a complexified motherhood, sexuality, otherness, agency, autonomy, and feminism in light of changes within patriarchal society. As a whole, the collection is strongly grounded in Second Wave Feminism with some inclusion of psychoanalytic interpretations and points to the value of applying theoretical perspectives that have been deemed by some to be part of the past. The insights of theorists such as Firestone, de Beaviour, MacKinnon, as well as Mulvey, Creed, Irigaray, and others offer useful building blocks and assist in contextualizing events and products, such as films and film characters, that are now part of our history.

Having said that, the politics of feminism have changed, and Western society has changed considerably over the last number of decades. The opportunities and limitations that young women see in their lives and the ways in which they see themselves are different in comparison to their mothers and grandmothers.

> Unlike their mothers' generation, who had to prove themselves, third-wavers consider themselves entitled to equality and self-fulfillment... even as they recognize continuing injustices. (Snyder 2008, 178)

These young women have grown up with and embrace a level of individual and societal contradiction that previous generations did not experience, and they accept the messiness of these contradictions (Snyder 2008). Their experiences with motherhood, sexuality, otherness, agency and autonomy seem far less problematic as they experience the complexity of each and refuse to maintain artificial boundaries that previous generations under patriarchy have created. This is not to imply that they fail to see the forces of patriarchy still at work but, rather, that they seem to recognize that an individual's action, rather than reaction of an individual does have power.

Recognizing this shift in the lives of young women, current scholars in feminist theory and film criticism have altered their approaches to reflect a more complex, pluralistic understanding of their subject matter. They draw our attention to the intersections of gender, class, race/ethnicity, sexuality, etc., and recognize the connections between biography and history in new, more complicated ways.[1]

Such an approach that embraces the complexity of lived experiences, I suggest, is an appropriate direction to go as a means of furthering our understandings of Ellen Ripley and characters like her. However, I suggest that adopting such an approach not be done at the expense of past insights that specifically call our attention to gender relations. At the end of *Alien Resurrection*, Ripley clearly is a complex, pluralistic being—white, female, sexual assault victim, former officer of the Company, mother to an alien queen, human-alien hybrid clone, and the list goes on. Her relationships with other humans and the aliens encourage images of victim/oppressed and aggressor/oppressor. She provides rich possibilities for explorations of intersectionality. With this in mind, there is no doubt that a more concentrated examination such as the collection offers of the first three films of Ripley in *Alien Resurrection*, whether adopting an intersectional approach or not, would also be beneficial. Exploration of her complexity and self-contradictions may improve not just our understandings of Ripley but also of how individuals within an ever-changing society interact with film.

I hope that there will be many female characters that will follow in Ripley's footsteps, giving us the opportunity to explore and debate further the issues of motherhood, sexuality, otherness, agency, autonomy, and feminism.

References

Baumgardner, J. and A. Richards. 2000. *Manifesta: Young women, feminism., and the future.* New York: Farrar, Straus & Giroux.

Henry, A. 2006. "Daughterhood is powerful": The emergence of Feminism's third wave. In *Not my mother's sister: Generational conflict and third-wave feminism,* ed. Heywood, 121-133. Bloomington: Indiana University Press.

Heywood, L. (ed.) 2006a. *The women's movement today: An encyclopedia of third-wave feminism,* vol. 1, *A-Z.* Westport, CT: Greenwood.

—. 2006b. *The women's movement today: An encyclopedia of third-wave feminism,* vol. 2, *Primary documents.* Westport, CT: Greenwood.

---

[1] For discussions of Third Wave Feminism, see Baumgardner and Richards (2000), Henry (2006), Heywood (2006a and b), Heywood and Drake, eds. (1997), and Snyder (2008).

Heywood, L. and J. Drake (eds.) 1997. *Third wave agenda: Being feminist, doing feminism.* Minneapolis: University of Minnesota Press.

Snyder, R. C. 2008. What is third-wave feminism? A new directions essay. *Signs: Journal of women in culture and society* 34(1): 175-196.

INTRODUCTORY NOTE TO APPENDICES A – D

Over the past three decades numerous versions of the four *Alien* films have been available to the public. There are scripts, storyboards, theatrical releases, and DVD versions of each film. It is often the case that in the existing literature an author does not clearly indicate to which version of a film s/he is referring. When only the Theatrical Releases were available to the public this absence of explanation was understandable; however, with the common availability of DVDs, of the Theatrical Releases and other versions, and Internet access to written versions of the films, all of which vary slightly to significantly from each other, the specific version of the film under discussion needs to be clear.

The contributors of this collection indicate what version to the films they refer to in their chapters. With only specified exceptions these authors have used either the Director's Cut/ Special Edition versions or the Theatrical Releases.

Appendices A – D offer the reader summaries of the box set, Collector's Edition DVD, Director's Cut/ Special Editions of the *Alien Quadrilogy*. At each point in which this version of a film differs from the Theatrical Release, a description of the difference is provided in italics. As indicated in the Introduction of the book, these appendices are meant to be used as a resource for those who are unfamiliar with the film, but more importantly they are designed to highlight the differences between the two most accessible versions of the films so that an interpretation of a particular version can be understood in its proper context.

APPENDIX A:

ALIEN SUMMARY

Characters

Ripley, Warrant Officer (Sigourney Weaver)
Dallas, Captain (Tom Skerritt)
Kane, Executive Officer (John Hurt)
Ash, Science Officer (Ian Holm)
Lambert, Navigator (Veronica Cartwright)
Parker, Chief Engineer (Yaphet Kotto)
Brett, Engineering Technician (Harry Dean Stanton)
The Alien (Bolaji Badejo)

Summary

Scene 1:
Opening title and credits.

Scene 2:
The spaceship Nostromo, viewed from beneath, comes from the top of the scene, and its size soon fills the picture as it moves slowly through deep space.

The follow overlay titles appear:

> commercial towing vehicle 'The Nostromo'
> crew: seven
> cargo: refinery processing
> 20,000,000 tons of mineral ore
> course: returning to earth

The film begins with the now famous opening of the camera panning through the empty corridors of a spaceship's interior. The camera scans instruments and equipment in the central control room, indicated by the control chairs and computer screens. The ship, if appearing uninhabited, nonetheless has small movements from a breeze that turns file pages and appears to move some lose components on the equipment. The camera's point of view is a single movement.

It comes to focus finally on a helmet propped before a dark computer screen. The screen suddenly comes to life, and the camera moves between the screen and the helmet's reflective surface to show a data stream filing by on the computer. Then the screen goes dark again.

Scene 3:

The lights flicker on now throughout the spaceship. It appears that the computer has reactivated the Nostromo and is bringing it on line. There are still no human beings visible through these early scenes. The camera, again moving down a corridor, comes to an airlock door which opens, and the audience enters a room in darkness. The lights here too come on, and we see a circular group of chambers like spokes in a wheel, cryotubes, we later learn, for hypersleep. The clear lids open automatically, and slowly, the inhabitants start to wake from hibernation.

The first to show any sign of life is Kane. He moves slowly as if unable to fully bring himself to life, and the others remain for a time unmoving; the effect is of a long hypersleep. One or two of the others show signs of life now, and the scene shifts to the galley.

Around the dining table there is a general murmur of conversations as the crew members smoke and discuss the food, notably the cornbread which Lambert doesn't seem to like. Parker and Brett with some unseen gestures bring up the "bonus situation," thinking they are soon to dock at earth and concerned that they are not getting "full shares" of the profits from the operation. Ash (only later exposed as a robot) breaks into the conversation to tell Dallas that "Mother" (the onboard computer) is signalling him. The conflict among various crew members becomes a major subtext from this point on.

Scene 4:

Dallas goes into the main chamber for "Mother," which is a cubical command post, it seems, for talking directly with the computer. To access this "inner sanctum" he must punch in some codes and retrieve an identity card for the door to the chamber to open. The effect is that the computer is restricted access to the captain of the ship. It reinforces the idea, continued from the opening scene, that the ship is somewhat under the control of "Mother."

Scene 5:

The scene shifts to the crew starting to take their posts on the bridge and determine their location and distance from home, earth. It becomes apparent that they are not where they thought they were, and after some debate which focuses on Ripley's and Lambert's differences about who knows their location, they determine that they are still in deep space, and months from where they should be. This scene parallels Dallas' time in the command module with "Mother," where he learns that they have been awakened for a particular mission. Ripley's voice in the background is "calling earth" and trying to make contact for landing instructions. The effect is to heighten our sense that they are, again, not near home, and isolated in the nether regions of the universe. Lambert finally finds their location, somewhere not yet to the "outer rim" while Ripley keeps sending a useless call to earth.

A short shot of the external view of the *Nostromo* silently sliding through space.

Parker and Brett are in the dark, half lit engine room complaining that none of the other crew every come down there, and continuing to complain about their wage. The tension between officer class and engineer class is made a central point.

The crew gathers in the galley, Parker reminding Ash as he enters that the seat Ash is in is his. Dallas informing them that "Mother" has interrupted the homeward hypersleep because they have received a signal of unknown origin, a "transmission," and the computer is actually set to awaken them if such a thing occurs. All seem surprised by this knowledge, and wonder about the transmission which yields at this point little information. Parker again brings up the "bonus situation," and Ash now explains to him that any transmission of intelligence must be investigated, and the penalty for not doing so is total loss of shares. Parker acquiesces.

Scene 6:

Director's Cut: On the bridge the crew discusses the unknown nature of the signal. Comments indicating that the signal was unlike anything they had ever heard. Lambert finally locates the signal on a small planetoid.

Theatrical Release: Crew's discussion about the nature of the signal is less detailed with no information about the planetoid.

Scene 7:

Outer view of the *Nostromo* approaching the planetoid. The crew, in the shuttle (officially named the "Narcissus" but more often referred to in the film as "the shuttle"), prepares to detach from the mother ship and head down to the planet. The landing is a bit rough, and there are minor fires on the bridge, put out with extinguishers. Parker and Brett in the engine room transmit up the damage report, Parker extending Brett estimation for time of repairs. Ripley on the intercom says she is coming down. The two men complain among themselves about Ripley's visit.

Scene 8:

Dallas, Kane and Ash discuss the signal, it's distance, and the possibility of walking out to it. Lambert, in the foreground for this scene, smoking a cigarette listening and looking anxious. Dallas decides to send a group out, and tells Lambert she will be part of it. She's noticeably unhappy about the situation.

The three member crew, Dallas, Kane and Lambert go out into a storm in spacesuits. Ash monitors their movements on a computer screen.

Scene 9:

Ripley is with Parker and Brett in the engine room, checking on damages. Parker asks her about the shares they are getting. She informs them that they are entitled to full shares like everyone else. The men, who don't seem to have known this, want more explanation. Ripley makes a remark as she exits the room about if they need more help she'll be on the bridge. Brett is amused, but Parker is noticeably angry.

Outside the ship and moving toward the signal, Lambert complains about not being able to see anything, and Kane tells her to stop complaining.

Scene 10:

When the sun rises, the storm ceases. They see in the distance the derelict ship, it's two tail fins in the air, having crash landed into the planet.

The camera view through this scene is full of static, as the audience is watching it though Ash's or Ripley's computer screen. The transmission from the outside crew gets broken up as they approach the derelict spacecraft. Ash loses contact with the group.

Scene 11:

Inside the derelict spacecraft we hear the heavy breathing of Dallas as the crew makes their way toward the center of the ship and pilot's seat. H. R. Giger's interior designs for the derelict ship are ribbed like an chest cavity, and there is a marked organic aspect to the ship's interior.

The three crew members must climb a wall to reach the level where the pilot of the ship sits, dead and fossilized. The creature is perhaps three times the size of a human.

The three look at the skeletal remains of the commander, whose chest has a hole in it, burst through from the inside. Kane finds a hole in the floor made by something that has burnt through to a lower level.

Back on the shuttle, Ripley has been trying to decipher, with "Mother's" help, the transmission. She tells Ash by intercom that it is not an S.O.S. but instead perhaps a warning. Ripley wants to go out after the crew, but Ash convinces her that by they time she finds them they will know one way or the other.

Scene 12:

Dallas and Lambert lower Kane into a cavernous inner chamber of either the spaceship or some auditorium sized cavity beneath it. Kane is lowered into the cavern along a line of what look like ribs, so that the entire chamber appears the interior of a body cavity. On the bottom are three-foot *eggs* covered with a mist. Kane falls among them as he is investigating, and as he comes close one opens and a crab-like creature (face-hugger) springs onto Kane helmet.

We are shifted immediately to an outside view of the spacecraft, and a moment later to the figures of Dallas and Lambert carrying Kane back to the shuttle.

Director's Cut: A short shot of Kane pulling back from the alien egg and reaching for his gun is added to the scene just before the facehugger attacks.

Scene 13:

From inside the shuttle, Ash watches the approach of the three, and Ripley becomes aware of their stepping onto the elevator to reach the airlock. Ash goes to the inner-lock hatch to meet them, while Ripley talks to the crew by intercom but refuses to let them back into the ship because of quarantine. There is an argument between Ripley and Dallas about opening the hatch, and Ripley stands firm on the fact that they cannot let Kane back into the ship with this apparent infection. Dallas orders her to open the hatch, but she refuses. An obviously difficult decision for her, Ripley here establishes both her authority and also reminds others of the quarantine laws. Ash, however, hearing her refusal by intercom, opens the hatch.

Scene 14:

In the infirmary, Dallas and Ash remove the helmet and outer layer of something solid from around the facehugger attached to Kane's face.

Director's Cut: The crew, Lambert, Parker and Brett are watching from behind a large glass pane. Ripley shows up, and Lambert immediately attacks her, slapping her; the men have to pull her off. She's upset that Ripley would have left them outside the ship. Parker makes his first suggestion that they freeze Kane.

Scene 15:

Dallas and Ash attempt to remove the "facehugger," but with its long tentacle like tail it wraps itself even tighter around Kane's throat. They scan it in the x-ray machine, and see that it has something down Kane's throat and is feeding him oxygen. Dallas is for removing it immediately; Ash attempts to convince him otherwise, using Kane's possible death as the reason. But Dallas is unswayed. Here, and earlier in more subtle ways, we see that Ash's concern focuses on the alien, and that he manipulates others, primarily Dallas, in his efforts to keep the specimen alive. When they attempt to cut one of the crab-like arms with a laser, it bleeds acid that immediately cuts through the floor. Dallas runs out, fearing it will "eat through the hull." Dallas and the rest of the crew, with the exception of Ash, climb down decks to find where the acid-blood will end. It finally stops two decks below. Parker remarks it is an "incredible defensive mechanism."

Brett and Parker are back working in the engine room repairing the damage from the landing. They complain about the fact that they had to take on this other mission.

Scene 16:

In the medical lab, Kane is on a table with the alien attached to his face and only Ash in the room. The camera pans the room to Ash, who is absorbed in his microscope and investigations of the alien. Ripley appears, asking about the alien. Ash shuts off the computer screen as if not to allow her access and asks her not to look in the microscope when she attempts this as well. Ash becomes reticent about what the alien is, but Ripley persists in her questions. Ash opens up finally when describing the alien, and Ripley suddenly wants to know why he let it onboard. They are vying for authority here. Ash argues Kane's life was at stake. Ripley says that she is in authority when Dallas is off the ship, and also that there are quarantine laws. They part without a resolution to the conflict.

Dallas is listening to classical music in the shuttle, obviously thinking, and Ash calls on the intercom to say he should take a look at Kane. Dallas calls Ripley to meet him in the infirmary.

Director's Cut: We hear Ripley over the intercom asking for Dallas, as we see him relaxing in the shuttle.

Scene 17:

Dallas, Ash and Ripley enter the infirmary through a locked door. Kane is on the operating table, but the alien is no longer attached to his face. They begin to look around the room for the alien. It finally falls from the ceiling area onto Ripley, and Dallas steps in to protect her, although the alien appears dead.

Scene 18:

In the medical lab, Ash, absorbed in probing the dead alien, argues that it must go back because it is a new species. Ripley wants to get rid of it. Dallas acquiesces to Ash's judgment, and this upsets Ripley. It is clear that Ash is playing to Dallas' sense of the right protocol on new species, while Ripley logically states that the alien, even though dead, may be pose a threat.

Ripley follows Dallas out of the lab arguing that they should get rid of this thing. Dallas says Ash has the authority which Ripley does not understand. Dallas explains that he just captains the ship everything having to do with science is under Ash's authority. Ripley wants to know why this new protocol. Dallas says because the Company has made it that way. Dallas asks about the ship's repairs which Ripley says are not quite done. But Dallas says the major things are fixed, and they should leave as soon as possible.

Scene 19:

The shuttle taking off from the planet. Inside, the ship shakes and the engineers are saying it will hold. There appears to be some anxiety about this for all are relieved when they finally gain some altitude.

In the galley, Parker again remarks that he thinks they should just freeze Kane and the alien (for the third time). Brett says, "right," as he does on most things, and there ensues a discussion started by Ripley about why he always simply goes along with whatever Parker says. Lambert tells them they are still ten months out and so will have to go back into hypersleep which no one is happy about.

Ash on the intercom suggests that Dallas needs to come and look at Kane. Ripley says they are on their way.

Scene 20:

Kane awake and seemingly okay, but remembering nothing of the events since he was in the alien ship. They decide to have one more meal before going back into hypersleep.

Around the dining table various conversations going on, and a discussion of the food. Parker makes a sexual joke about eating something else, to which Lambert responses with a nervous smile. At about this instant, Kane starts choking. All are concerned, with the exception of Ash, who studies Kane expressionlessly as his goes into convulsions. Attempting to hold Kane down on the table where they have been eating, with Lambert watching behind, suddenly there is a blood spurt from Kane's chest. All of them are shocked and stop for an instant.

The alien bursts through Kane's chest, killing him instantly. The creature, now resembling a thick snake with a exoskeletal head (often referred to as the "chestburster" or in phallic terms), and about six inches high, surveys the crew around the room from something of a standing position in the middle of Kane's chest. The crew don't move, but then Parker grabs a table knife and makes to attack the alien. Ash steps in and tells him not to touch it. The alien escapes across the room and all stand transfixed but Ash, who looks on with seeming scientific interest and curiosity.

There are voices are they look for the alien, but nothing is found.

Back on the bridge, the remaining crew look on at the computer screen as Kane's body has been wrapped for burial in space. Dallas asks if anyone wants to say anything, and no one speaks. Kane's body is jettisoned into space. There is a parting shot of the ship silently moving through space.

Scene 21:

Brett explains to the crew about the cattle-prod type devices he has made to hunt the alien. Ash says he has devised a way to track it with a hand-held locator which Ripley wants explained. With some frustration over always being questioned by her, Ash explains that the device keys on changes in air density. Dallas breaks the crew into two teams, Dallas, Ash and Lambert, and Ripley, Parker and Brett. He warns Parker about his tendencies to display heroics.

Scene 22:

Ripley's team enters a dark corridor, and Parker and Brett attempt to fix the lighting which they thought was already fixed. Beyond a door Ripley picks up a sound on the locator, making a comment about how she doesn't believe Ash's explanation of the equipment, suspecting perhaps he has been planning for more than he has told the crew. They determine the noise is from within a locker, and when they open it, Jones (the crew's cat) springs out and escapes. Brett allows it by his net, and the others scold him and say now they have to catch it again. Brett goes off looking for Jones.

Scene 23:

Brett is off looking for Jones, calling for him and going slowly through what appears to be the warehousing area of the ship's lower levels. He hears Jones cry and finds him once, only to lose him as Jones escapes through a door into another area. Brett finds something that looks like a snake's shed skin and goes on. He finally finds Jones hiding behind some machinery. The alien, now nearly seven feet tall, descends from the upper area behind Brett. Brett turns around, amazed at this full-grown alien, and freezes. The alien, whose jaw houses another projectile-like jaw within it extends this inner set of teeth slowly and then strikes, something like a snake, and picks up Brett.

Director's Cut: Parker and Ripley come rushing in calling above for Bret. The dripping water has turned to blood and it covers Parker. Jones watches unmoved.

Scene 24:

Parker is telling the others with some disbelief on his part that the thing has grown and is the size of a man now. They determine it is using the air ducts to move around. Lambert wants to know if Brett could be alive, and Ripley says no. Dallas' plan is to use the air ducts to drive it into the airlock and send it out into space. Parker continues to be amazed that it has grown so large, and Ash seems clinically interested in this, quietly identifying the alien as Kane's son. Ripley calls on Ash to help them fight the alien as he has remained for the most part in the background, and he suggests fire as animals tend to be afraid of fire. Lambert asks who gets to go into the vent and drive it on, and Ripley says she does. But Dallas says no, he will go. Ripley gives him a long steely look which suggests Dallas is putting himself in harms way, out of the normal procedure for next in command, perhaps because she is a woman.

Theatrical Release: Dallas consults "Mother" regarding destroying the alien and asks what the chances are of success. There is no response from "Mother" except, "Unable to compute. Available data insufficient."

Scene 25:

Ripley and Ash tracking Dallas in the vents, and Lambert using one of the locating devices to follow his movements. Dallas in the vent with a flamethrower, just barely able to stand crouched, going junction by junction in the vent, having them close the hatches down as he moves through. Lambert locates the alien on a movement locator, near the third junction which Dallas moves toward.

Scene 26:

Ripley on the intercom with Dallas; Ash watching detached by her side. Lambert says she has lost the signal but that the alien must be around there somewhere. Dallas, getting nervous wants out, and Lambert says it is now moving directly toward him. We see Dallas in the vent wondering which way to go, not knowing where the alien might be. Lambert tells him to get out quick. Dallas descends a ladder, and turning, finds himself face to face with the alien. The computer screen and audio link go dead.

Scene 27:

Parker with the others, slams down a flamethrower and says this was all they found of Dallas. Ripley says they should go ahead with Dallas' plan. Lambert says they should get in the shuttle and abandon the Nostromo. But the shuttle won't take four. Parker says he wants to kill it in any case. Ripley, now in charge, attempts to take control and lay out the plan, but Parker is raging. She yells at him to shut up in order to proceed. She asks Ash if he can help; Ash says he is "still collating," with "Mother"; Ripley complains that he has done nothing. She has access to "Mother" now and will find out for herself she says.

Scene 28:

Ripley entering the inner chamber of the computer "Mother." She accesses the computer through a keyboard and screen and asks for answers. She wants to know how to neutralize the alien, but the computer does not understand. She finds only "Special Order 937" after overriding the classification "Science Officer's Eyes Only." She finds the Company's order: "Priority One, Insure Return of Organism for Analysis. All Other Considerations Secondary. Crew Expendable." At some point during the previous moments, Ash has entered the chamber and is next to her. He says there is an explanation, but Ripley grabs him by the shirt front and pushes him up against the computer wall, crying and angry.

Scene 29:

Ripley, leaving the computer chamber, calls for Parker and Lambert on the intercom but gets no answer. When she attempts to leave the central area, Ash closes the doors. When she tries to get by him, he grabs her by the hair and takes away a handful. With extraordinary strength, he throws her across the quad and knocks her semi-unconscious. Looking a bit disoriented, moving mechanically, and sweating white liquid, Ash throws Ripley into one of the cubicles off the main area, and attempts to choke her to death with a rolled up magazine. The cubical is full of pin-up pictures of nude women; the "oral rape" becomes a key image in Ash's final moments and his conflict with Ripley. At this moment, Parker and Lambert arrive. Parker tries to pull Ash off, but Ash grabs him with one hand crushing his chest, as he continues to jam the rolled magazine down Ripley's throat. But now Parker hits him from behind with a canister, perhaps a fire extinguisher. Ash, short-circuited, begins to roll around the room in jerking and antic motions, spraying while liquid. With another blow from the canister, Parker dislocates Ash's robotic head which hangs by a single shoulder muscle. As Ash subsides finally, Parker repeats again, in disbelief, that Ash is a robot. Ash, nearly beheaded, is yet active and grabs Parker wrists and won't let go. Lambert, with one of the prods, now stabs Ash repeatedly and electrocutes him.

Scene 30:

Ripley working on the mechanics of Ash's remains, reconnecting him so they can find out how to kill the alien. She realizes that the Company has sent him to bring back just such specimens, and she thinks this is perhaps for their "bio-weapons" division. Ash is reactivated, or his head is; he reaffirms that they are all expendable. He says they can't kill it, and then goes into a monologue about the uniqueness of this "perfect organism" without the "delusion of morality." They pull the plug on him, and Ripley now repeats Lambert's earlier suggestion that they abandon the ship, take the shuttle, and blow up the ship with the alien in it. Parker torches Ash's robotic corpse on the way out.

The three remaining crew members head down the corridor to prepare the shuttle and get supplies. Ripley heads to the shuttle, and the others go to get coolant for the trip.

Scene 31:

Ripley on the bridge hears Jones while she is preparing the shuttle.

Lambert and Parker, in the lower level supply area, start grabbing canisters of coolant and placing them on a cart. Parker guards with the flamethrower as Lambert collects bottles. Switching between the bridge with Ripley looking for Jones now and the supply area with Lambert and Parker, the audience anticipates the alien's reappearance.

Scene 32:

Ripley can hear Parker and Lambert on the open intercom. Ripley keeps calling "Jones" and searching. Jones, frightened, jumps from a chair, and Ripley screams. Ripley catches him at last, and places him in a carrier.

Lambert shuffling oxygen or coolant metal bottle to Parker is covered in a descending shadow; she suddenly stops.

Scene 33:

The alien has descended between them. Lambert, seemingly frozen with fear, cannot move as the alien approaches her. Parker keeps yelling for her to "get out of the way" so he can use his flamethrower, finally charging in and being knocked by the alien's serpentine tail and then held as the alien's inner jaw appears, striking and killing Parker. Ripley has heard some of this on the intercom.

Intermittently with the above scene, we see Ripley, now with Jones in a carrier, climbing down to the lower level to come to their aid.

Finished with Parker, the alien turns back to Lambert who has still not moved, even as the alien's sharpened tail beings to slowly climb around her leg and upward.

The view from Ripley's perspective now, running down a corridor, and in the background we hear first Lambert's screams, excited breathing, a screech of some kind, and then silence. Ripley shows up to find Parker dismembered on the ground and Lambert dangling from above; all of her we see is a single, naked leg.

Scene 34:

Again at first from the perspective of Ripley running down corridors toward the main controls to set the ship to self-destruct. She must disengage the cooling system on the nuclear reactor, and this takes three or four steps, including raising the cylinders which perhaps hold the nuclear fuel. The speaker comes on with a standardized warning that the ship has been set to self-destruct in five minutes.

Scene 35:

Director's Cut: Ripley climbs down with her flamethrower toward the shuttle. She comes upon a strange, organic wall of combs which include, embedded within them, Dallas, only his face showing, and Brett. They appear to be hived and are only just alive. Dallas starts crying "kill me," and Ripley with some trepidation fires on the combs.

Ripley's head appears slowly out of a ladder tube as she climbs up toward the shuttle level, searching in every direction for the alien. With Jones again in tow in the carrier, and with flamethrower slung from her shoulder, she runs, looking back. The computer comes on to say that there are three minutes left before the five minute warning. When she stops to breathe and peers around the corner, Ripley finds herself face to face with the alien between her and the shuttle.

As the alien's head begins to emerge from around the corner in her direction, Ripley runs back the way she has come, leaving Jones in the carrier.

Director's Cut: View from within the carrier; a side view of Jones looking out.

Scene 36:

Ripley races back down the way she has come, climbing down to the level of the self-destruct mechanism. In the midst of steam and pressure releases, we heard the computer calmly informing her and the audience that the five-minute self-destruct timer will start in "t minus one minute." At 30 seconds, the computer starts counting down to zero. Ripley just manages to get the fuel rods back into the coolant and to throw the two main power switches as the countdown ends. Ripley addresses "Mother" and tells her that she has turned the cooling units back on, but the computer states the ship will destruct in five minutes. Ripley calls "Mother" a bitch and smashes the flamethrower into a computer console.

Director's Cut: the scene is extended with longer shots of Ripley preparing the Nostromo to self-destruct.

Scene 37:

Ripley returns for Jones now, slowly searching to see if the alien is still about. In the background, a loud horn signals the final moments. Making it to the shuttle, the computer tells her she has one minute until the ship's destruction. Working steadily, Ripley prepares the "drop" of the shuttle from the Nostromo, and straps herself in. The computer counts down from 30 seconds. The shuttle clears the ship with about ten seconds, and then in the distance we see a mega-explosion with a burn that repeats three times and spreads in a giant disc. All goes quiet, and Ripley, obviously exhausted, lies back in the chair and says "I got you, you son of a bitch."

Scene 38:

Ripley lying back in her chair for a long moment, then gets Jones out of his carrier and prepares him for hypersleep. She puts him into one of the cryotubes after calming him a bit with some affection. Ripley undresses, preparing herself for hypersleep; stripping down to her underwear as she throws a few switches and sets other gages.

In setting one gage next to the shuttle's walls of tubing and metallic ducting the alien's hand falls out in front of her. She screams and runs into the locker with the spacesuits, hiding behind one.

Scene 39:

From inside the locker she watches the alien, which has not moved from its hiding spot among the tubes and duct work. Slowly, Ripley emerges. The alien, now moving very slowly for some reason, is still sideways in among the duct work. Ripley, realizing she is in the spacesuit compartment, slowly climbs inside one of the suits. We see the alien's inner jaw slowly emerging and retracting, as Ripley climbs under a space helmet and fastens it on. Taking something like a grappling gun from the rack inside the closet, and loading it with a short bolt and line, she emerges from the locker.

Singing in a frightened, breathy voice, "You are my lucky star," she slowly straps herself into the command chair. Opening a control panel, she selects a few buttons, searching for the one that will release pressure right where the alien is hiding. Finally, the pressure dislodges the alien, now screaming, from its hiding place, and it appears to fall out onto the shuttle's deck. Still singing, but facing away from the alien, she waits for it to reach her. When she sees it out of the very edge of her helmet, she screams and hits a button to open the shuttle's outside door. The alien is sucked out, but manages to catch both sides of the portal frame. Ripley shoots it with the grappling gun, and the hook hits it in the chest and knocks it out, but the door closes catching the gun and leaving the alien connected to the shuttle by a tether. The alien is either pulled into the shuttles engine, or climbs in, and Ripley, watching from the window of the shuttle, hits the button to fire the engines. The engines ignite and propel the alien finally out into space.

Over the glow of the engines from outside, we hear Ripley making her final report. She lists the dead of the crew, and states that the ship and its cargo are destroyed. She notes that she should reach "the frontier" in about six week and will hopefully be picked up by the "network." She signs off as "Ripley, the last survivor of the Nostromo." Her final remark is to Jones, who is out again, and the final picture is of Ripley, in white, asleep in the cryotube.

Scene 40:
The credits follow over a view of deep space.

APPENDIX B

ALIENS SUMMARY

Characters

Ripley, Warrant Officer (Sigourney Weaver)
Rebecca Jorden "Newt" (Carrie Henn)
Corporal Hicks (Michael Biehn)
Carter J Burke (Paul Reiser)
Bishop (Lance Henriksen)
Private Hudson (Bill Paxton)
Lieutenant Gorman (William Hope)
Private Vasquez (Jenette Goldstein)
Sergeant Apone (Al Matthews)
Private Frost (Ricco Ross)
Private Drake (Mark Rolston)
Corporal Dietrich (Cynthia Scott)
Corporal Ferro (Colette Hiller)
Private Spunkmeyer (Daniel Kash)
Private Crowe (Tip Tipping)
Private Wierzbowski (Trevor Steedman)
Van Leuwen (Paul Maxwell)
ECA Rep (Valerie Colgan)
Insurance Man (Alan Polonsky)
Med Tech (Alibe Parsons)
Doctor (Blain Fairman)
Cocooned Woman (Barbara Coles)
Alien Warrior (Carl Toop)
Power Loader Operator (John Lees)

Summary

Scene 1:
    Opening title and credits. The slow drift of the darkened space shuttle, Narcissus, toward the viewer.

Scene 2:

The interior now, instruments and equipment covered with a thin crystalline shine, as the camera pans to Ripley asleep in her cryotube. The computer onboard comes to life with a screen reading "Proximity Alert," and from the outside we see the shuttle being pulled slowly upward into a much larger spacecraft.

A robotic arm cuts through the thick shuttle door with a laser in a few seconds. A second robotic arm enters, scanning the interior with a camera eye and thin beam of light. Men in oxygen masks and rubber suits follow. They determine that the bio-readings are all "in the green" on Ripley. One pulls his mask off to expose a human face, and says "There goes our salvage, guys." The outline of Ripley's sleeping face becomes the outline of a blue planet.

Scene 3:

Above the earth, a space station, and then moving to the interior, a medical lab. Ripley wakes, and the nurse tells her she is at Gateway Station. Burke enters the room holding Jones, the cat. Ripley, happy to see the cat, ignores Burke until he sits and introduces himself, making a joke about "working for the Company" and asking that she not hold that against him. Ripley is immediately suspicious. Burke says she is suffering from the effects of "such a long hypersleep." Ripley, not recognizing the station, wants to know how long she was out there. Fifty-seven years, Burke finally tells her, and begins to explain that she derived through the "core systems" and a salvage team found her only out of luck.

Within this scene Ripley transitions to a dream state, where, still hearing Burke explain, she begins to imagine something within her chest. Jones hisses. Ripley goes into convulsions and as Burke, the nurse and others try to hold her down, an eruption from her chest seems imminent. Ripley pleads "kill me" and then suddenly wakes from her dream in the infirmary at night.

Scene 4:

The nurse comes on the monitor ask if she is having bad dreams again. But Ripley seems comforted perhaps only by the presence of Jones.

Special Edition: Ripley is sitting on a bench in a garden, listening to the birds. As the camera pans around her, we see that she is still actually at the station, and she turns off the simulation of the garden. Burke arrives, and Ripley immediately asks about "her daughter." Burke tries to keep her focused on Company business and the inquire she must face shortly, but she persists. Burke gives her a picture, and tells her that her daughter died, at age 66, two years ago. The audience becomes aware of the incredible disconnection for Ripley in this her new world. Ripley remembers telling her she would be home for her birthday.

Scene 5:

The court of inquiry, with a conference table and screen where Ripley is looking at data records for the crew on the Nostromo from the first *Alien* film. Ripley, noticeable frustrated that the committee seems only concerned with the cost of the destroyed ship, tells them that they should be thinking about the total devastation if just one of the aliens makes it to earth. Ripley challenges the ECA Rep, a woman, when she thinks the aliens were indigenous to the planet, now identified as LV-426. Realizing they are going to try and make her out as mentally unstable, she yells at them that Kane saw thousands of "eggs" down there.

Special Edition: Van Leuwen levels the committee's judgment: Ripley has acted with "questionable judgment' and is no longer fit to be an flight officer on a starship. Ripley's license is suspended indefinitely. And she must undergo regular psychometric evaluations.

As the conference room empties, Ripley corners Van Leuwen and tells him to check out LV-426. He tells her that there's been a colony on the planet for twenty years, with a plant that produces breathable atmosphere, and sixty or seventy families terra-farming. She repeats his final word: "families."

Scene 6:

Special Edition: View of storm on LV-426 and a sign reading: "Hadley's Hope, Pop. 158." An all-terrain vehicle enters the compound, and we move inside the command center of Hadley's Hope.

A technician catches Al, the supervisor, on his way through the room with a report that a "mom and pop survey team" Al had sent to the planet's outer regions has called in and want to know if their "claims" will be honoured on anything they find. Al sent them out to that specific region on Company orders, a fact that suggests Ripley's information about the location of the alien eggs has not gone completely unnoticed. The technician's kids are playing along the grid walks of the corridor, where later Newt will be hiding, and are told to stay off "this level." The scene ends with a view of a sign in the compound that reads: Weyland-Yutani Corp. "Building Better World."

Scene 7:

Special Edition: Outer regions of LV-426 and an all-terrain vehicle with the survey term: mother, father, and a young son and daughter. They approach the derelict spacecraft, the view through their windshield similar to the Nostromo's first glimpse of the alien ship in Alien. The father sees this as possibly making them rich, and doesn't want to "call it in" until they know more. Leaving the kids in the all-terrain vehicle, the parents venture into the ship.

Newt is worried they have been gone a long time, when the mother opens the door and calls in an emergency on the radio. The father with an alien "face-hugger" attached to his face is lying next to the vehicle. Newt screams.

Scene 8:

Special Edition: Ripley in her room, smoking and staring into space.

Burke and Lieutenant Gorman arrive and ring her bell. Burke tries to introduce Gorman, but Ripley shuts the door on them. Burke calls through the door that they have lost contact with the colony on LV-426. Ripley can't believe they want her help after all they did to her. They want her to escort the Marines back out to the planet. Ripley repeatedly refuses to go back. She is suspicious of Burke's motives for going out, but he offers her full reinstatement as a flight officer, with the Company picking up her contract, if she will agree to return with them. She's been working on the cargo docks, running a loader (a robotic suit with forklift capabilities), since her demotion. Determined in her decision not go out there again, Burke urges her to face up to her fears. He is aware of her nightmares about the alien. He leaves her with his card.

Ripley wakes from another nightmare.

Scene 9:

In the predawn, she calls Burke on the video phone. She only wants to know if he is going out there to kill the alien, not bring it back. He gives her his word, and she accepts the mission, and hangs up. Jones, she says, is staying behind.

Scene 10:

Special Edition: View of the Marine's spaceship, the Sulaco, moving through deep space.

Inside the Sulaco, much as with the opening scene of the original *Alien*, the camera pans an empty ship, the "garage" lower level here, full of equipment. Certain geometric toys are moving on countertops, and there is a similar light breeze, but no humans. The camera arrives at the cryotubes; a computer comes on, lists the tubes' inhabitants as the lights come on and the tubes open. We see Ripley and the others slowly starting to come back to life. Sergeant Apone opens his eyes and immediately sticks a cold cigar in his mouth. Others rise more slowly. Apone starts a pep talk about another day in the Corp as the others complain about waking from hypersleep. The group gathers at the lockers and dresses.

Private Vasquez asks Corporal Ferro about "Snow White" (Ripley), and they make fun, along with Private Hudson, of the fact that Ripley has seen "an alien." Vasquez makes a joke about Hudson's masculinity, and we see there is a bond between her and Private Drake, the two more aggressive Marines.

Scene 11:

At the mess, Apone and Hudson make sexual jokes about the mission, and remembering sex with other species, some sexually difficult to define. Ripley is noticeably concerned that no one is taking this mission too seriously. There are complaints about the cornbread (echoing similar in the original *Alien*). Hudson convinces Bishop to "do the thing with the knife." Bishop's knife trick is to stick the point between the fingers of a hand held down on the table, in rotation and with increasing speed. Drake grabs Hudson's hand for the trick this time, and Hudson no longer finds the trick funny. Corporal Hicks makes a comment that the new Lieutenant is too good to eat with the rest of them. Bishop has cut his finger, and white liquid oozes out. Ripley, seeing this, realizes he's an android, and wants to know why no one told her an android was on this mission. Burke explains to the others that it was an android (Ash) who "malfunctioned" on the first mission. Bishop, preferring to be called "an artificial person," understands the problems with the earlier models, and states that he could never harm a human being.

Scene 12:

In the staging area of the Sulaco, the crew gathers for Gorman to brief them on the specifics of mission. Not knowing the group well, he calls Hudson by the wrong name. Hudson complains about their being sent on a "bug hunt." Ripley tries to explain what she knows of the alien, gets nervous remembering the events, and is interrupted by Vasquez who says she's ready to exterminate anything. Still frustrated with their attitudes toward the mission, Ripley tells them that just one of alien wiped out her whole crew. Gorman, irritated with the crew's attitude, gives them prep order and all complain.

Scene 13:

Apone riding hard on the crew to get the Armoured Personal Carrier (APC) and other equipment ready. Ripley comes looking for someway to help, and Hicks and Apone are impressed that she can run a loader with the best of them (preparing us for the scene where she battles the Queen from inside one of these).

Scene 14:

The Sulaco coming into orbit around the planet, the Marines gear up and load the APC onto the shuttle. Apone is giving the crew another pep talk, as the adrenaline level rises. Locked into the APC within the shuttle, they prepare to "drop" from the Sulaco. Ferro pilots the "drop-ship" as it free falls at a tremendous rate of speed down into orbit. Gorman, obviously having a rough time of the flight, is asked by Ripley how many drops this is for him, and Vasquez wants to know how many combat drops. This is his second.

Special Edition: Hudson goes into a performance about being the "ultimate badass," listing the weaponry they carry and trying to convince Ripley that there is nothing to fear when they are on the job.

Burke talks about the Atmospheric Processor, which is turning the planet inhabitable. They circle the complex but see no signs of life.

Scene 15:

The APC deploys immediately upon touch down with the Marines in it, and they disperse and approach the entrance to the compound in a pouring rain.

Ripley, Gorman, Bishop and Burke remain in the APC on the video monitors watching the deployment. From the APC Gorman gives commands through Apone's headset.

On Gorman's commands the two squads reach the compound door. Inside the compound things are in disarray, with water leaking from the ceiling gashes and hanging wires. They search two levels of the compound but encounter nothing, but evidence of a battle. And nothing shows on the motion detectors.

Special Edition: Hudson and Vasquez get a signal on their tracker and enter a room, only to find some lab mice in cages.

Ripley sees something through Hick's helmet camera and has him back up. It's a hole burned through the steel grid of the corridor flooring, where an alien must have bled. Burke repeats "acid for blood" in recognition. They find more evidence of alien burns.

Apone says they found nothing, and second squad also; Gorman says the area is secured, but Ripley objects. Hudson jokes about feeling saver because Gorman is coming in.

Scene 16:
Special Edition: the four left on the APC now enter the building, with Ripley looking worried and uncertain. Hicks, aware of her hesitancy, comes back to ask if she is okay.

It appears the terra-farmers put up a last stand near operations, sealing off the doors at both ends. Hicks is becoming more sensitive both to Ripley's fears and the fact that what they are up against may be more than they had thought as he surveys the farmer's "last stand" against the aliens.

Scene 17:
Ripley finds a lab with alien "face-huggers" in glass canisters. One strikes the glass close to Burke's face. Bishop finds the log and reads: two are alive, but the human hosts were killed taking them off.

Scene 18:
One of the motion detectors goes off, and Drake leads the way prepared to fire at the first chance. In the corridor, the signal gets stronger. Hicks just manages to raise the barrel of Drake's "smart-gun" (modeled on a German machine gun) so he doesn't kill a child who has scurried across the corridor and disappeared into the steel grids. Hicks calls Ripley up to help, and they find a little girl, dishevelled and clinging to a doll.

While the other watch, Ripley dives into a small air duct after her, and comes upon a small room in the ducting, where Newt has made a "nest" of clothes, memorabilia, and foodstuffs. Before she can escape out the other side, Ripley grabs her and repeatedly tells her it will be alright. Newt finally becomes catatonic. Ripley finds a photo of the girl from a second grade citizenship award she'd won, looking much different, and we discover her name is Rebecca Jorden ("Newt").

Scene 19:

In operations, Gorman starts to grill Rebecca for information about what has occurred. Rebecca, obviously in shock, stares blankly ahead of her. Ripley tells him to give it a rest. When the others leave, Ripley feeds Rebecca some hot chocolate, taking the opportunity to clean off her face with a towel, and smoothing her with a bit of motherly-like care.

Hudson and Burke are scanning a monitor for PDT (Personal Data Transmitters) which the terra-farmers all had implanted.

Ripley is telling Rebecca that she is one brave kid for surviving this long, reflecting perhaps on her own experience. Rebecca finally speaks, whispering that her name is "Newt," opening more to Ripley's quiet interest. Ripley asks about her brother, Timmy, and her parents, working up to finding out what has happened to everyone. Newt suddenly reacts sharply by stating they are dead, and asking if she can go. Ripley asks her if she doesn't think she'd be saver with the troops, and Newt shakes her head no. To Ripley's remark that they are soldiers, she says "it won't make any difference."

In the lab, Bishop is dissecting one of the alien "face-huggers," and when disturbed by Private Wierzbowski, seems distracted (mirroring Ash's absorption in the "face-hugger" of the original film), calling the specimen "magnificent."

Hudson locates the inhabitants, all together in the processing station, under the cooling towers. Gorman and Apone gather the squads to head out.

Scene 20:

In the APC, Newt comforts her doll. Inside the processing station, the two squads deploy, with motion detectors leading them toward the signals. In the APC, Gorman, Ripley and Newt watch on the screen. The squads enter a corridor that looks like the interior of a skeletal cavity, much like H. R. Giger's designs for the original derelict spacecraft. Apone warns them that they are looking for civilians, and to watch their fire, and they identify the hive walls as some kind of "secreted resin."

Ripley realizes that the team is now under the "primary heat exchangers," and it takes some prompting from Burke for Gorman to realize that a wrong shot could rupture the cooling system and set off a fusion reaction. Gorman, frustrated, calls Apone and tells him no one is to fire their weapon, only flamethrowers, and to collect cartridges from everyone. Angry at being disarmed, Vasquez pulls two extra cartridges from her vest, and gives one to Drake after the Captain collects rounds. Hicks pulls out his rather low tech shotgun.

Scene 21:

The team finds humans "hived" in comb-like structures and suspended from the walls and ceiling.

When they appear on the monitors, Ripley sends Newt up to the front the vehicle so she won't' see this.

Corporal Dietrich finds one of the hived humans still alive. The woman trapped in the resin repeats "kill me."

Ripley, from inside the APC watching through a helmet camera, starts to grab her own chest as a newborn alien break through the woman's chest. Apone turns a flamethrower on the woman.

Scene 22:

The flamethrower seems to awaken the hive, and suddenly aliens are climbing out of the woodwork, descending on the team. Hudson says the movement on the motion detector is all around them.

Gorman starting to lose control, can't see what has happened, and Ripley tells him to pull his team out.

The team still can't see the aliens, until one suddenly grabs Dietrich, whose flamethrower goes off and torches Private Frost, who falls over the stairwell railing. Hick's grabs Wierzbowski to try and save him from an explosion of Frost's ammo belt burning on the deck. But Private Crowe is caught in the explosion. Wierzbowski is grabbed by an alien as Hicks is tending Crowe. At this point, Vasquez and Drake open up with their smart-guns.

In the APC, Gorman has lost control of the team, but tries to maintain a nervous calm as he repeats orders that no one inside hears. As he tells Apone to "fall back," the Sergeant is grabbed by an alien and disappears. The helmet cameras are going dead one by one.

Ripley starts yelling to get them out of there. Gorman tells her to shut up, She gets on the helmet intercoms and tries to tell them herself. Gorman can't find anyone to give orders to finally. Ripley keeps yelling at him to do something.

Scene 23:

Ripley straps herself in and pilots the APC, burning rubber and heading into the hive to save the remaining team members. Gorman tries to stop her, but Burke gets in his way saying he had his chance. Hicks leads the few remaining Marines in retreat, and Ripley reaches them, running the APC through the hive wall. Drake and Vasquez are firing, when Drake is sprayed with acid-blood and disappears as the others squeeze inside the APC. Vasquez refuses to leave him behind but is held back by Hicks. Hicks in an attempt to shut the APC door must shoot an alien, whose acid-blood sprays on his arm. Gorman is knocked out by falling hardware from a shelf. And Ripley struggles with an alien that has landed on the front of the APC, braking to dislodge it and running over it finally. Once broken through the station doors she keeps racing the engine, and Hicks has to tell her to let up, they have made it.

Ripley's immediate concern is Newt; others tend to Gorman who is unconscious. Vasquez wants to kill Gorman, and Hicks has to pull her off. Two of the others are not dead, according to their monitors, Hudson says, and Vasquez wants to go back in. Ripley says no, they are being cocooned now like the others. Hudson, losing it, can't believe what is happening.

Scene 24:

Vasquez says they have enough nerve gas to wipe out the hive. Ripley, in a moment reflecting her final decision on the Nostromo, says they should lift off and nuke the whole site. Burke argues the cost of the facility, and that this is a unique species they are talking about exterminating. Ripley points out that Hicks is next in command, and must decide. Burke insults him by calling him a grunt, and Hicks, repeating Ripley's words, says they'll nuke the site, "the only way to be sure."

Scene 25:

Outside, the they carry Gorman on a stretcher and set up flares, waiting for the military shuttle.

Ferro calls to Private Spunkmeyer, who is relieving himself outside the shuttle, to get a move on. He climbs aboard, but finds some sticky substance on the side of the ramp as he enters.

Ferro, getting angry with Spunkmeyer, turns to find herself face to face with an alien, its inner jaw just emerging.

On the ground, Ripley notices the shuttle swaying, as it loses a landing gear on a rock projection. She screams "run," as it just misses the group and explodes into the processing station. Hudson starts to lose it again. Hicks has to confront him. Burke gets sarcastic. Newt says to Ripley that they should get inside, as the aliens mostly come at night. Inside operations, the window shutters go up.

Scene 26:

The remaining Marines gather what weapons they have to take store. Hicks goes through the list, pulse rifles, grenades, but nothing in abundance.

Special Edition: The one things they do have are four robot sentries.

Ripley asks how long after they are overdue can they expect a rescue. Hicks tells her seventeen days. Hudson starts to lose it again, and Ripley has to yell at him that Newt survived longer than that without any weapons or training. Ripley forces Hudson to "start dealing with it," and sends him on mission to find floor plans and blueprints of the compound. Bishop says he'll be in med lab, continuing his analysis, an echo of Ash, in the original *Alien*, always stating that he is "still collating," and Ripley reacts similarly as well, suspicious of his motives.

The service tunnel is how they are moving in, Ripley decides on the blue prints. On a light table, they discuss sealing the tunnel.

Special Edition: Placing one of the robot sentry guns in the tunnel is suggested.

Ripley suggests sealing two tunnel accesses, to limit the way they can get in. Hicks agrees, and suggests then all they have to do is wait.

Special Edition: Hicks setting up the remote for the robot sentries. Hudson and Vasquez in the tunnel set up the guns, and test them.

They re-seal the barricades, and carry in supplies. Hicks gives Ripley a locator watch, so he can find her anywhere in the compound. She smiles, but he says it doesn't mean their engaged or anything.

Special Edition: One of the sentry guns panning the tunnel.

Scene 27:
Ripley carries Newt into the infirmary and places her on a bed. Ripley says she should sleep, but Newt is afraid of nightmares. Newt asks why her mother told her there were no monsters, and Ripley says most of the time it's true.

Special Edition: Newt asks if an alien went inside her mother, and wonders if that isn't how babies come. Ripley says, no, it is different, and tells her she had a daughter. Ripley says she's gone; Newt says you mean dead.

Ripley gives Newt the locator watch that Hicks had given her. Newt is afraid to be alone, but Ripley promises not to leave her, a promise she will later be fulfill when Ripley makes them return for Newt.

Scene 28:

Bishop is explaining the acid-blood neutralizes when dead. Ripley is impatient and wants options, and they discuss where the many eggs might be coming from, something they have not seen.

Special Edition: Hudson says it might be like an ant hive, and Vasquez corrects him, "bees." He says one female, and Bishop says, yes, "the Queen."

Ripley says she wants the specimens destroyed. Bishop says Burke gave him orders to keep them in stasis, to be returned to the Company labs.

Burke explains to Ripley that the specimens are worth millions, and they can both be heroes and get rich. Ripley says he'll never get them passed ICC quarantine, for she will expose him. It is here that Ripley confronts Burke with the fact that she will report his responsibility for the deaths of the colonists. She's checked the log and read that he sent them out there to find the ship without warning them. Burke was afraid he would lose his exclusive rights if everyone knew, and calls it a "bad call." Ripley throws him up against a wall screaming about his "bad call" that killed 150 people. She promises he will pay for this one. He says he expected more from her. Burke is noticeably worried.

Scene 29:

Special Edition: The warning siren goes off, and the Marines and Ripley gather around Hicks on the sentry gun computer. The computer shows the rounds dropping as the guns are fired. One of the guns runs out. They hear them now, and Ripley says they are at the pressure door.

Scene 30:

Bishop with the others at a window, shows them the "emergency venting" of the reactor. Hicks asks how long, and Bishops says four hours. Bishop says an overload was inevitable because of the damage the shuttle crash did, and the impending blast will have a radius of 30 kilometres. Hudson starts up again, saying he only had four weeks of service left. Ripley says there must be a way to get the other drop-ship on remote from the Sulaco. She says the colony transmitters will have to be manually aligned, after Hicks suggests using them. Hudson says no one will go. Bishop volunteers, saying he is the only one who can "remote pilot the ship," but that he's not stupid and doesn't really want to die out there.

They torch through a conduit, and Bishop climbs inside. Vasquez hands him a gun, but he gives it back. Ripley says the time will be close, with all Bishop must do to get the shuttle down. Inside, we see Bishop shouldering his way along the conduit. They seal him in.

Scene 31:

Special Edition: The remaining robot sentry guns, B and C, are firing. Hicks counts off the last rounds. We get a few shots from inside the tunnel with the guns firing rapidly and numerous aliens getting blown apart. B gun runs out. Hicks grabs his weapon. The aliens retreat just as the last gun has 10 rounds left. Hicks says next time nothing will stop them; Ripley suggests they are probably already looking for other ways in.

Hicks sends Hudson and Vasquez out to walk the perimeter. Ripley makes Hicks promise that he's kill her before he lets her get taken by the aliens, and he promises to kill them both.

Bishop shouldering his way through the conduit.

Hicks then shows Ripley how to use the pulse rifle, and when she asks for all aspects of it, he trains her briefly in the weapons.

Scene 32:

Returning to Newt, Ripley meets Gorman who is conscious again. He tries to apologize, but she won't hear it. Entering the infirmary, Newt is not on the bed, but Ripley finds her sleeping beneath it. She curls up with her.

Bishop has made it to the uplink and starts to remote the second shuttle for drop.

Scene 33:

Ripley wakes under the bed and realizes that two glass canisters that held aliens "face-huggers" are open on the floor. She reaches for her pulse rifle which she left on the bed, but it is gone. One of the aliens flies at her face, and she catches it between the bed and the wall. The door is locked, and they try to open it. The aliens have hidden.

We see the monitors with Ripley trying to get Hicks' attention, but Burke shuts them off before anyone sees. Newt suggests breaking the glass of the window, and Ripley tries with a chair, but it is unbreakable. Ripley sets off the fire alarm by lighting an overhead detector.

Hicks sees the fire alarm in the medlab, and tells Hudson and Vasquez to meet him there. An alien springs at Ripley, and she knocks it away, crawling along the floor until her back is against the wall. It jumps again, and wraps its tentacle tail around her neck, trying to go down her throat. At the same instant, Newt sees the other alien crawling up from the other side of a table behind her and pins it between the table and the wall.

Hicks yells for Hudson to shoot out the window, and then dives through. He grabs the alien trying to get at Ripley's face, and Hudson saves Newt by shooting the other alien. It takes two to pull the alien lose and throw it across the room where Vasquez shoots it. Ripley, barely able to breath, says it was Burke.

Scene 34:

The group surrounds Burke in operations. Ripley explains that Burke thought he could get an alien through quarantine if one of them were impregnated, but only if he killed the others by sabotaging their cryotubes on the return trip. Ripley says she doesn't know which species is worse, as the aliens don't kill each other for a percentage. Hudson and Hicks decide Burke should die, but Ripley says she he must go back.

Scene 35:

The lights are cut by the aliens. Hudson picks up a signal on the motion detector, inside the perimeter. Ripley has them retreat to operations, and they seal the door. Ripley says they must have missed something, some way in. Hudson counts off the meters, but the reading is in the room with them. Finally, Ripley looks up and Hicks checks the overhead suspended ceiling to find an army of aliens coming in. They fire as the aliens drop into the room. Ripley says "get to medical," but Burke slips out and locks the door. There is a long battle, and Hudson is grabbed from beneath the floor and dragged down. Hicks cuts through the lock, but Burke has locked another door. In escaping through the next, however, he runs straight into an alien. Locked between rooms, Newt tells Ripley they must go into the air ducts (a place she knows well), and all follow Ripley in.

In the air ducts, Newt leads Ripley toward the landing field, the others follow. Vasquez is last, firing and covering their retreat. Hicks calls Bishop, who says the ship will be there in sixteen minutes. Newt, in her excitement, runs ahead of Ripley. Vasquez catches an alien and kills it but is scorched by acid-blood. Gorman sends Hicks ahead and returns for Vasquez, and they are trapped between aliens on both ends at last. Vasquez calls him an asshole, as he has pulls the pin from a grenade, and they die huddled together.

At the same time, Newt has reached a fan in the air duct, and would climb over it. The blast from Gorman's grenade makes Newt lose her balance and fall into the fan, which cycles her downward. Ripley grabs her by the jacket sleeve, but she slips away down a vertical air duct to a lower level.

Ripley and Hicks go after her with the locator for her wrist tracker.

Scene 36:

Newt in the flooded lower level calls for Ripley, looking around fearfully and hanging desperately on to her doll. Ripley and Hicks descend along a steel walkway and find her beneath. But Hicks must torch through the walkway to reach her. Ripley's tracker detects an alien close, as Hick's works against the clock. Just as he cuts through, Newt turns to face an alien rising up out of the water. Ripley would go down after her, but Hicks says they have to go, now. The doll's head is left floating in the water. They make it to the elevator, doors closing, as an alien reaches through. Hicks shoots it but gets acid-blood on his armour, which they strip off him, but he's wounded.

Ripley half carrying Hicks now asks Bishop how much time as he works on the remote, and she tells him they are not leaving.

Scene 37:

In the shuttle now, Bishop pilots into the processing station, as Ripley gears up, duct taping together a pulse rifle and flamethrower, and grabbing a handful of grenades.

Bishop finds a platform and lands. Ripley tapes the tracker with Newt's signal to the top of the pulse rifle. Bishop warns her in nineteen minutes everything blows. Ripley says "she's alive" and tells Hicks not to let him go. Hicks says they aren't leaving.

Special Edition: Ripley says "See you, Hicks," and he replies, "Dwayne."
She says, simply, "Ellen."

Scene 38:

Ripley descending into the processing station, by freight elevator, down to the hive. The computer speaker tells us they have fifteen minutes to reach safe distances (echoing the Nostromo's countdown to self-destruction in the original *Alien*). Ripley straps on her double weapon ensemble, takes a deep breath and waits for the elevators doors to open.

Tracking Newt with the locator, she moves down through the complex, using the flamethrower to clear her way, and dropping flares as markers for her return trip. Deep in the hive, she checks the tracker to find that she should be there, and finds the watch locator on the ground.

Newt, webbed into a comb so that she cannot move, wakes to see an alien egg open, and a "face-hugger" slowly emerge. She screams, and Ripley, exasperated having thought she lost her, hears the scream and arrives just in time to blast the alien "face-hugger," and a couple others that appear. Ripley breaks Newt out of the webbing, and has her cling to her neck, carrying her as they make their escape.

Scene 39:

They come through a passage and Ripley realizes they are stand among hundreds of alien eggs. Turning slowly, she sees the giant, translucent egg-sac, producing new eggs, attached to the abdomen of the Queen alien. Seeing Ripley, she hisses, from what appears to be a double set of inner jaws. Ripley, looking at the eggs, shoots the flamethrower above them, warning the Queen of her intentions. The warrior aliens retreat back into hiding at the Queen's signal, in her effort to protect her eggs. In retreat, Ripley stops with Newt at the doorway, and deciding differently, sprays the field of eggs with the flamethrower, shooting grenades into a few for good measure.

The Queen, distraught at the destruction of her offspring, literally pulls herself loose from her own egg sac, and follows Ripley and Newt.

Scene 40:

Carrying Newt, Ripley follows her own trail of flares, running toward the elevators. The compound is collapsing through all of this, and the computer now calls out that they have four minutes to reach a safe distance. At the elevators, they must wait for one to descend. Ripley suddenly sees the Queen emerge from the smoke behind them, just as the elevator arrives. She keeps the Queen back with the flamethrower long enough for the elevator to ascend.

Ripley and Newt reach the platform but Bishop and the shuttle are gone. Ripley curses Bishop, as she realizes that the other elevator is ascending. The compound starts to explode around them, as the elevator opens and the Queen emerges. Ripley tells Newt to close her eyes. At this instant, the shuttle appears at the edge of the platform with its ramp open, and the two climb onboard.

Bishop pilots the shuttle through the processing station, as it collapses around them, and into clear space, moments before the compound explodes.

Scene 41:
Everything goes quiet. Ripley, holding Newt, says "we made it," and Newt replies, "I knew you'd come."

Checking Hicks when they land, Bishop says he had to given him another shot to put him out.

Scene 42:
Climbing down from the shuttle, Bishop is explaining that the platform was too unstable to remain, and he had to lift off and hope he could pick them back up. Ripley, finally convinced of Bishop's loyalty, tells him he did okay. At the same instant, he looks down to see acid-blood burning a hole in the floor, and the Queen's tail sticking through his chest. Ripley pushes Newt away, as Bishop rises on the tail, and the Queen rips him in half, discarding his two parts.

Ripley tells Newt to move, run, and distracts the Queen to herself. Newt hides in the flooring of the garage level, and Ripley escaped under a closing bay door. Half of Bishop watches, unable to help. Queen stalks Newt now, lifting a section of the steel flooring where she's hiding. Newt scurries under the steel grid, but is cornered by the Queen. At this moment, the bay door reopens and Ripley emerges in a loader. Ripley tells the Queen to "get away from her, you bitch."

The battle begins, with Ripley in the loader and the Queen trying to hit her with her tail. Ripley grabs her with the loader's hydraulic vice grips, and they struggle. Opening a vertical shaft to the "Outer Doors" with a button on the loader, Ripley uses a blow torch to keep the Queen's jaw from reaching her. Finally, lifting the Queen with two hydraulic arms, Ripley throws her into the open shaft. But at the last instant, the Queen grabs the loader and pulls it and Ripley down the shaft on top of her.

Ripley extricates herself from the loader and starts up a ladder, but the Queen, still pinned beneath the loader, catches her foot. Ripley throws a lever to open the outer doors, and the vacuum begins to suck out everything not fastened down. Hanging on to the ladder, with the Queen dangling now from her foot, Ripley struggles to hold on. Finally, her tennis shoe gives way, and the Queen and loader are jettisoned into space.

Newt has been sucked to the very edge of the shaft by the decompression, where Bishop has caught her with one hand, as he hangs onto the flooring grid with the other, saving her life. Ripley crawls from the shaft and hits a button to close the upper door. When she reaches the others, Newt throws herself into Ripley's arms, calling her "mommy." Bishop has the last line, and says "not bad, for a human."

Scene 43:

Inside the Sulaco's cryotube room, Newt looks on the half of Bishop that has been put to sleep already. She asks Ripley if they will sleep all the way home, and if she can dream. Ripley says they both can dream now. The final shot is of the two peacefully asleep next to each other in two cryotubes.

Scene 44:

Final credits.

Special Edition: Credits include those for Newts parents and others who are included in this version of the film.

APPENDIX C

ALIEN³ SUMMARY

Characters

Ellen Ripley (Sigourney Weaver)
Jonathan Clemens, Chief Medical Officer (Charles Dance)
Andrews, Superintendant (Brian Glover)
Aaron (Ralph Brown)
Dillon (Charles S. Dutton)
Morse (Daniel Webb)
Golic (Paul McGann)
Boggs (Leon Herbert)
Rains (Christopher John Fields)
David (Pete Postlethwaite)
Murphy (Christopher Fairbank)
Kevin (Philip Davis)
Arthur (Dhobi Oparei)
Eric (Niall Buggy)
Frank (Carl Chase)
Junior (Holt McCallany)
Jude (Vincenzo Nicoli)
Troy (Paul Brennen)
Vincent (unidentified extra)
Williams (Clive Mantle)
Gregor (Peter Guinness)
Bishop (Lance Henriksen)
Bishop 2 (Lance Henriksen)

Summary

Scene 1:
 Opening title and credits. Ripley asleep in a cryotube. The Sulaco drifting through space. Interior: an opened alien egg attached to the cryotube chamber wall. The alien climbing a cryotube; the sound of

breaking glass. The picture of a facehugger attached to someone's face. The computer speaking: "Warning, fire in cryogenics compartment," which repeats. The computer says that personnel will be transferred to the escape vehicle. On a monitor, the bio-scan of an alien attached to a human face and with its tentacle down its throat. Blood is soaking through a paper blotter. Ripley semi-conscious, with red emergency lights flashing. A ball of fire in the lab. Ripley's cryotube is automatically transferred to EEV Unit.

Scene 2:
Ripley tossing but asleep while the emergency EEV detaches from the Sulaco and drops toward the planet. On screen titles:

> Fiorina "Fury" 161
> Outer-Veil Mineral Ore Refinery
> Double Y Chromosome-Work Correctional Facility

The vehicle meteors through the sky, viewed from inside the facility, and crashes into the sea.

Scene 3:
The series of events at this point radically revises the storyline between the Theatrical Release and the later Special Edition.

Theatrical Release: The men together find the EEV and the prisoner Gregor discovers Ripley is still alive. Murphy's dog, riding the EEV as it is lifted by crane and carried back, sees an alien facehugger crawling inside. The dog then is the host for the alien in the Theatrical Release. Hicks and Newt are found dead, but physically intact.

Special Edition: The coastline of Fury 161, with abandoned loading cranes and large shipping structures. A solo figure Clemens, Chief Medical Officer, walks among the ruins. He sees the vehicle sticking from the surf, and finds a burned and blacked body (Ripley) on the shore.
Clemens running through the port landscape with Ripley's body, and entering an underground facility. He enters a room where three men are working and sends them up to the beach in case there are others. Clemens revives Ripley who spits up water. On the beach, half a dozen men are running.

On a monitor: Fury 161 Class C Prison Unit Iris – 12037154 Report EEV Unit 2650 Crash. One Survivor: Lt. Ripley (with Superintendant Andrew's face reflected as he writes).
Ripley is being put onto a stretcher.
Outside, the men find CPL Hicks (from Aliens*) dead, and Andrews at the same time types it onto the computer screen. Outside, Gregor looks into the escape vehicle and sees the body of Newt (from* Aliens*), erupted through by an alien (the absence of this scene in the Theatrical Release changes the plot considerably). On the screen Andrews records a dead female approximately 10 years old.*
Ripley getting oxygen on the stretcher. On the computer screen: Request Energ, Evac Soonest Possible-Await Response-Supt. Andrews.
The men on the beach are unloading the bodies and cargo from the EEV Unit. Oxen have been used to pull the EEV Unit onto the shore.
On the monitor, Weyland Yutani Corp acknowledges message received.
The sun sets around the side of the planet.

Scene 4:

Special Edition: Aaron, second in command at the facility, calls the group of prisoners to order to hear the group's leader, Dillon, who opens with a prayer.

Andrews informs the group about the crashed EEV and the sole survivor, a woman, to which the men immediately react. Morse reminds Andrews that they all have taken the vow of celibacy, which Dillon confirms by saying that any outsider is a threat to the harmony of their group. Andrews says he has requested a rescue team which he expects within a week. Clemens says Ripley will survive. Andrews suggests that she not be allowed out of the infirmary and tells the group that they stick to their routines.

Scene 5:

Clemens prepares to give the sleeping Ripley a shot, but she wakes, suspicious, wanting to know where she is. Clemens fills her in and says she really ought to shave her head because of lice. Jolted out of hypersleep, she expects to be sick for a couple weeks. This may be why she doesn't immediately realize she carries an alien inside her. She learns the others are dead. She immediately gets up, naked, saying she must get to the ship. Clemens suggests clothes as the all-male population hasn't seen a woman in years.

Scene 6:

Once five thousand convicts, there are now only a custodial crew of twenty-five. On the dock, they lower in the damaged EEV. Ripley is suspicious that Clemens knows her name; he himself starts to get a little suspicious because of her suspicions.

In the EEV, Ripley asks about the others. The pieces of Bishop are on the garbage pile; Hicks was impaled by a safety support; and "the girl" drowned in her cryotube. Clemens says he doesn't think she was conscious; Ripley, moved, suddenly catches sight of an acid burn on the side of the cryotube and says she has to see "what is left of her."

Scene 7:

Special Edition: Clemens asks her why. Ripley says she has to be sure how she died. Clemens says it is clear she drowned and asks if the girl was Ripley's daughter.

In the morgue, Ripley asks to be alone with Newt's body. Clemens and prisoner Kevin stand down the hall as Ripley begins to feel around the girl's chest and mouth. Clemens returns, and Ripley says they have to do an autopsy. Clemens knows it was drowning, but Ripley persists. She needs "to see inside." She makes the excuse of possible contagion: cholera. Clemens says there hasn't been any cholera for two hundred years but relents when he sees that Ripley is desperate to know.

Clemens performs an autopsy, showing no infection. Ripley insists they open her chest which shows that the lungs are full of fluid. Clemens says he's not an idiot; he wants Ripley to tell him what they were really looking for.

Andrews and Aaron arrive, and Clemens maintains Ripley's story about a contagion and says the autopsy had to be performed quickly. Andrews' concern is that Ripley not "parade around" among the male prisoners. Ripley wants the body cremated which Andrews rejects. Clemens supports her with mention of cholera which scares Andrews enough to consent to the cremation. Andrews makes it clear that they have twenty-five "double Y chromos; thieves, rapist, murders" in the facility, and just because they've found "religion," doesn't mean they are less dangerous. His main concern is to not "upset the order" by offending the prisoners or having a woman walking around, "giving them ideas."

Scene 8:

Special Edition: The prisoners Murphy and Frank are hauling in the carcass of an ox. They discuss how they would "seduce" Ripley, given the chance, mentioning a good deal of violence. They don't know how the oxen died, but when Frank has left, Murphy finds the discarded skin of a facehugger on the oxen, but thinks nothing of it.

Scene 9:
The group is gathered above the furnace for the cremation of the "child and the man," as Andrew refers to them in the context of his biblical references on death. This scene is inter-spliced with that of the oxen moving, starting to give life to the alien inside it.

Special Edition: The alien is born of this oxen.

Theatrical Release: The alien is born of Murphy's dog, Spike.
However, it appears that the same footage was used of the alien once it emerges.

We watch with the others as the mummy wrapped bodies of Hicks and Newt are dropped from a height into the burning furnace.

Dillon asks, "why the innocent are punished," referencing the girl's death. And, ironically, he suggests hope that "within each seed is the promise of a flower." A drop of blood comes from Ripley's nose.

Special Edition: The scene showing the birthing of the alien from the ox carcass.

Ripley is in front of a mirror having just shaved her head.
Ripley's showering while Clemens guards the outer door for her, and we hear voices saying how strange a woman was the only survivor, and how she changes everything.

Scene 10:
The cafeteria in the prison with men at various tables.

Special Edition: Dillon sits with prisoners Boggs and Rains and asks what the rumours are about. They turn out to be about Golic, with whom they refuse to work because he smells bad and is crazy.

Scene 11:
Ripley appears in the doorway. The men all become tense. She takes a tray of food over to the table with Dillon. She tries to thank Dillon for his comments at the funeral, but he tells her she does not want to know him

for he's a rapist and murder. Her rebuttal is that she "must make him nervous." Dillon tells her they have a lot of faith here, enough even for her and, until now, no temptation.

Scene 12:

One of the men overhears Clemens telling Ripley about the facility, how the prisoners embraced an "apocalyptic millenarian Christian" fundamentalism five years earlier. When the Company wanted to close the mining operation, Dillon and the rest asked to stay and were left as custodians. Ripley asks Clemens how he ended up here, and he changes the subject. Clemens confronts her about what she was looking for in Newt's body. Ripley deflects the question by asking if he is attracted to her sexually as she's been in space a long time.

Special Edition: Clemens replies "So have I."

Scene 13:

Murphy is cleaning a fan-tunnel and discovers the discarded skin of an alien facehugger, and when he looks deeper into a hole in the shaft, the alien strikes and he falls backward into the fan.

In bed, Clemens persists in his question about what Ripley was looking for in the girl. Ripley will only mention a nightmare in hypersleep, and suggests she has broken the rules by fraternizing with a prisoner; she's seen the barcode on his neck. Clemens promises an explanation.

Andrews calls on the intercom to tell Clemens that one of the prisoners has been killed. Ripley hears the news and is suspicious.

In the shaft, Clemens and others identify Murphy splattered all over the fan shaft by his sole remaining boot. Clemens finds a burn hole on the side of the shaft which he cannot identify. Andrews demands to see Clemens in his quarters.

Scene 14:

Ripley rummages through the EEV, looking for the flight recorder. Clemens finds her, and she wants to know about how Murphy died. Clemens says he found something at the accident: "a mark, a burn." He identifies it as like the one Ripley found on the girl's cryotube. Clemens tries to convince her to confide, but she says she must access the flight recorder and needs the remains of Bishop to do so.

Special Edition: Boggs, Rains and Golic head out on their mission to survey the tunnels.

Scene 15:

Special Edition: Clemens enters Andrews office, with Aaron there. Andrews politely offers Clemens tea, dismisses Aaron, and then tears into Clemens.

Andrews tells him that he has received a "high level communication," the first ever from the Network, that Ripley is a priority and must be watched. Andrews blames Ripley for stirring up the men. Andrews reminds Clemens of his past, and Clemens attempts to leave, but is commanded back because Andrews threatens to tell Ripley.

Special Edition: Andrews complains that he doesn't like Clemens and grills him on what Ripley is doing. Clemens can tell him little.

Scene 16:

Ripley is in the garbage area for the facility looking for the remains of Bishop. With Bishop slung over her shoulder, she runs into three of the men, obviously waiting for her, and then runs directly into prisoner Junior. The four men attempt to rape Ripley, but Dillon appears. Making sure she is okay, he proceeds to "re-educate some of the brothers" with a piece of pipe. Ripley gives one parting shot to Junior in the jaw.

Scene 17:

Special Edition: Boggs, Rains and Golic in the tunnel; Golic finds a cigarette machine no one has pillaged and loads up.

Surveying the lower levels, and leaving a trail of candles Boggs must send Rains to find out why a couple of the candles have gone out. Rains finds the alien and is attacked. From a distance, Boggs and Golic see the alien ravaging Rains and run. With one flare left to find their way, they come on Rains again whose head has been caved in by the alien. The alien grabs Boggs next and drags him upward, piercing his head finally with his inner jaw which splatters blood over Golic's face. Golic, in shock, runs.

Scene 18:

Ripley with Bishop, secluded in the medical lab, wires him to the flight recorder. Bishop seems to be unaware of his condition at first and says he likes Ripley's new haircut. He then accesses the data on the flight recorder.

Special Edition: Golic is in the cafeteria having a bowl of cereal, his face still covered with blood.

Bishop repeats data about "stasis interrupted," because of the fire and at last confirms that there was an alien onboard which landed with them in the EEV.

Special Edition: Golic is captured by the other men.

Bishop tells Ripley the Company knows everything that has happened. He asks to be disconnected rather than rebuilt. Nothingness, he says, is better than being second rate.

Scene 19:
Dillon and Clemens now enter the infirmary carrying Golic without seeing Ripley. Golic, now bound, is saying "It was a dragon," killed the other two who were "slaughtered like pigs." Andrews suggests he has murdered them, but Dillon refuses this. Ripley steps out from behind the curtain and says he is "telling the truth."

In his office, Andrews is sceptical of Ripley's story about an alien, with "acid for blood." Ripley asks what weapons they have, and Andrews tells her it is a prison, and so there are no weapons. Ripley concludes they are doomed. Andrews does not believe her and orders that she be quarantined.

Scene 20:
Special Edition: Ripley and Clemens are in the infirmary with Golic discussing the fact that there is no way to escape the planet.

Clemens tells Ripley, however, they are sending someone to pick her up. Ripley still refuses to tell Clemens about the alien. Ripley is now feeling poorly with a sore throat and bad stomach.

Special Edition: Golic rambles about there being "no perfect human" and how to survive the sane man must appear insane in an insane world (the perfect human idea echoes Ash's admiration for the alien as the "perfect organism" in the original Alien.*).*

Golic asks if Ripley is married and reminisces about girls he knew back home. He suddenly predicts that Ripley is "going to die too." Clemens asks if she's married. Then Ripley wants the truth about his tattooed barcode. Clemens finally tells Ripley the story of his medical student days, being addicted to morphine, getting drunk one night after a long shift and then being called back, prescribing the wrong dosage of painkiller that inadvertently killed eleven accident victims, and of his seven-year imprisonment. Clemens stayed on with the prisoners as the medical officer after serving his time there among them.

Scene 21:

Special Edition: The alien appears, with Golic terrified, and quietly descends to the floor behind Clemens. Also intermittent fragments of footage here as the alien's inner jaw strikes through Clemens's skull.

The alien grabs Clemens head in its hands, and drops his dead body at Ripley's feet. Ripley backs against the wall, and the alien comes up right next to her face but does not attack her. Rather, it grabs Clemens body and disappears into the ceiling, leaving a trail of blood.

Special Edition: A final comment by Golic as the alien ascends: "magnificent." Ripley runs down a hall. Dillon is praying over the men in the cafeteria and then raging at them about all the trouble that has happened and how they must stand together.

In the cafeteria, Andrews gives his version of events: Murphy's accident with the fan, the missing Boggs and Rains, and the possibility of Golic's involvement. At which point he asks for volunteers for a search party. Inter-spliced with this scene are flashes of Ripley running in desperation toward the cafeteria.

Ripley appears saying "it's here," and that Clemens is gone. Andrew orders her back to the infirmary, seconds before he himself is picked up by the alien and pulled into a ceiling hole, leaving a trail of blood. Everyone is now aware of the alien's presence in the facility.

Scene 22:

Special Edition: The apocalypse is upon them, Dillon tells the gathered men. Who is in change now, one asks.

Aaron says he guesses he's in charge, and Morse makes a sarcastic comment about "85." Aaron begins a eulogy about Andrews having been a good man, but Dillon interrupts to ask Ripley to take command as she is an officer. The men want Dillon, but he refuses to take charge himself. One asks if the alien is going to try for them all, and Ripley says yes.

Ripley says she "hasn't seen one like this before," but the others were afraid of fire. Ten miles of tunnels makes it impossible to close off the area, and the video monitors don't work. Morse confronts Ripley about being the one responsible for the alien's presence and suggests shoving Ripley's head through the wall.

Special Edition: Ripley replies, "Sounds good to me."

Scene 23:
Ripley and Aaron look at a map of the complex. Ripley suggests they flush it out; she says it will nest nearby because, like a lion, it sticks close to the zebras. Aaron says they have no working batteries for the flashlights, but Ripley says all humans have fire.

Aaron shows Ripley an old nuclear waste tank where they might trap the alien.

David, Aaron, and Ripley survey the storage area for the Quinitricetyline. Ripley wants to know why David keeps calling Aaron "85," and he confides that they saw his personnel file and it's his I.Q.. David warns that they must handle the Quinitricetyline carefully because it is highly explosive.

Dillon repeats that Ripley wants to "burn it out of the pipes" and trap it in the nuclear waste tank. He asks why the "y chromo" boys should help her, and she tells him they are already part of this.

Scene 24:
The men in the tunnels preparing to paint the Quinitricetyline on the walls.

Special Edition: Two men sitting around checking to see if any of the batteries work. There are also intermittent shots of the men mopping and brushing the Quinitricetyline onto the floors and walls.

Dillon asks if she misses Clemens, and Ripley says he's been spying. Dillon has surmised a sexual liaison. Ripley starts to show signs of being sick.

Special Edition: Dillon says she doesn't look okay to him.

Scene 25:
Aaron is telling the men not to light the fire until he gives the signal.

Special Edition: Frank climbs a ladder into a narrow passage between levels. This scene and that with the ensuing fire are inter-spliced with extra footage.

Frank drops his firing cap and lands precariously on the rim of the passage. He manages just to retrieve it before climbing back up and encountering the alien. As the alien grabs him, he drops his bucket of Quinitricetyline and the firing cap which fall in slow motion to the lower level where the cap ignites the tunnel. The tunnels explode in flame, and Dillon screams they must find the sprinklers and help these men.

Special Edition: Dillon tries to get the sprinklers turned on but fails. Aaron runs off and leaves Gregor burning after an explosion. Ripley helps put out the fire, but Gregor continues to struggle hysterically in fear.
  Junior is cut off from the others by the alien in the tunnel. Cursing the alien, he leads it into the waste tank, and Ripley manages to close the door. The alien has been captured. Dillon hits the sprinkler button and the fires subside. In slow motion, the men begin to depart the scene of carnage.

Scene 26:
Special Edition: Dillon gives a eulogy for the dead, released now he says to achieve a higher place.
  Aaron and Ripley talk quietly, standing on a level above and away from the others. Aaron confides that he is not religious; Ripley seems to understand that he does not have the capacity. He reports that the rescue team will be there within six days, and that one message said she was "top priority." She asks "what if they don't want to kill it." Aaron can't believe it.

Scene 27:
Special Edition: In the infirmary, Golic is trying to convince Morse to let him loose, and when he does, Golic knocks him out, and leaves to find the alien.

Scene 28:
Special Edition: Aaron and Ripley on the computer contacting the Company about the alien. Ripley, suspicious of the Company's intentions, asks for permission to kill it. Her request is denied.

Scene 29:
Special Edition: Golic finds the waste tank guarded by Arthur and kills him to get to the alien which he takes as some kind of mission from God. The alien immediately kills him and escapes.

In a cell, Dillon refuses to help Ripley kill the alien and is unconcerned when she tells him the Company wants to take it back with them. Morse comes to say the alien has escaped.

At the waste tank, with the men arguing, Ripley starts feeling ill. She tells them she must get to the EEV and use the neuroscanner. Dillon has Morse gather the men in the assembly hall.

Scene 30:
Riley runs the neuroscanner in the EEV. Aaron finds her and helps her scan herself on biofunctions. To her disbelief, and Aaron's, they discover an alien inside her. She has him freeze the screen and looks for herself.

Scene 31:
Special Edition: Dillon tells the men they should stay in the assembly hall and guard the doors. Dillon argues they must fight it until the rescue team arrives. They decide to head to the furnace for safety.

Scene 32:
Communicating with the Company again, Riley wants Aaron to tell them that the whole facility has "gone toxic." Aaron won't as he wants to be rescued and says he has a family. Ripley tries to convince him this is a threat to humanity, but he does not understand, and shuts off the screen before she can get the access code.

Special Edition: Ripley tells Aaron it won't kill her because she's carrying the new queen.

She says maybe she'll go look for it down there in "the basement" which she must explain to Aaron is "a metaphor." When she's left, the monitor reads that a medivac tem will arrive in two hours, and they want Ripley quarantined until arrival.

The Company's spaceship moves toward Fury 161.

Scene 33:
Ripley searches alone for the alien, suggesting, ironically, that it is not there when she needs it (to kill her). She says she's "part of the family" now. Among old sewage pipes, she sees what she thinks is the alien

hiding. She asks it to do something for her now and hits it with a piece of pipe. But it turns out to be only an unused sewage line that breaks open and is full of maggots. The alien shows up right before the scene shifts. Ripley finds Dillon to tell him that it won't kill her.

Special Edition: Ripley tells Dillon that they won't kill their own. She just saw it, stood next to it, and it wouldn't touch her. She says it won't because it knows she is carrying its future.

She tells Dillon she's carrying an alien within her, that she saw it on the CAT scan. It's "an egg layer" and can make "thousands more." Dillon refuses to believe.

Special Edition: Ripley says now she gets to "be the mother of the thing."

Ripley tells Dillon she needs him to kill her.

Special Edition: The one inside her can "wipe out the whole universe," she tells Dillon, and so has to die.

Preparing herself to die, Ripley places her head against the bars of the prison cell. With a fire axe, Dillon prepares to crush her skull. But at the last moment, diverts his swing. He tells her that if she wants to save the universe, she will have to help kill the one out there. He says if it won't kill her then perhaps they can use that to fight it.

Special Edition: Dillon tells her if she wants to die to kill herself.

She makes him a deal; if they "waste this thing," then Dillon will kill her.

Scene 35:
Special Edition: In the assembly hall, Ripley argues that they should kill it because it has killed so many of them. Aaron argues that the rescue team is almost there. Ripley and Dillon convince the others that the Company cares only about the survival of the alien. Dillon calls Aaron a "Company man" (echoing Ash's role in the first film).

Dillon says this is as good a place and time to die as any, and Ripley tells them that they will probably be killed by the Company simply because they have seen the alien. She lays it out for them: "When they first heard of this thing, it was crew expendable. The next time they sent in

Marines. They were expendable too. What makes you think they are going
to care about a bunch of lifers, who found God at the ass end of space?"
They must lure it into the lead works and drown it in hot lead, Dillon says.

*Special Edition: Dillon tells them: "We're all going to die; the only
question is when."*

He declares that he "ain't much for begging," and convinces the others
they should fight this thing to the death. Aaron alone seems uncertain.

Scene 36:

They prepare to stoke up the lead works but are uncertain after all these
years if the piston will work. Dillon explains: they must lure it into where
Ripley can pull the switch so the piston will drive it into the mould and
lead can be poured on top of it. He says they have only one chance to do it.

*Special Edition: The men preparing the maze of corridors into the piston
chamber. David calls to the others; they can hear each other but can't tell
from where. Morse's door closes only half way down.*

Scene 37:

Suddenly, there's a scream. Kevin comes upon the alien finishing off
Vincent, and yells at it to come after him. We see from the alien's
perspective as it chases Kevin through the tunnels. Elsewhere, Dillon says
it has started. The others start closing doors to block its retreat. Safe
behind a door, Kevin yells that the alien is "really pissed off."

*Special Edition: David finds Vincent or what he thinks are the remains of
Vincent.*

Prisoner Troy, just escaping, shuts the door but looks through the small
window, and the alien's tail breaks through, just missing him.

Scene 38:

*Special Edition: The men return to the piston chamber too early and
scatter. Ripley says what are we doing, and Dillon says "improvising."*

The Company's spaceship prepares to land.
David, looking for the alien to chase him, sees it on the ceiling, throws
his flare at it and runs. We now have the alien's view, upside down,
running along the ceiling. David's door jams, but closes just in time.

Gregor and Morse run into each other coming from different directions in a tunnel.

Dillon calls to all of them all but without reply.

As David peers through one of the small windows of a closed door, the alien lowers itself silently behind him and attacks.

Ripley stops Eric from throwing the piston switch after the alien runs through the chamber. They must catch it inside.

External picture of the crew of the Company's spaceship. They have landed and are approaching the facility.

Kevin is attacked from above as he walks along a tunnel.

Dillon comes upon him being carried above and pulls him down. Then Dillon tries to save him by dragging him along a corridor as the alien chases them. In the piston chamber, Ripley and Dillon tend Kevin as the alien appears in a doorway. The piston is started, but the alien escapes with Kevin's body. Dillon says they have five minutes to get it back in.

Ripley goes after the alien as Dillon closes off of the piston chamber.

Jude now runs from the alien, but all the doors he attempts to close jam halfway. Dillon yells to run as fast as he can and not to look back, but he is killed with one foot in the piston chamber.

External shot of the Company's medical team entering the facility from the planet's surface.

Aaron has been waiting at the door for the team. He reports, but the team leader wants only to know about the location of "Lieutenant Ripley" and if she is alive. We see the shadowy figure of a man in the doorway, who has heard this news that Ripley is in the lead works with the beast.

Scene 39:

Morse and Gregor run into each other in a corridor and start laughing. The alien suddenly attacks Gregor. Morse is splattered in blood and crawls off to escape and comes up on Ripley standing with a flare, looking at the alien. Riley approaches it and hits it with the flare.

Elsewhere, Dillon yells that they are running out of time.

Trying to grab the alien, Ripley cannot move it. Dillon shows up and pulls her back, and the alien follows them. Dillon yells at Morse to shut the door when they have it in the chamber.

Aaron is showing the medical team to the lead works.

Scene 40:

Now, Ripley and Dillon back up slowly into the mould, and the alien follows.

Morse climbs above to open the lead flow.

Ripley says she is staying there in the mould with the alien, but Dillon says no, their deal was that the alien dies first. He gets her to climb out, but then as the alien starts to follow her, he diverts it to himself and stays in the chamber. Dillon tells Ripley that he has to hold it there, and God will take care of her now. Dillon and the alien fight. Ripley calls to Morse to pour the lead. He releases it into the mould, drowning Dillon and the alien in molten lead.

Scene 41:

The alien leaps from the liquid lead and climbs toward Ripley. Morse calls to her to hit the sprinkler above her. Hanging from the sprinkler chains, Ripley dowses the alien who shatters into pieces as the cold water hits the hot lead.

Scene 42:

The team arrives just as Ripley and Morse are stepping off the platform. Ripley tells them not to come any closer, but Bishop now takes off his glasses and approaches. Bishop says he is here to help her; promises that he is not another android, but the designer of them, sent by the Company to show her a friendly face. Ripley still does not trust him. But he says he is there to take it out of her. "Everything they know would be in jeopardy" if it were to live he says. Ripley asks if it is true they don't want to take it back. They have a medical lab on the rescue ship to remove it from her he says.

Special Edition: The team leader tells her it would be a simple operation of two hours.

Bishop says she can still have a life with children, and she'll know the alien is finally dead. Ripley wants to know what guarantee she has, and Bishop says she must trust him. At last, she says no. She closes the gate between them and Morse immediately swings the platform back out over the furnace and lead works. One of the guards shoots Morse in the leg.

Aaron, seeing Morse shot and Ripley refusing help, picks up a wrench and hits Bishop over the head. A guard turns on him and shoots him repeatedly.

Special Edition: Bishop grabs his head where Aaron has hit him, an entire ear hanging from the side of his skull, and bleeding, and calls in a hoarse voice that he is "not a droid."(This footage makes it much clearer that Bishop is not, indeed, an android, but human.)

Theatrical Release: Bishop does not react to the blow to his head and continues on with his ear hanging from the side of his head.

Scene 43:

Bishop is calling to Ripley on the platform saying: "Think of all we could learn from it. You must let me have it. It's a magnificent specimen."

Special Edition: Bishop holds his wounded ear, bleeding, and yells at a cameraman, somewhat under his breath, "no pictures."

Ripley swings out onto the platform again over the furnace with Morse's help.

Special Edition: Ripley has a moment of doubt and pain, looking down into the furnace.

Bishop asks what she is doing and then yells "No" as Ripley lets herself fall slowly backward off the platform down toward the furnace.

Special Edition: Ripley falls into the flames of the furnace and disappears.

Theatrical Release: A chestbuster alien breaking through her chest as Ripley falls into the furnace. She grabs it with both hands and carries it into the flames with her.

The furnace goes dead.

The sun breaks from around the planet's edge. The facility is locked up, and Morse, the solo survivor, is marched off to the waiting ship.

In the garbage area for the facility, we hear the voice of Ripley on the voice recorder from the Nostromo's shuttle, repeating her words from the end of the film *Alien*: "...last survivor of the Nostromo, signing off."

On a computer monitor we read that Weyland-Yutan has closed and sealed the work prison of Fury 161 and will sell the equipment as scrap.

Scene 44:

Final credits run over a view of deep space.

APPENDIX D

ALIEN RESURRECTION SUMMARY

Characters

Ripley, Human-alien hybrid clone (Sigourney Weaver)
Annalee Call (Winona Ryder)
Dr. Mason Wren (J. E. Freeman)
D. Jonathan Gediman (Brad Dourif)
General Martin Perez (Dan Hedaya)
Frank Elgyn (Michael Wincott)
Johner (Ron Perlman)
Vriess (Dominique Pinon)
Christie (Gary Dourdan)
Sabra Hillard (Kim Flowers)
Vincent Distephano (Raymond Cruz)
Larry Purvis (Leland Orser)
Carlyn Williamson, anesthesiologist (Carolyn Campbell)
Scientist (Marlene Bush)
Surgeon (David St. James)

Summary

Scene 1:
Special Edition: Close up of sharp, jagged teeth. The camera pulls back and we see a bug that is quickly squashed by a man who then scraps the bug into a drinking straw and blows it at a window. Opening credits appear as the camera pulls back to reveal a spacestation.

Theatrical Release: Distorted images appear and disappear. The camera slowly pulls back to reveal that the images are close-ups of alien and human body parts. The image of a spaceship moving toward a spacestation appears.

Scene 2:

Inside the spacestation USM Auriga is a set of guarded doors. They open and reveal scientists working inside. A glass tube with a young, naked and unconscious Ripley is in the room with the scientists. As the camera centres on her, we hear the voice of Ripley is heard saying, "My mother always said there were no monsters. No real ones. But there are."

Scene 3:

Drs. Wren and Gediman, with others, operate on Ripley to remove an alien. Initially they have no interest in Ripley, but as they start to disperse Wren decides to keep her alive.

Special Edition: As the scientists begin to disperse, one of them prepares to close Ripley's incision. Ripley awakens, grabs his arm and pulls him close to her.

Scene 4:

Ripley is alone, lying on the floor in a circular cell. She is enclosed in gauze type material. Slowly she breaks through; she looks at the scar on her chest and the number 8 tattooed on her arm.

In a medical facility Gediman examines Ripley who is sitting on a table in restraints. When Wren enters the room, Gediman tells him of her amazing progress. Wren moves in close to Ripley, and she breaks free of her restraints, attacking him. A soldier shoots her with an electrical charge to end her attack.

Scene 5:

A scientist holds up flashcards while Ripley, in restraints, and with an armed guard nearby, states the appropriate word for each image.

General Perez, Wren, and Gediman observe her by video monitor as Perez expresses his desire that she be terminated while the scientists disagree.

Special Edition: As the scientist holds a flashcard with the picture of a little girl Ripley looks sad but also smiles.

Perez, Wren, and Gediman leave the observation room and begin walking through the corridors, continuing their conversation until they reach another observation room from which they can see the alien queen that was removed from Ripley's chest. Their conversation shifts to the queen and the cargo that is needed for the next stage of their work.

Scene 6:

Sitting in a cafeteria, Ripley is told by Gediman that she is a clone of Ripley (the Ripley who died with an alien queen inside her in *Alien³*).

Special Edition: Gediman's explanation is more detailed.

Wren joins them. Ripley asks about the alien queen and the Company. Wren tells her that the Company no longer exists.

Special Edition: He tells her it was bought out by Wal-Mart.

Wren explains that the work they are doing is for the military. She laughs at the idea that the military is preferable to the Company or that it will be able to control the alien.

Scene 7:

A spaceship, the Betty, approaches Auriga. The following overlay appears:

The Betty
Commercial Freighter
Standing crew: 6
Unregistered

In the remainder of this scene segments are organized differently in the Special Edition and Theatrical Release.

Special Edition: Elgyn and Hillard are on the bridge of the ship. A voice from the Auriga requests a code in order to allow the ship to dock. Elgyn says his code is "EATME." He then makes sexual comments to Hillard. (In the Theatrical Release this segment follows the segment below in which Johner threatens Call in the cargo bay.)

Special Edition: Elgyn walks over to Hillard and, as he asks her if she wants anything, he puts his hand on her breast. She asks for coffee.

Special Edition: Elgyn gives Hillard instructions for docking on the Auriga. Over the intercom, he informs Vriess that they will be docking soon and the cargo needs to be ready. (In the Theatrical Release this segment follows sexual comments to Hillard, above.)

Vriess and Call are busy securing the cargo.

Special Edition: Vriess stops working to tell Call a sexual joke. Call smirks.

Special Edition: Elgyn and Christie discuss going to the military facility and the fact that the Betty needs repairs while Christie tests his weapons. (In the Theatrical Release this segment follows the external shot of the Betty, above.)

Acting like a gorilla, Johner stands on a platform above Call and Vriess. He lobs a knife into one of Vriess's paralyzed legs. Call looks up and carps at Johner. Vriess curses and throws a tool at him but misses. Call yells at Johner, pulls the knife out of Vriess's leg and snaps the blade. Johner threatens her and alludes to her being a new member of the crew.

Scene 8:

The Betty docks on the Auriga. The crew disembarks and "FA-TH-UR," the Auriga's computer greets them and explains that certain levels on the spacestation are off limits to civilians. The crew walks toward a group of soldiers who are waiting conduct a security search. The crew complies. Johner shows the soldier his flask when it sets off the sensors. Elgyn calls up to Perez, who stands on a platform above them, and mocks him for taking such security precautions with the Betty's crew. Vriess's wheelchair sets off the security scanner, but the soldier allows him to proceed.

Special Edition: Vriess tells Call that they need to start associating with a better class of people.

Scene 9:

Perez pushes a stack of money across the table to Elgyn. He indicates that it was difficult to get cash. Elgyn implies that the same can be said of the cargo he has delivered. As they chat, the conversation turns to Call with both men indicating they find her sexually attractive. Elgyn notes that she was very interested in the transaction between the Betty's crew and Auriga. He says the crew would like to stay on Auriga for a couple of days to relax and do some ship repairs. Perez consents.

Special Edition: Perez explains two conditions of his consent. The crew of the Betty must stay out of restricted areas and not fight.

Scene 10:

The cargo is being unloaded from the Betty. It is a number of cryotubes with unconscious humans inside them. Wren and a few soldiers wait at a set of doors inside Auriga as Call and Christie electronically move the cargo. When they reach Wren, Call hands the remote control to him and he proceeds with the cargo into a restricted area.

Close-up of an unconscious man with his head secured by metal strapping. We then see an alien egg in front of him. Pulling back further, the camera reveals six other individuals similarly situated. Wren, Gediman, and a female scientist watch from behind glass as the eggs open. One man awakens and upon seeing the opening egg in front of him begins to scream.

Scene 11:

In an exercise facility Ripley is playing with a basketball when the crew of the Betty enters. Making sexual innuendos Johner asks her for a game. Ripley smiles and toys with him by keeping the ball just out of his reach. When, standing behind her, Johner becomes more insistent, Ripley bounces the ball between her legs, hitting him in the groin and then back-fists him across the face. The crew attempts to attack her but is unsuccessful with the exception of Christie who makes contact once, hitting Ripley in the face with a barbell, making her nose bleed. Ripley promptly knocks him down and casually throws the basketball into the net. Observing this, Wren and Gediman smile and agree that she is quite the predator. Wren calls Ripley and there is a visible reaction on Call's face to the name. Ripley flicks the blood from her nose onto the floor, and it begins to bubble and burn a hole.

In private sleeping quarters, Elgyn rubs Hillard's feet while she lies on her stomach wearing nothing but a thong.

Perez heats shoe polish and begins to spit-polish his boots.

Vriess moves through the storage area of the Auriga, stealing various things as he goes.

Call, Johner, and Christie sit at a table watching a television and drinking Johner's home-brew.

Scene 12:

From a mobile observation station in the centre of a large room lined with large containers, Gediman inspects the alien warriors that are confined in the containers. Using the controls at his location, Gediman brings one of the containers close to his observation window. There are three warriors inside. One approaches the window. After Gediman mimics its behaviour and kisses the window, the warrior attempts to attack him but hits the glass of the window. Gediman punishes this behaviour by pushing a button to release a gaseous substance that makes the warrior scream. The warrior threatens to retaliate, but when Gediman puts his hand over the button the warrior refrains.

Scene 13:

Call, Johner, and Christie are still watching television, but Call appears to be drunk. Johner becomes hostile when she spills her drink (she is wearing boxing gloves). She staggers out of the room. Once the door is closed behind her, she no longer appears to be drunk. She makes her way to the cell where Ripley is held and enters. Ripley appears to be asleep. Call is there to kill Ripley but hesitates when she sees the scar on Ripley's chest. Ripley startles Call when she opens her eyes and begins to talk. While it is clear that Call is too late to prevent the birth of the alien, she offers to release Ripley through death. Ripley rejects the offer as she forces the knife that Call is holding through the palm of her hand causing the blade to smoke. Call reveals to Ripley that she was created so the military could extract the alien from her body and then asks Ripley to help her destroy the alien. Ripley tells her it is too late and that Call should leave because "they're looking for you."

Scene 14:

In the hall outside Ripley's cell an angry Wren with the assistance of soldiers captures Call and demands to know where the rest of the Betty's crew can be found.

In the mess hall, soldiers point their weapons at Elgyn, Johner, Hillard, and Christie as Wren enters holding Call by the base of her neck. Elgyn demands to know what is going on. Wren accuses the crew of being terrorists like Call and says they will all die with her. The Betty's crew pulls out the smuggled weapons they have with them, and a shoot-out ensues. The crew, Wren, and one soldier, Distephano, are left standing.

Scene 15:

In his mobile observation station, Gediman has witnesses the shoot-out on a computer monitor. He unsuccessfully attempts to inform security.

Elgyn threatens to kill Call if she doesn't explain what is going on.

In the container Gediman had been observing prior to the gunfight, two alien warriors attack a third, killing it.

In her cell, Ripley looks up.

When Gediman and a female scientist hear a noise coming from the container they had been observing they turn away from the screen showing the gunfight to investigate. They discover the blood and body parts of the dead alien warrior burning a hole through the floor of the container. Before Gediman can prevent it, the other warriors in the container have escaped. Gediman then goes into the container to examine the hole. As he leans over it, an alien hand comes up through the hole, grabs Gediman's head and pulls him down out of sight.

In the mess hall, Call explains what the military is doing with Ripley and the aliens but stops when everyone hears an alarm.

Perez sits up in his bed when he hears "FA-TH-UR" announcing that there is a security breach.

A soldier enters the container with the dead alien warrior. On the other side of the window, in the observation station, an alien pushes the button that releases the gaseous substance, freezing the soldier to death.

Ripley, in her cell, looks up and smiles as she hears the growl of an alien warrior.

In the mess hall, Elgyn grabs a gun and says that Wren and Distephano should guide them to the Betty. Johner and Christie gather up the weapons. Hillard voices her concern over Vriess's absence.

Scene 16:

Vriess enters a hallway and hears "FA-TH-UR" announce that some of the aliens have escaped.

In the docking bay, Perez and his soldiers clamour to evacuate the spacestation.

Ripley sits in her cell as an alien warrior attempts to break down the door.

In the docking bay soldiers quickly enter multiple-person escape shuttles which Perez then launches remotely.

Using a gun constructed of parts of his wheelchair, Vriess shoots an alien that is in the grated ceiling above him.

Ripley breaks into the electrical panel that controls the doors of her cell. While the alien warrior continues its efforts to break into her cell, Ripley manages to open a different door and escape.

Alien acid falls on Vriess from above. He shoots at the alien he sees when he looks up.

Perez continues the evacuation. Just before the hatch to one shuttle closes an alien warrior enters. Perez tosses a grenade into the shuttle just as the hatch closes. He launches the shuttle and detonates the grenade. As he salutes the soldiers who have just died, an alien warrior attacks him from behind.

The group, composed of Elgyn, Christie, Johner, Call, Hillard, Wren, and Distephano, makes its way through the spacestation.

Scene 17:

Elgyn stops to collect more guns he sees in a side corridor. He bends down to pick up a hand gun and discovers that it is covered with slime. As he begins to stand, an alien beneath him pulls the grated floor out from under him. Elgyn falls but only to his armpits. Before he can pull himself up the alien warrior kills him.

Scene 18:

The group finds Elgyn. They try to pull his body out of the hole but stop and draw their weapons when they see an alien warrior.

Special Edition: Johner pulling Call back.

The group runs. The alien follows them but stops and returns to Elgyn's body. As it leans over him a gun barrel comes up through the hole in his chest and shoots the alien. Elgyn's body is tossed aside by Ripley as she climbs up through the floor. The group has returned and watches her climb up. Ripley hands her weapon and the ammunition she took from Elgyn's body to Hillard.

The group realizes that it is on its own and there are twelve more aliens running loose on the spacestation. Ripley says there will be more and sarcastically asks who she has to fuck to get off the spacestation. Call tries to convince everyone to leave Ripley behind but Christie says "she comes." He suggests that in order to survive they need to work together. The group starts to move out. Ripley leans over the dead alien, rips out its tongue, and offers it to Call as a souvenir.

Scene 19:

Walking through the corridors, Call reveals her shock that Ripley would kill an alien. Ripley expresses her indifference by saying "It was in my way." Hearing a sound everyone stops and aims their weapons at the source—a door. As they watch, the door opens to reveal Vriess on the other side aiming a gun in their direction. While Wren says that the aliens will remain in a location away from the Betty, Ripley simply says they will follow the meat (the group). Distephano explains a possible escape route. When they realize the spacestation is moving, Wren and Distephano explain that it is standard procedure for the spacestation to go to earth when there are any serious problems, and given the time when they began to move they should arrive in about three hours. Everyone is angry. Call wants to destroy the spacestation. Christie says only after they get off.

Ripley is at the front of the group with Johner who asks her how she handled the aliens when she encountered them in the past. She laughs and tells him that she died.

Scene 20:

As the others walk passed her, Ripley stops in front of a door labelled "1-7." She looks at the "8" tattooed on her arm, opens the door and goes inside. It is a lab with six dead and deformed Ripley-alien hybrid clones enclosed on glass tubes. Ripley closely examines each one and then hears something further inside the lab. There is a seventh clone, still alive, strapped to a table. The clone looks at Ripley and with difficulty says, "kill me." Call hands Ripley a flame-throwing gun. Crying now, Ripley fires the gun, burning the clone. She slowly backs out of the lab burning each of the other clones as she goes. She moves out of the lab, turns and aims her gun at Wren, but instead of firing she throws the gun at his feet and walks away. Call punches Wren in the face. As everyone begins to walk away, Johner looks in the lab, and in his comments to Christie, reveals his confusion over what Ripley has done.

We see the spacestation moving.

Scene 21:

Inside, a door opens. The group walks through to discover the bodies of the human cargo delivered by the Betty's crew. They have been used as hosts for the aliens. All have holes in their chests where the aliens have burst out. Ripley finds one man, Purvis, still alive. He starts to scream, waving around a pipe. He calms down, drops the pipe and asks what is going on. There is disagreement about whether Purvis should go with the group, especially when Ripley reveals that he has an alien inside him. Purvis wants to know what she is talking about.

Special Edition: Wren tells him that he has a parasite in his chest.

Ripley explains in more detail. After listening, Purvis asks her who she is, and she tells him that she is the monster's mother.

Special Edition: More discussion about whether Purvis should go with them.

They agree to take Purvis with them.

Special Edition: Wren stretching out his arm in invitation.

Scene 22:

The group opens a hatch and descends a ladder to a hallway below that is filling with water. Vriess is strapped to Christie's back. Wren explains that they have to get to the elevator on the other side of the kitchen which is completely under water. No one is happy but they move forward.

Special Edition: Distephano shows an interest in Christie's disposable gun. Call makes a joke about taking a deep breath.

Individually they dive into the water and begin to swim across the kitchen. Johner yells when he sees two alien warriors coming toward them. He fires his weapon and kills one of the aliens. The group swims frantically as the other alien chases them. It grabs Hillard's ankle and pulls her back into the water until she disappears. Distephano opens an elevator door at the end of the kitchen and holds it as the other swim through. They swim up the elevator shaft toward the surface, but there is something covering the surface, and they struggle to break through it.

Above the surface is an alien nest. As the group breaks through they see the alien eggs surrounding them. A facehugger leaps out of one of the eggs and attaches to Ripley's face. Struggling against it she goes under water. Other eggs begin to open. The group descends under the water, and Christie fires his weapon causing an explosion in the nest area. An alien warrior is swimming toward them. Ripley manages to remove the facehugger from her face. With the eggs destroyed everyone swims back to the nest area and quickly gets out of the water.

They begin to climb the ladder in the elevator shaft. The door at the upper level is jammed. Wren asks Call for her gun so he can shoot the control panel. She hands it to him. Wren turns the gun on her and fires. Call falls into the water below and disappears. Vriess yells and tries to shoot Wren but misses and his gun jams. Wren turns and opens the elevator door, escaping, and the door closes behind him.

The alien warrior that was chasing them in the water has reached the surface. It leaps up onto the ladder and begins to climb up behind Christie and Vriess who is strapped to Christie's back. Vriess sees the alien approaching. He warns Christie and tries to shoot but his gun is still jammed. Then Christie shoots at the alien but misses. The alien hits Christie in the face with acid that it has expelled from its mouth. Christie loses his grip on the ladder, but Vriess grabs it. The alien grabs Christie's foot. Johner leans backward and shoots the alien. The alien is dead but continues to hang on to Christie's foot. Vriess struggles not to lose his grip. Christie unbuckles and cuts the straps holding him to Vriess and falls into the water. A buzzer sounds. Everyone looks as the elevator door opens to reveal Call standing there. They are shocked to see her alive.

Scene 23:

As what is left of the group gathers in a hallway, they question how Call survived Wren's attack. Pushing back Call's jacket, Ripley discovers that Call is a robot. The others begin to talk about her as a thing. Call hangs her head.

As Purvis and Distephano try to open a door Ripley points out that if Wren gets to the main computer before them the group could be in trouble. Although they are not near any computer terminals, they realize that, as an android, Call can patch into the computer manually and take control of the spacestation.

Scene 24:

Call and Ripley enter a chapel. Ripley unplugs an electronic bible and hands the cable to Call. Reluctantly Call takes the cable and plugs it into her arm. She becomes the voice of the space station's computer, detailing the status of the spacestation. She discovers that they have used too much power and she is unable to activate the space station's self-destruct program. Ripley tells her to crash the spacestation.

Purvis, Distephano, with Johner, continue their attempts to open the door. When Purvis stops, coughing and grabbing his chest, Johner and Distephano point their guns at him. But, it is a false alarm.

Still patched into the computer Call programs the spacestation to crash into an uninhabited sector of earth. At Ripley's suggestion she then programs the computer to open a series of doors throughout the spacestation so that the group will have a clear path to the Betty.

Doors begin opening, and the Betty is turned on.

Call discovers that Wren is getting close to the Betty.

Wren tries to open a door to the docking bay. The door jams. He commands "FA-TH-UR" to assist him. A door behind him opens and he hears Call's voice saying that "FA-TH-UR" is dead. Wren then hears Call inviting the aliens to move to his location, and he runs.

Ripley smiles. Call disconnects from the computer. She cringes with the pain of her gunshot wound. Ripley looks at the wound and pushes wires back into Call's body. Call expresses her self-loathing for not being human. She tells Ripley how she discovered what the military was doing on Auriga by accessing the mainframe and that because she is programmed to care for humanity her mission was to destroy Ripley and the aliens in order to protect humanity. Ripley laughs at her and refers to her as the asshole model of androids.

Special Edition: Ripley goes on to explain that in the past she understood the desire to save humanity and makes reference to a specific little girl.

Distephano enters the chapel saying, "Guess we're almost there" and, as he turns to leave, Ripley and Call stand up, preparing to follow.

Special Edition: Ripley tells Call about her alien dreams as they walk out, saying that they no longer scare her because reality is always worse.

Scene 25:

The group runs through the hallways toward the Betty, pausing when they step in slime. Ripley suspects that they are near an alien nest. Vriess wants to change direction but there is no time now that the spacestation is programmed to crash instead of land. Johner gets angry and threatens Call. Ripley intervenes and offers to rip out his tongue for Call, as she had done to the alien earlier. Distephano says they are about a hundred yards from the Betty. Everyone starts to run.

Ripley stops and drops to her hands and knees. Call tries to get her to follow the others, but Ripley says she can hear the aliens below and that the queen is in pain. As Ripley stands, alien hands reach up from below and pull the floor grate out from under her. She falls, landing in an unidentifiable mass of alien tentacles. Call yells. Purvis comes to Call's side. They look down and watch Ripley disappear into slimy darkness. Purvis and Call rise and run after the group.

Images of an alien warrior embracing and carrying Ripley fade in and out.

Scene 26:

We see the spacestation approaching earth.

The group reaches the Betty.

Vriess, Call, Johner and Purvis are on the bridge of the Betty. As Call gets up to leave the bridge, she suggests to Johner that it is time to put Purvis in the freezer.

A gunshot is heard. Purvis is hit. As Johner and Distephano aim their guns, Wren enters with Call as a hostage. He wants to land on earth. Call refuses to change the computer's programming. Purvis, slouched on the floor with a bullet wound shows signs that the alien inside him is about to burst out of his chest. He gets to his feet and runs at Wren. Wren releases Call and begins shooting at Purvis, hitting him a number of times. Purvis does not stop. He attacks Wren, beating him mercilessly. Then, grabbing Wren from behind by the shoulders, Purvis holds Wren so that Wren's head is directly in front of his own chest. The alien breaking through Purvis's chest bursts right through Wren's head. Call, Johner and Distephano fire their weapons, killing the alien.

Scene 27:

Gediman and a number of others are cocooned in alien resin. Although the others appear to be unconscious or dead, Gediman is talking about the biological changes in the alien queen; she no longer lays eggs. She has a human womb which is a consequence of the cloning process. As he is talking the camera reveals Ripley lying semi-conscious on the floor nearby, next to the queen. The alien queen is about to give birth, and as she screams, Ripley sits up. The queen's abdomen rips open from the inside out. The newborn looks at the queen and suddenly knocks off most of her head. The newborn then turns to Ripley and approaches her. It snarls and sniffs and licks Ripley's face. Gediman indicates his delight. When the newborn sees Gediman it goes to him and with little hesitation bites off his head. As this is happening Ripley climbs up and out of the nest.

Scene 28:

The Betty is about to disembark.

Ripley runs toward the docking bay.

Seeing Ripley on the monitor, Call opens the door to the Betty. Ripley leaps a few metres into the ship and closes the hatch behind her.

Ripley arrives on the bridge. Everyone welcomes her back. Vriess says the hatch is open so Call goes back to the cargo area to close it.

Scene 29:

Call tries to close the hatch.

Ripley yells to Call over the intercom to make her hurry.

As Call is struggling to close the hatch, the newborn appears behind her and closes the hatch.

Ripley works to manoeuvre the Betty away from the Auriga.

Call runs from the newborn.

The ship is shaky so Johner tells Distephano to go help Call turn on an auxiliary pump.

The newborn is on the floor, trying to grab Call who has rolled under some grating just out of its reach. Distephano enters the cargo area. The newborn sees him, and Call yells out to warn him. Distephano comes face-to-face with the newborn that grabs his head and smashes it while Call watches.

Vriess yells at Johner to complete his repair off to the side on the bridge. Then Vriess yells over the intercom for Call to return to the bridge. When she does not respond, Ripley gets up to go and check on her, leaving Vriess and Johner alone to fly the ship.

Scene 30:

The newborn touches Call's head and puts its fingers in her abdominal wound. Ripley appears and orders the newborn to release Call. It complies and tosses Call aside. Call watches, and Ripley and the newborn approach each other and embrace. Ripley intentionally cuts her hand on the newborns teeth and throws her blood at a window. As her acid blood burns a hole in the glass Ripley grabs strapping used to secure cargo. The force of decompression created by the hole in the window pulls the newborn toward that hole. Call secures herself to the ship as the force of the decompression pulls at her. Ripley watches as the newborn's flesh is sucked through the hole and released into space. She lowers her head and begins to cry. The newborn is sucked into space. Call and Ripley reach out to each other for support against the pull of the decompression.

"FA-TH-UR," counts down the seconds to the space station's crash on earth. There are empty hallways and a close-up of alien warrior teeth.

The Auriga explodes as it crashes into the earth's surface.

Ripley and Call hold onto each other in the cargo area.

The Betty, falling apart, as it descends toward earth.

Johner and Vriess scream because the Betty is on fire.

Flames shoot into the cargo area.

After entering the earth's atmosphere, the fire on the outside of the Betty dies.

Scene 31:

Call and Ripley look out the window to a sunrise in the clouds.

Johner grabs Vriess, kisses him on the lips, and puts his arm around him as they look out the window of the bridge.

The Betty is hovering above the earth.

Special Edition: The Betty sets down on a post-apocalyptic looking earth.

Ripley and Call sit on a rock as they discuss earth and what they should do next.

From behind Ripley and Call, the camera pulls back revealing what appear to be the ruins of Paris.

Scene 32:

The credits roll over the image of Paris.

APPENDIX E

AVP: PREDATORS AND PREQUELS TO RIPLEY

Four films associated with the *Alien Quadrilogy* move away from the focus of this book—Ellen Ripley; however, a brief description of each film seems appropriate. The four films are: *Predator, Predator II, Alien versus Predator,* and *Alien versus Predator: Requiem.*

In 2004, director Paul Anderson, along with writers Dan O'Bannon, Ronald Schusett, Jim Thomas, and John Thomas attempted to merge the *Alien Quadrilogy* with *Predator* films by creating *Alien versus Predator.* Then, in 2007, directors Colin and Greg Strause, with writers Shane Salerno and Dan O'Bannon presented the public with *Alien vs. Predator: Requiem.* The films act as sequels to the two *Predator* films and prequels to the *Alien Quadrilogy.* While fans eagerly anticipated such a merger for many years, sparked in large part by the *Dark Horse* comic book series, both films are generally thought to have been box office and critical failures (For example, see Harvey 2004, and Booker 2006). However, consideration of the films as a series allows us to examine the development of female characters who encounter the alien across fictional time. For those who are unfamiliar with the *Predator I* and *II, Alien versus Predator,* and *Alien vs. Predator: Requiem,* this appendix offers a brief summary of these films with specific attention to the female characters.

The first *Predator* film was released in 1987 and is situated in that time period. Dutch, the main character, played by Arnold Schwarzenegger, is the leader of an army commando team. Dutch and his team are hired by the CIA for what they believe is a rescue mission in Central America but is actually an unofficial mission to collect military intelligence. While making their way through the jungle to the location of the supposed guerrilla terrorists who are holding the hostages, the team encounters the bodies of another military team, in some cases finding bodies that had been skinned and in other cases finding skulls with the spinal column still attached. Initially, they believe that the deaths are the work of the guerrillas but come to realize that something else is responsible. Following their total destruction of the guerrilla camp, they realize that the CIA has lied. There is one survivor from the camp, Anna, played by Elpidia Carrillo. She is the only female character in the film. During the journey out of the jungle, members of the team are killed off one at a time. Anna is with the first soldier when the predator attacks him. When the team finds her, she is covered in blood and in shock. Eventually, Anna tells them what happened and what she knows about the predator which she describes as the jungle coming alive and killing men. They come to realize that the team is being hunted by some other-worldly creature, a creature of immense strength and advanced technology that makes it almost invisible. One by one, the members of the team are killed until only Dutch and Anna remain alive. In traditional hero fashion, Dutch sends Anna out of harm's way to meet the helicopter that the team had originally arranged to meet. Dutch engages in battle with the predator in true Rambo style. He ultimately kills the predator and is picked up by the helicopter that Anna had met with earlier.

Predator II, also written by Jim and John Thomas, was directed by Stephen Hopkins. It was released in 1990 and situated in that time period. Lieutenant Mike Harrigan, a police officer in Los Angeles, played by Danny Glover, is the main character. Similar to *Predator*, there is only one female character that has more than a walk-on part in this film. Maria Conchita Alonso, played by Leona Cantrell, is a police officer who works with Harrigan. In this film, Harrigan, Alonso and the rest of their police team are dealing with a turf war among drug dealers in Los Angeles. Initially, when they begin finding bodies skinned and hanging from the ceiling they believe it is the work of rival drug dealers. The FBI enters the picture and claims jurisdiction because, as we find out later in the film, they know the murders are the work of an extraterrestrial being. Similar to the first *Predator* film, the police team members are killed by the predator, one by one. At one point in the film, Alonso and one of the male team members are confronted by the predator. While the man is quickly killed by the predator, Alonso is spared. The predator seeing her with its heat-sensing vision, recognizes that she is pregnant and the audience is led to believe that is the reason that she is allowed to survive. Harrigan, becoming increasingly confrontational in his interactions with the FBI, believes they know something more than they are saying about the killings. In the latter part of the film, the leader of the FBI team reluctantly explains to Harrigan that the predator is the same creature that attacked a team of army commandos in Central America a few years before, as we see in the first *Predator* film. The FBI sets a trap to capture the predator, believing that the information they could acquire from it would be invaluable for combat situations. Their trap fails, and Harrigan, a stereotypical masculine hero, takes it upon himself to go in and destroy the predator. In the end, he is successful but finds himself surrounded by a group of predators. However, they do not attack him. Instead, the film ends with the predators collecting the body of the dead predator and offering Harrigan a trophy (an antique hand gun) indicating their respect for him as a successful hunter as well as the fact that they have been hunting on earth for many years.

In 2004, *Alien versus Predator* was released. Written by Paul Anderson, who is also the director, Dan O'Bannon, and Ronald Shusett, the film is situated in Antarctica in 2004 where a satellite of the Weyland Corporation, the same "Company" as in the first three *Alien* films, has found an unidentified heat source beneath the earth's surface. The Corporation's CEO, Charles Weyland, has assembled a team of experts in archaeology, engineering, environmental technology and guiding, and mercenaries/soldiers to investigate the site. Charles Weyland believes the satellite has found an ancient pyramid that predates Aztec and Egyptian pyramids. The central character, Alexa Woods, played by Sanaa Lathan, is the environmental technician and guide for the team.

When the team arrives at the designated coordinates they find an old abandoned whaling station. (The audience learned at the beginning of the film that 100 years earlier something sinister happened there.) As the team begins to work, a predator ship lands undetected, and the predators watch the humans. The unknown source of heat identified by the satellite is 2,000 feet below the ice surface. The team begins to drill and taps into an existing tunnel that takes them to the structure below. It is a pyramid, and the hieroglyphs noticed by the team members look like images of aliens and predators fighting. By entering the pyramid, the humans have unknowingly activated a trigger that unfreezes and awakens an alien queen, presumably held prisoner by the predators in the pyramid for the past 100 years. Team members are systematically separated and the predators begin attacking them. One group from the expedition team finds a sacrificial chamber full of human skeletons. An inscription in the chamber reads, "They gave their lives so that the hunt may begin." The alien queen, now awake, has begun to lay eggs, a number of which rise up through the floor in the sacrificial chamber. The humans trapped in the chamber are attacked by alien facehuggers, but when they regain consciousness they do not realize what has happened to them until the first chestburster erupts through the chest of the only woman other than Woods in the film.

As Woods and the others with her try to find their way out of the pyramid, they begin interpreting the hieroglyphs inside the structure. The hieroglyphs tell the story of predators coming to earth for thousands of years, teaching humans to build, and being worshipped as gods. Every 100 years the predators would return and require human sacrifices to breed the predators' ultimate prey, aliens. Adolescent predators would battle the aliens to prove themselves worthy hunters. If the predators failed in the hunt, they destroyed everyone - themselves, the aliens, and the humans.

When Woods and Sebastian, the archaeologist, realize that the predators will destroy everyone if they are unable to defeat the aliens, they decide that they must prevent the aliens from reaching the surface. Shortly after this Sebastian is taken by an alien warrior and Woods is left alone. She manages to kill an alien, saving a predator. The predator is about to leave her, but she protests. It returns, makes a shield out of the alien head and a spear out of its tail and hands them to Woods. The predator begins to leave again and does not disapprove when Woods follows. Only these two are now left to fight the aliens.

Woods and the predator enter a room and find members of the expedition team cocooned by the aliens. Sebastian is among them, conscious and infected by an alien facehugger. Woods shoots him, and the predator is intrigued by her action. They move on and the predator indicates to Woods that it is setting a bomb to destroy the aliens. They begin to make their way to the surface. Woods kills an alien that attacks the predator. She and the predator make it to the surface and run away from the whaling station just as the bomb goes off. They stop and the predator takes off its helmet. The predator then takes a piece of an alien that it has on its belt and indicates to Woods that it is going to give her the mark of the hunter on the side of her face, the practice of the predators when they have killed an alien. She nods in agreement, and using the acid blood of the alien the predator burns two lines into the side of Woods face. Just as this ritual is finished, the queen alien bursts through the ice and attacks the predator. Woods stabs the queen from behind. Woods and the predator work together to force the queen off the edge of a cliff. The queen fatally injuries the predator before she falls. As Woods kneels beside the dead predator, other predators appear, and then their ship appears. They see the mark of the hunter on her face. Four of them take the dead predator into the ship. One stays behind and moves closer to Woods and hands her retractable spear and then returns to the ship. As the ship takes off, Woods is left standing alone on the surface. From inside the ship, we see the dead predator laid out in front of a window that looks out to earth. Then, suddenly, in the final scene of the film, a chestburster that is half alien and half predator emerges from the predator's chest.

In 2007, *Alien versus Predator: Requiem* was released and begins with the final scene of *Alien versus Predator*. On board the predator ship, an alien-predator hybrid explodes through the chest of the dead warrior who fought along side Alexa Woods. The hybrid kills the crew and the ship crashes to earth, landing near a small town in the mountains of Colorado. Receiving information that the ship has crashed, a predator solider makes its way to earth to investigate and destroy evidence of the predators. The facehuggers that were on the ship escape and their first two victims are a father and young son hunting team. More people are attacked by the facehuggers and alien soldiers begin to emerge from the chests of the victims. A variety of human characters are gradually introduced as those events unfold but no one emerges as the clear leader. There is Dallas, played by Steven Pasquale, returning home following his release from the state penitentiary; Morales, played by John Ortiz, a onetime trouble-maker, now sheriff; Kelly, played by Reiko Aylesworth, who has just returned from her tour of duty in Iraq; Kelly's husband and daughter; Dallas' brother, Ricky; Jesse, the romantic interest of Ricky; and Jesse's boyfriend, Dale; along with a variety of other town's-people and military personnel.

The predator that has arrived in the area begins to hunt the aliens and most importantly the alien-predator hybrid. While humans are not its targets, they are quickly eliminated by the predator if infected with a chestburster or simply in the way of the hunt. More than any of the other films, this film is about other-worldly creatures battling each other with the humans generally relegated to the secondary status of victims caught in the cross-fire. Once military officials realize what is happening they adopt an attitude similar to that of the predator—the aliens must be destroyed, and the humans who will be killed in the process are expendable. A small number of humans flee the town in a helicopter just before the massive destruction. They crash in the woods and are found by members of the military.

Most reviewers and critics have concluded that the attempts to merge the stories of aliens and predators were critical and box office failures. The films act as sequels to the two *Predator* films and prequels to the *Alien Quadrilogy*. While fans eagerly anticipated such a merger for many years, sparked in large part by the *Dark Horse* comic book series, both films are generally considered to have been box office and critical failures, with much of the disappointment coming from *Alien* fans. As John Gholson (2010) explains:

> the *Predator* series, while cool, is a macho B-movie action franchise...
> When you mix Alien with Predator, you don't get a highbrow Predator
> film, you get a dumb actioner with Aliens in it.

For additional examples, see Harvey (2004) and Booker (2006).

Whether failures or not, these films depart significantly from the path of depicting a strong, central female character laid out by the *Alien Quadriolgy*. However, the release of films such as *Underworld, Underworld: Evolution, Aeon Flux, Resident Evil: Apocalypse*, and *Ultraviolet* with female protagonists similar to Ellen Ripley means that explorations of identity, gender, and feminism in science fiction will continue.

References

Alien Quadrilogy, DVD. 2003. Includes *Alien, Aliens, Alien³, Alien Resurrection*. Los Angeles: Twentieth-Century Fox Home Entertainment.

Alien vs. Predator, DVD. 2004. Los Angeles: Twentieth-Century Fox.

Aliens vs. Predator: Requiem, DVD. 2007. Los Angeles: Twentieth-Century Fox.

Booker, M. K. 2006. *Alien*. In *Alternate Americas: Science fiction film and American culture*, 141-155. Westport, Connecticut: Praeger.

Gholson, J. 2010. Does Ridley Scott's new "Alien" Need 3-D? http://www.cinematical.com/2010/03/05/does-ridley-scotts-new-alien-need-3-d/. (accessed 10 March 2010.)

Harvey, D. 2004. Review of *Alien vs. Predator*. *Daily Variety*, August 16.

Predator, DVD. 2007. Twentieth Century Fox Home Entertainment.

Predator2, Special Edition. 2004. Twentieth Century Fox Home Entertainment.

SELECTED BIBLIOGRAPHY
ON THE *ALIEN* SERIES

Abbott, Joe. "They Came from Beyond the Center: Ideology and Political Textuality in the Radical Science Fiction Films of James Cameron." *Literature Film Quarterly* 22, no. 1 (1994): 21- 27.

"AFI Rates Hollywood's Best Heroes, Villains." *USA Today* June, 2003.

Alex K. "The Aliens Series Just Went Up a Notch!" Amazon.com (2005), http://www.amazon.com/gp/cdp/member-reviews/A2T2MYZEB81 NOQ/002-4099377-7946448?ie=UTF8&display=public&page=12 (accessed April 26, 2010).

Alleva, Richard. "Alienated: Ripley's Believe It or Not." *Commonweal* 17 (July 1992): 18-19.

Ambrogio, Anthony. "*Alien*: In Space, No One Can Hear Your Primal Scream." In *Eros in the Mind's Eye: Sexuality and the Fantastic in Art and Film,* ed. Donald Palumbo, 169-179. Westport, CN: Greenwood Press, 1986.

Anderson, Craig. "*Alien*." In *Science Fiction Films of the Seventies.* Jefferson, NC: McFarland, 1985.

Ansen, David. "Saint Ripley and the Dragon." *Newsweek,* June 1, 1992." Bad Movies, not Tough Heroines, Turn Filmgoers Away." *USA Today.* September 26, 2005.

Barale, Michele A. "When *Lambs* and *Aliens* Meet: Girl-Faggots and Boy-Dykes go to the Movies." In *Cross-purposes: Lesbians, Feminists, and the Limits of Alliance,* ed. Dana Heller, 95-106. Bloomington: Indiana University Press, 1997.

Bell-Metereau, Rebecca. "Woman: The Other Alien in *Alien*." In *Women Worldwalkers: New Dimensions of Science Fiction and Fantasy,* ed. J. B. Weedman, 9-24. Lubbock Texas: Texas Tech Press, 1985.

Berenstein, Rhona. "Mommie Dearest: *Aliens, Rosemary's Baby* and Mothering." *Journal of Popular Culture* 24, no. 2 (1990.): 55-73.

Bergeron, Danielle. "Aliens and the Psychotic Experience." In *Lacan, Politics, Aesthetics,* ed. W. Apollon and R. Feldstein, 305-314. Albany: State University of New York Press, 1996.

Bick, Ilsa. J. "*Alien* Within, *Aliens* Without: The Primal Scene and the Return to the Repressed." *American Imago* 45, no. 3 (1989.): 337-358.

—. "'Well, I Guess I Must Make You Nervous': Woman and the Space of *Alien³*." *Post Script* 14, no. 1-2 (1994): 45-58.

Billy, Ted. A. "A Curious Case of Influence: *Nostromo* and *Alien(s)*." *Conradiana: A Journal of Joseph Conrad Studies* 21, no. 2 (1989): 147-157.

—. "'This Whole Place is a Basement': The Gnostic/Existentialist Vision of *Alien³*." *Journal of Evolutionary Psychology* 16, no. 3-4 (1995): 229-35.

Blackmore, Tim. "'Is this going to be Another Bug Hunt?': S-F Tradition Versus Biology-as-Destiny in James Cameron's *Aliens*." *Journal of Popular Culture* 29, no. 4 (1996): 211-226.

Booker, M. Keith. "*Alien*." In *Alternate Americas: Science Fiction Film and American Culture*. Westport, Connecticut: Praeger, 2006.

Bowman, James. "Alien Menace: Lt. Ripley is Hollywood's Mythical Woman–Butch and Ready to Kill." *National Review*, January 26, 1998.

Briggs, Scott. D. "Alien: Trilogy of Terror." *Other Dimensions* 3(1996): 12-24.

Brooker, Will. "Internet Fandom and the Continuing Narratives of *Star Wars*, *Blade Runner* and *Alien*." In *Alien Zone II: The Spaces of Science Fiction Cinema*, ed. A. Kuhn, 50-72. London: Verso, 1999.

Bueno, Eva. P. "Writing the Mother, The Mother Writing: The Space of Motherhood and Feminine *Ecriture* in *Alien* and *The Matrix*." *Acta Scientiarum, Language and Culture Maringa* 32, no. 1 (2010): 73-82.

Bundtzen, Lynda. K. "Monstrous Mothers: Medusa, Grendel, and Now Alien." *Film Quarterly* 40, no. 3 (1987): 11-17.

Byars, Jackie. "Introduction to Some Ideological Readings of *Alien*." In "Symposium on Alien," ed., C. Elkins. *Science-Fiction Studies* 7, no. 3 (1980): 278-282.

Byers, Thomas. B. "Kissing Becky: Masculine Fears and Misogynist Moments in Science Fiction Films." *Arizona Quarterly* 45, no. 3 (1989): 77-95.

—. "Commodity Futures." In *Alien Zone: Cultural Theory and Contemporary Science Fiction Cinema*, ed. A. Kuhn, 39-50. London: Verso, 1990. Previously published in *Science Fiction Studies* 14, no. 3 (1987): 326-339.

Canby, Vincent. "Screen: *Alien* Brings Chills from the Far Galaxy." *New York Times*, May 25, 1979.

—. "*Alien³*; HAL, If You're Still Out There, Here's a Computer Friendly Sequel." *New York Times*, May 22, 1992.

Cantin, Lucie. "Aliens or Staging the Trauma." In *Lacan, Politics, Aesthetics*, ed. W. Apollon and R. Feldstein, 315-323. Albany: State University of New York Press, 1996.

Carveth, Donald, and Naomi Gold. "The Pre-oedipalizing of Klein in (North) America: Ridley Scott's *Alien* Re-analyzed." *PSYART: A Hyperlink Journal for the Psychological Study of the Arts* (1999), www.clas.ufl. edu/ipsa/journal/1999_carveth03.shtml Accessed 26 April 2010.

Chien, Joseph. "Containing Horror: The *Alien* Trilogy and the Abject." *Focus Magazine* 14 (1994): 7-17.

Christopher, Renny. "Negotiating the Viet Nam War through Permeable Genre Borders: *Aliens* as Viet Nam War film; *Platoon* as Horror Film." *Literature, Interpretation, Theory* 5, no. 1 (1994): 53-66.

Clough, Patricia. T. "'The Final Girl' in the Fictions of Science and Culture." *Stanford Humanities Review* 2, no. 2-3 (1992): 57-69.

Cobbs, John. L. "*Alien* as an Abortion Pparable." *Literature/Film Quarterly* 18, no. 3 (1990): 198-201.

Colwell, C. Carter. "Primitivism in the Movies of Ridley Scott: *Alien* and *Blade Runner*." In *Retrofitting Blade Runner: Issues in Ridley Scott's Blade Runner and Philip K. Dick's Do Androids Dream of Electric Sheep?* ed. Judith B. Kerman, 124-131. Bowling Green, Ohio: Bowling Green State University Popular Press, 1991.

Constable, Catherine. "Becoming the Monster's Mother: Morphologies of Identity in the *Alien* Series." In *Alien Zone II: The Spaces of Science Fiction Cinema*, ed. A. Kuhn, 173–202. London: Verso, 1999.

Creed, Barbara. "Horror and the Monstrous feminine: An Imaginary Abjection." *Screen* 27, no. 1 (1986): 44-71. Revised versions appear in *The Dread of Difference: Gender and the Horror Film*, ed. B. K. Grant (Austin: University of Texas Press, 1996), 35-65, and *Feminist film theory: A Reader*, ed. S. Thornham (New York: New York University Press, 1999), 251-66.

—. "*Alien* and the Monstrous feminine." In *Alien Zone: Cultural Theory and Contemporary Science Fiction Cinema*, A. Kuhn, ed. 128-141.London: Verso, 1990.

—. *The Monstrous feminine: Film, Feminism, Psychoanalysis*. New York: Routledge, 1993.

Dargis, Manohla. "*Alien³* and its Metaphors." *The Village Voice*, June 30, 1992.

Davis-Genelli, Lynn and Tom Davis-Genelli. "*Alien*: A Myth of Survival." *Film/Psychology Review* 4, no. 2 (1980): 235-242.

Detora, Lisa "Ridley Scott's Epic: Gender of Violence." In *Heroes of Film, Comics and American Culture: Essays on Real and Fictional Defenders of Home*, 281-300. Jefferson, North Carolina: McFarland & Company, Inc., Publishers, 2009.

Doherty, Thomas. "Genre, Gender, and the *Aliens* Trilogy." In *The Dread of Difference: Gender and the Horror Film*, ed. B. K. Grant, 181-199. Austin: University of Texas Press, 1996.

Duda, Heather. "The Advent of The Female Monster Hunter." In *The Monster Hunter in Modern Popular Culture*, 101-141. Jefferson, North Carolina: McFarland & Company, Inc., Publishers, 2008.

Eaton, Michael. "Born Again." *Sight and Sound,* December, 1997.

Edelstein, David. "Mother of the Year." *Rolling Stone*, August, 1986.

Edmonds, Lisa. "Here there be Monsters: Ellen Ripley Redefines the Science Fiction Hero(ine)." In *The Image of the Hero in Literature, Media, and Society*, ed. W. Wright and S. Kaplan, 126-130. Pueblo, CO: Colorado State University, 2004.

Eisenstein, Alex. "*Alien* Dissected: Anatomy of a Monster Movie." *Fantastic Films* 13 (1980): 51-63.

Elkins, Charles, ed. "Symposium on *Alien.*" *Science-Fiction Studies* 7, no. 3 (1980): 278-304.

Ferreira, Aline. "Artificial Wombs and Archaic Tombs: Angela Carter's *The Passion of New Eve* and the *Alien* Tetralogy." *FEMSPEC* 4, no. 1 (2002.): 90-107.

Fitting, Peter. "The Second *Alien.*" In "*Symposium on* Alien," ed., C. Elkins. *Science-Fiction Studies* 7, no. 3 (1980): 285-293.

Fitzgerald, Lauren. "(In)Alienable Rights: Property, Feminism, and the Female Body from Ann Radcliffe to the *Alien* films." *Romanticism on the Net: An Electronic Journal Devoted to Romantic Studies* 21 (2001), http://www.erudit.org/revue/ron/2001/v/n21/005961ar.html (accessed April 26 2010).

Floyd, Nancy. *She's Got a Gun*. Philadelphia: Temple University Press, 2008.

Flynn, John. F. *Dissecting Aliens: Terror in Space*. London: Boxtree, 1995.

Frank, Alan. "*Alien.*" In *The Science Fiction and Fantasy Handbook*, 10-11. London: Batsford, 1982.

Freer, I. "Alien Procrastination." *Empire*, December 1997.

Gabbard, Krin. "*Aliens* and the New Family Romance." *Post Script* VIII, no. 1 (1988): 29-42.

Gabbard, Krin and Glen O. Gabbard. "*Alien* and Melanie Klein's Night Music." In *Psychiatry and the Cinema*, 2nd ed., 226-239. Arlington, VA: American Psychiatric Publishing, 1999.

Gallardo C., Xemina and C. Jason Smith. *Alien Woman: The Making of Lt. Ellen Ripley*. New York: Continuum, 2004.

George, Susan. A. Not Exactly "'Of Woman Born:' Procreation and Creation in Recent Science Fiction Films." *Journal of Popular Film and Television* 28, no. 4 (2001): 176-83.

Gibson, Pamela C. "'You've Been in My Life so Long I Can't Remember Anything Else': Into the Labyrinth with Ripley and the Alien." In *Keyframes: Popular Cinema and Cultural Studies*, ed. M. Tinkcom and A. Villarejo, 35-51. London, England: Routledge, 2001.

Goldberg, Lee, Randy Lofficier, Jean-Marc Lofficier, and William Rabkin. *Aliens* (1986). In *Science Fiction Filmmaking in the 1980s: Interviews with Actors, Directors, Producers, and Writers*, 7-22. Jefferson, NC: McFarland, 1995.

Goodall, Jane R. "*Aliens.*" *Southern Review* 23, no.1 (1990): 73-82.

Goodman, Walter. "Film: Sigourney Weaver in *Aliens.*" *New York Times*, July 18, 1986.

Gould, Jeff, "The Destruction of the Social by the Organic in *Alien.*" In "Symposium on *Alien*," ed., C. Elkins. *Science-Fiction Studies* 7, no. 3 (1980): 282-285.

Graham, Paula. "Looking Lesbian: Amazons and Aliens in Science Fiction cinema." In *The Good, the Bad and the Gorgeous: Popular Culture's Romance with Lesbianism*, ed. D. Hamer and B. Budge, 196-217. San Francisco: Pandora, 1994.

Grant, Barry. K. *The Dread of Difference: Gender and the Horror Film*. Austin: University of Texas Press, 1996.

Greenberg, Harvey R. "Fembo: *Aliens'* Intentions." *Journal of Popular Film and TV* 15, no. 4 (1988): 165-171.

—. "Reimagining the Gargoyle: Psychoanalytic Notes on *Alien.*" In *Close Encounters: Film, Feminism, and Science Fiction*, ed. C. Penley et al., 83 – 104. University of Minnesota Press, 1991. Previously published in *Camera Obscura* 15 (1986): 87-108, and as "The Fractures of Desire: Psychoanalytic Notes on *Alien* and the Contemporary 'Cruel' Horror Film," in *Psychoanalytic Review* 70, no. 2 (1983): 241 – 267.

Hantke, Steffen. "In the Belly of the Mechanical Beast: Technological Environments in the *Alien* Films." *Journal of Popular Culture* 36, no. 3 (2003.): 518-546.

Harmetz, Aljean. "A Sequel to *Alien* Ready to go into Production." *New York Times*, July 9, 1985.

Harris, Hilary. "Queer White Woman as Spectator." *Media International Australia* 78 (November 1995.): 39-47.

Hermann, Chad. "'Some Horrible Dream About (S)Mothering': Sexuality, Gender, and Family in the *Alien* Trilogy." *Post Script: Essays in Film and the Humanities* 16, no. 3 (1997): 36-50.

Hill, Walter and David Giler. *"Alien"* Final Shooting Script (1978), http://www.dailyscript.com/scripts/alien_shooting.html (accessed April 26, 2010).

Hills, Elizabeth. "From 'Figurative Males' to Action Heroines: Further Thoughts on Active Women in the Cinema." *Screen* 40, no. 1 (1999): 38-50.

Hinson, Hal. *"Alien³."* *Washington Post*, May 22, 1992.

Hocker-Rushing, Janice. "Evolution of 'The New Frontier' in *Alien* and *Aliens*: Patriarchal Co-optation of the Feminine Archetype." In *Screening the Sacred: Religion, Myth, and Ideology in Popular American Film*, ed. J. W. Martin and C. E. Ostwalt Jr. Boulder: Westview Press, 1995. Previously published in *Quarterly Journal of Speech* 75, no. 1 (1989): 1-24.

Hochman, David. "Beauties and the Beast." *Entertainment Weekly*, December 5, 1997.

Hofler, Robert. "Sigourney Weaver: The *US* Interview." *US*, June 1992.

Howe, Desson. *"Alien³."* *Washington Post,* May 22, 1992.

Hurley, Kelly. "Reading like an Alien: Posthuman Identity in Ridley Scott's *Alien* and David Cronenberg's *Rabid."* In *Posthuman Bodies,* ed. J. Halberstam and I. Livingston, 203-224. Bloomington: Indiana University Press, 1995.

James, Caryn. "Sequels Battle Monsters, Villains and Burnout." *New York Times*, May 31, 1992.

Jamison, Stewart. "Three Times a Lady: Part 1." *Starburst* 168 (August 1992): 36-39.

—. "Three Times a Lady: Part 2." *Starburst* 69 (September 1992): 44-46.

Jeffords, Susanos. "'The Battle of the Big Mamas': Feminism and the Alienation of Women." *Journal of American Culture* 10, no. 3 (1987): 73-84.

Jennings, R. "Desire and Design: Ripley Undressed." In *Immortal, Invisible: Lesbians and the Moving Image*, ed. Tamsin Wilton, 193-206. London: Routledge, 1995.

Jones, Gwyneth. "Patricia Meltzer, Review of *Alien Constructions: Science Fiction and Feminist Thought." Science Fiction Film and Television* 1, no. 2 (2008): 327-340.

Kael, Pauline. "*Aliens*". In *Hooked* (film reviews), 192-194. New York: Penguin, 1989.

Kavanaugh, James H. "Feminism, Humanism and Science in *Alien*." In *Alien Zone: Cultural: Theory and Contemporary Science Fiction Cinema*, ed. A. Kuhn, 73-81. London: Verso, 1990.

Kaveney, Roz. *From Alien to The Matrix: Reading Science Fiction Film.* London: I.B. Tauris, 2005.

Keane, Colleen. Ambiguity, Perversity and *Alien Resurrection*. *Metro* 116 (1998): 30-35.

Kendrick, James. "Marxist Overtones in Three Films by James Cameron." *Journal of Popular Film and Television* 27, no. 3 (1999): 36-44.

Kimball, A. Samuel. "Conceptions and Contraceptions of the Future: *Terminator 2*, *The Matrix*, and *Alien Resurrection*." *Camera Obscura 50* 17, no. 2 (2002): 69-107.

Knapp, Laurence F. and A. Kulas. *Ridley Scott Interviews*. Jackson: U Press of Mississippi, 2005.

Korpivaara, An. "Roll Over, Rambo." *Ms*, September 15, 1986.

Kuhn, Annette, ed. *Alien Zone: Cultural Theory and Contemporary Science Fiction Cinema*. London: Verso, 1990.

—. ed. *Alien Zone II: The Spaces of Science Fiction Cinema*. London: Verso, 1999.

Lee, Clayton. "Cognitive Approaches to *Alien*." In "Symposium on *Alien*," ed., C. Elkins. *Science-Fiction Studies* 7, no. 3 (1980): 299-302.

Lev, Peter. "Whose Future?: *Star Wars*, *Alien*, and *Blade Runner*." *Literature-Film Quarterly* 26, no. 1 (1998): 30-37.

Lippert, Barbara. "Hey There, Warrior Grrrl." *New York*, 30, no. 48 (1997).

Magid, Ron. "*Alien³*: In Space, They're Still Screaming." *American Cinematographer* 73 (July 1992): 52-58.

—. "Speeding up the Screams in *Alien³*." *American Cinematographer* 73 (December 1992): 70-76.

Maslin, Janet. "Ripley, Believe It or Not, has a Secret, and It's not Pretty." *New York Times* November 26, 1997.

Matheson, T.J. "Triumphant Technology and Minimal Man: *The Technological Society*, Science Fiction Films, and Ridley Scott's *Alien*." *Extrapolation* 33, no. 3 (1992): 215-229.

McIntee, David. *Beautiful Monsters: The Unofficial and Unauthorised Guide to the "Alien" and "Predator" Films*. Tolworth: Telos Publishing, Ltd, 2005.

Melzer, Patricia. *Alien Constructions: Science Fiction and Feminist Thought*. Austin: University of Texas Press, 2006.

Miles, Geoff and Carol Moore. "Explorations, Prosthetics and Sacrifice: Phantasies of the Maternal Body in the *Alien* Trilogy." *CineAction!* 30 (1992): 54-62.

Miller, Mark "You Say You Want a Resurrection? Done." *Newsweek*, June 9, 1997.

Mullhall, Stephen. *On Film: Thinking in Action*. London: Routledge, 2002.

Murdock, Andrew. and Rachel Aberly. *The Making of "Alien Resurrection"*. New York: HarperPrism, 1997.

Murphy, Kathleen. "The Last Temptation of Sigourney Weaver." *Film Comment* 28, no. 4 (1992): 17-20.

Naureckas, Jim. "*Aliens*: Mother and the Teeming Hordes." *Jump Cut*, 32 (April2006 [1987]): 1, 4, http://www.ejumpcut.org/archive/online ssays/JC32folder/aliens.html (accessed April 26, 2010).

Neale, Stephen. "Issues of Difference: *Alien* and *Blade Runner*." In *Fantasy and the Cinema*, ed. James Donald, 213–223. London: British Film Institute, 1989.

Newton, Judith. "Feminism and Anxiety in *Alien*." In *Alien Zone: Cultural Theory and Contemporary Science Fiction Cinema*, ed. A. Kuhn, 82-87. London: Verso, 1990. Previously published in "Symposium on *Alien*," ed., C. Elkins. *Science-Fiction Studies* 7, no. 3 (1980): 293-297.

Nicholls, Peter. "*Aliens*." In *The Encyclopedia of Science Fiction* edited by John Clute and Peter Nicholls, 19. New York: St. Martin's Griffin, 1993.

Nolan, Steven. "Worshipping (Wo)men, Liturgical Representation and Feminist Film Theory: An Alien/s Identification?" *Bulletin of the John Rylands University Library of Manchester* 80 (Autumn 1998): 195-213.

O'Bannon, Dan and Ronald Shusett. "*Alien*" Script, 1976. http://www.dailyscript. com/scripts/alien_early.html (accessed April 26, 2010).

Peary, Danny. "Playing Ripley in *Alien*: An Interview with Sigourney Weaver." In *Omni's Screen Flights/Screen Fantasies: The Future According to Science Fiction Cinema*, 154-166. New York: Doubleday, 1984.

—. "Directing *Alien* and *Blade Runner*: An Interview with Ridley Scott." In *Omni's Screen Flights/Screen Fantasies: The Future According to Science Fiction Cinema*, 293-302. New York: Doubleday, 1984.

Penley, Constance. "Time Travel, Primal Scene and the Critical Dystopia." *Camera Obscura* 15 (1986): 66-85. A slightly revised version appears in *Alien Zone: Cultural Theory and Contemporary Science Fiction Cinema*, ed. A. Kuhn (London: Verso, 1990), 116-127.

Picart, Caroline J. S. *Remaking the Frankenstein Myth on Film: Between Laughter and Horror.* Albany: State University of New York Press, 2003.

—. "Ripley as Interstitial Character: White Woman as Monster and Hero in *Alien Resurrection.*" *P.O.V: A Danish Journal of Film Studies* 16 (2003): 26-41.

—. "The Third Shadow and Hybrid Genres: Horror, Humor, Gender and Race." *Alien Resurrection. Communication and Critical/Cultural Studies* 1, no. 4 (2004): 335-354.

Pimley, Daniel. "Representations of the Body in Alien: How can Science Fiction be seen as an Expression of Contemporary Attitudes and Anxieties about human biology?" 2003. http://www.pimley.net/documents/thebody inalien.pdf (accessed April 26, 2010).

Ramirez Berg, C. "Immigrants, Aliens and Extra-Terrestrials: Science Fiction's Alien 'Other.'" *Cineaction* 18 (Autumn 1989): 3-18.

Rapping, Elayne. "Hollywood's New 'Feminist Heroines.'" *Cineaste* 14, no. 4 (1986): 4-9.

Reider, John. "Embracing the Alien: Science Fiction in Mass Culture." *Science-Fiction Studies* 9, no. 26 (1982): 26-37.

Rizzo, Teresa. "The *Alien* Series: A Deleuzian Perspective." *Women: A Cultural Review* 15, no. 3 (2004): 330-344.

Roberts, Robin. "Adoptive versus Biological Mothering in *Aliens.*" *Extrapolation* 30, no. 4 (1989): 353-363.

Robertson, Robbie. "The Narrative Sources of Ridley Scott's *Alien.*" In *Cinema and Fiction: New Modes of Adapting, 1950-1990*, ed. J. Orr and C. Nicholson, 171-179. Edinburgh: Edinburgh University Press, 1992.

Safford, Tony. "Alien/Alienation." In "Symposium on *Alien*," ed., C. Elkins. *Science-Fiction Studies* 7, no. 3 (1980): 297-299.

Schemanske, Mark. "Working for the Company: Patriarchal Legislation of the Maternal in *Alien 3.*" In *Authority and Transgression in Literature and Film*, ed., B. Braendlin and H. Braendlin, 127-135. Gainesville: University Press of Florida, 1996.

Schickel, Richard. "Help! They're back!" *Time*, July 28, 1986.

—. *"Alien Resurrection"* (review of film). *Time*, December 1, 1997.

Schwartzbaum, Lisa. "Reborn to be Wild." *Entertainment Weekly*, December 5, 1997.

Scobie, Stephen. "What's the Story, Mother: The Mourning of the Alien."
    Science-Fiction Studies 20, no. 1 (1993): 80-93.
Shay, Don. "*Aliens.*" *Cinefex* 27 (August 1986): 4-67.
"Sigourney Weaver is offered $15million to Star in *Alien* Movie." *The
    Times (United Kingdom)*, February 17, 2001.
Slattery, Dennis. P. "Demeter-Perspehone and the *Alien(s)* cultural body."
    New Orleans Review 19, no. 1 (1992): 30-35.
Sobchack. Vivian. "The Virginity of Astronauts: Sex and the Science
    Fiction Film." *Shadows of the Magic Lamp*, ed. G. E, Slusser and E. S.
    Rabkin. Southern Illinois University Press, 1985. A slightly revised
    version appears in *Alien Zone: Cultural Theory and Contemporary
    Science Fiction Cinema*, ed. Λ. Kuhn (London: Verso, 1990), 103-115.
Speed, Louise. "*Alien*[3]: A Postmodern Encounter with the Abject."
    Arizona Quarterly 54, no. 1 (1998): 125-151.
Stacey, Jackie. "She is not Herself: The Deviant Relations of *Alien
    Resurrection.*" *Screen* 44, no. 3 (2003): 251-276.
Stein, Ruthe. "Weaver Stands Alone as Female Action Hero."
    SFGate.com, February 18, 2005.
    http://sfgate.com/cgi-bin/article.cgi?file=/chronicle
    /archive/2005/02/18/DDGIMBCKG01.DTL (accessed April 26, 2005).
Strick, Philip. "*Alien*[3]." *Sight and Sound*, August 1992: 46-47.
Syonan-Teo, Kobayashi. "Why Sigourney is Jesus: Watching *Alien*[3] in the
    Light of *Se7en.*" *Vidiocy*, 1992. http://inkpot.com/film/alien.html
    (accessed April 26, 2010).
Taubin, Amy. "Invading Bodies: *Alien*[3] and the Trilogy." *Sight and Sound*,
    July-August 1992: 8-10. Reprinted in longer form as "The *Alien*
    trilogy: From feminism to AIDS." In *Women and Film: A Sight and
    Sound Reader*, ed. P. Cook and P. Dodd, 93-100. Philadelphia: Temple
    University Press, 1993.
Taylor, Henry. "From *Alien* to *The Matrix*: Reading Science Fiction Film."
    Journal of Popular Film and Television 37, no. 4 (2009): 199-199.
Thomson, David. "The Bitch is Back." *Esquire*, 6 (December 1997): 56.
—. *David Thomson on the Alien Quartet*. New York: Bloomsbury, 1998.
Torry, Robert. "Awakening to the Other: Feminism and the Ego-Ideal in
    Alien." *Women's Studies* 23 (1994): 343-363.
Tremonte, Colleen. "Recasting the Western Hero: Ethos in High-Tech
    Science Fiction." *JASAT* 20 (1989): 94-100.
Vaughn, Thomas. "Voices of Sexual Distortion: Rape, Birth, and Self-
    Annihilation Metaphors in the *Alien Trilogy.*" *The Quarterly Journal
    of Speech* 81, no. 4 (1995): 423-435.

Weise, Matthew and Henry Jenkins. Short Controlled Bursts: Affect and Aliens. *Cinema Journal* 48, no. 3 (2009): 111-116.

Whitney, Cindy. *"She's Got a Gun* by N. Floyd" (review). *Gender & Society* 23 (2009): 414-416.

Williams, Anne. "Inner and Outer spaces: The Alien Trilogy." In *Art of Darkness: Poetics of Gothic*, 249-252. Chicago: University of Chicago Press, 1995.

Williams, Eric "Birth Kills, Abortion Saves: Two Perspectives by Incongruity in Ridley Scott's *Alien.*" In The Rhetoric of Alien abduction. *E-Clectic* 4, no. 2 (2006). http://abacus.bates.edu/eclectic/vol4iss2 /pdf/troaaewf.pdf (accessed April 26, 2010).

Wloszczyna, Susan. "In Search of a Serious Protagonist." *USA Today,* June 24, 2005.

Wood, Robert. E. "Cross Talk: The Implications of Generic Hybridization in the *Alien* films." *Studies in the Humanities* 15, no. 1 (1988): 1-12.

Young, Robert. M. *"Alien³." Free Associations* 4, no. 31 (1994): 447-53.

Zanger, Anat. *Film Remakes as Ritual and Disguise: From Carmen to Ripley.* Amsterdam: Amsterdam University Press, 2006.

Zwinger, Linda. Blood Relations: Feminist Theory Meets the Uncanny Alien Bug Mother. *Hypatia: A Journal of Feminist Philosophy* 7, no. 2 (1992): 74-90.

CONTRIBUTORS

Sarah BACH holds a Bachelor's Degree (Honours) in Cinema Studies from the University of Toronto. She has presented papers at the American Culture Association, San Diego. Her research includes representations of female sexuality in the *Alien* films as well as the examination of the viewing subject as masochist in cinema. Having completed her education, Bach is currently working at a web hosting company managing the Quality Assurance department.

Eva DADLEZ is professor of Philosophy at the University of Central Oklahoma. Her work is mainly on the philosophy of literature, and on topics at the intersection of aesthetics, ethics and epistemology. She recently received an NEH award enabling her to participate in a Seminar on the Aesthetics of the Scottish Enlightenment. She is the author of a number of articles in aesthetics and applied ethics, as well as *What's Hecuba to Him? Fictional Events and Actual Emotions* (1997) and *Mirrors to One Another: Emotion and Value in Jane Austen and David Hume* (2009). She is also a feminist ethics dilettante.

Elizabeth GRAHAM is an Assistant Professor of Sociology and Gender and Women's Studies at Brandon University. Her background is in the areas of women's health, feminism, and Symbolic Interactionism. She has presented numerous conference papers that centre on the relationship between the individual and society, including two presentations on Ripley. She has co-authored a book chapter with J. Low entitled, "Bodies out of Time: Women's Reproductive Firsts" in *Sociology of the Body: A Reader* (2008). However, with an interest in research methodologies, Symbolic Interactionism, and Second Wave Feminism, her substantive interests have moved into the area of the individuals' sense of self and experience with specific projects on adult participation in Taekwondo and as well as graduate students and new faculty expectations and experiences.

Jessica LANGER received her PhD in 2009 from Royal Holloway, University of London. Her dissertation focused on science fiction and postcolonialism. Jessica is the author of a number of articles and book chapters addressing the intersections and interactions between science fiction and postcolonialism in literature, film and video games, including

"Three Versions of Komatsu Sakyo's Japan Sinks" (2009) and a forthcoming article, "The Shapes of Dystopia: Boundaries, Bridges and Hybridity" (2010). She is currently a Research Associate at Royal Holloway.

George MOORE teaches English Literature at the University of Colorado, Boulder, the Sewall Academic Program and the Honors Resident Academic Program. His numerous works include a book length study, *Gertrude Stein's The Making of Americans: Repetition and the Emergence of Modernism* (1998), "Beyond Cultural Dialogues: Identities in the Interstices of Culture in the Poetry of Jimmy Santiago Baca" in *Western American Literature* (1998; reprinted in *Poetics*, 2001). As a poet, he has also produced the collections *Headhunting* (2002) and the e-Book, *All Night Card Game in the Back Room of Time* (Pulpbits.com), and his poetry has appeared in national and international publications. He has been nominated for numerous awards including two Pushcart Prizes, two "Best of the Web" (2009), and the Rhysling Poetry Award for 2010.

Peter WOOD holds a Master's in Theatre History from the University of Maryland and is currently working toward a PhD in Theatre Arts at the University of Pittsburgh. In addition to issues of gender, his research interests include the history of the Living Theatre, zombie performance, and the Japanese dance form of Butoh. His recent production work includes sound design for Brown University's New Play Festival and Perishable Theatre. His play, "Movie Time" was chosen as a finalist for the 2009 Heidemann award. A chronicle of his time and work as a PhD student can be found at http://thisthus.com. He has dedicated his chapter in this collection to Dr. Joan Dagle, who was there at the very beginning of Peter's journey with Ripley.

INDEX